Dear Reader,

Thank you for choosing *3D Animation Essentials*. This book is part of a family of premium-quality Sybex books, all of which are written by outstanding authors who combine practical experience with a gift for teaching.

Sybex was founded in 1976. More than 30 years later, we're still committed to producing consistently exceptional books. With each of our titles, we're working hard to set a new standard for the industry. From the paper we print on, to the authors we work with, our goal is to bring you the best books available.

I hope you see all that reflected in these pages. I'd be very interested to hear your comments and get your feedback on how we're doing. Feel free to let me know what you think about this or any other Sybex book by sending me an email at nedde@wiley.com. If you think you've found a technical error in this book, please visit http://sybex.custhelp.com. Customer feedback is critical to our efforts at Sybex.

Best regards,

NEIL EDDE
Vice President and Publisher
Sybex, an Imprint of Wiley

To my wife, Heather, and my boys, Ollie and Max,
thank you for all of the patience you have shown me
during all of my fretting and for picking up my slack
around the house to allow me to complete this project.

ACKNOWLEDGMENTS

This book allowed me to write out in a formal form information I am asked about weekly as a professor at Ball State University—questions such as *What kind of jobs are there in 3D animation?* and *Where will I have to move to, to work in 3D animation?* To the prospective students and their parents who have been asking these questions, this book is for you.

I would first like to thank my fantastic wife for supporting me during the writing of this book. Also I would like to thank Mariann Barsolo for giving me the chance to write this book and for helping me through the whole process. Thanks to Candace English, my development editor, for helping me make this book understandable and worth reading. Thank you to my technical editor, Keith Reicher, for helping me keep it real and correct. I would like to thank Larry Richman for giving me a recommendation that started this whole endeavor and for giving me my start in the education world. I would also like to thank the entire Sybex production team for making this book look great. I would like to thank everyone who helped me by talking about his book and creating images for me to use. They look good.

ABOUT THE AUTHOR

Andy Beane is an animation artist who has been teaching and working in the field since 2002. He currently oversees the animation major at Ball State University in Indiana and previously taught animation at the Art Institute of California–Orange County. His production experience includes a children's television show pilot with Xzault Studio, "Coming Undone" music video, and *Barnyard* from Paramount Pictures. He wrote curriculum for the Autodesk Animation Academy 2010 and is also a board member of the MG Collective, an Indiana-based motion graphics and animation community group. He has an MFA in computer animation from the Academy of Art University in San Francisco.

CONTENTS AT A GLANCE

Contents

CHAPTER 3   **Understanding Digital Imaging and Video**   **55**

CHAPTER 4   **Exploring Animation, Story, and Pre-visualization**   **83**

CHAPTER 5   Understanding Modeling and Texturing   135

CHAPTER 6   Rigging and Animation   177

CHAPTER 7   **Understanding Visual Effects, Lighting, and Rendering   213**

CHAPTER 8   **Hardware and Software Tools of the Trade   249**

INTRODUCTION

What is 3D animation? What kind of jobs are there in the field? How does 3D animation get created? What is the future of 3D animation? These are all questions that are asked by someone who is looking to pursue 3D animation as a career or hobby and are reasons this book was written. The answers to these questions are not always easy to find and definitely not in one location, so this book can be used as a reference to answer your personal questions about the animation industry.

   This book looks at the history of the computer and how its evolution has driven and continues to drive computer graphics and 3D animation, and at the same time how computer graphics have driven developments in computer hardware and software. 3D animation is an industry that borrows from many other fields, including film, art, photography, sculpting, painting, and technology. In this book, you will look at up-to-date techniques and practices related to those realms and also take a look at what is coming up in the near future.

Who Should Read This Book

This book is for anyone who is at all interested in anything related to 3D animation. For students graduating from high school (and for parents of high-school students), this book can give you insight into the industry of 3D animation and allow you to better understand basic job functions, basic terminology, and 3D animation techniques. For students already in college or undergoing some other kind of formal training, this book can give you insight into future concepts you may need to learn to make you more marketable in the 3D animation industry. Finally, for people looking to change careers, this book will teach you the basics so you can figure out what part of the industry you might be interested in breaking into.

What You Need

This book is about concepts and techniques, so you really do not need any particular program to complete this book. But if you want to jump in and try some

3D animation techniques, you can get demo versions of 3D animation software from various software companies, including the following:

Autodesk Maya, 3ds Max, Softimage, Mudbox, and MotionBuilder at http://usa.autodesk.com/ and http://students.autodesk.com/

Blender at www.blender.org

Maxon Cinema 4D at www.maxon.net

NewTek LightWave 3D at www.newtek.com/lightwave.html

Side Effects Software Houdini at www.sidefx.com

Luxology modo at www.luxology.com/modo/

What Is Covered in This Book

You will learn the essentials of the 3D animation industry, including a history of the industry, how 3D animation projects are created, basic computer-graphics principles, basic animation, story and film theory, the core concepts of each of the job functions of a 3D artist, what hardware and software tools are available today, and what the future of 3D animation may have in store.

Chapter 1: 3D Animation Overview   What is 3D animation? This question is answered in Chapter 1. This chapter also explores the different industries that utilize 3D animation in various ways. The history of 3D animation is presented, along with the history of the computer, as the two are tied together inextricably.

Chapter 2: Getting to Know the Production Pipeline   Almost all 3D animation is created in a team setting, and this chapter breaks down the steps that a studio uses to create 3D animated projects. You'll learn about the preproduction, production, and postproduction stages of the production pipeline and get a high-level view of the specific jobs in each of the stages.

Chapter 3: Understanding Digital Imaging and Video   Almost all 3D animation is viewed via computer monitors, projectors, or TV screens, and all 3D animation is created on computers. So an understanding of digital imaging and video is a must. This chapter breaks down the digital image to its most basic form—the pixel—and then explores the other elements that make up a digital image.

Chapter 4: Exploring Animation, Story, and Pre-visualization   All 3D animation must tell a story. This chapter presents basic 3D animation methods worked out through traditional 2D animation, basic storytelling theory, and film and pre-visualization techniques with cameras.

Chapter 5: Understanding Modeling and Texturing   This is the first of three chapters that provide detailed looks at the individual job roles in the 3D modeling profession. Chapter 5 breaks down the basic principles, terminology, and techniques of modeling and texturing. When you're finished with this chapter, you'll understand what's behind polygons, NURBS, UVs, shaders, and more.

Chapter 6: Rigging and Animation   This chapter digs into the specifics of the closely linked animation and rigging roles to give you a good idea of their interrelatedness and the fundamentals behind the jobs, such as deformers, inverse and forward kinematics, and keyframes.

Chapter 7: Understanding Visual Effects, Lighting, and Rendering   Here you'll learn about visual effects, lighting, and rendering through discussions of particle systems, light types and options, raytracing, global illumination, and more.

Chapter 8: Hardware and Software Tools of the Trade   Many tools are available to 3D animators today, including the computer, monitor, and human interface tools such as a mouse and tablet options. This chapter covers those plus storage options and solutions that make 3D animation possible with the large amount of data the files will create and files that will need to be shared by different artists at one time. This chapter also presents the software options 3D animators have so you can figure out what packages make the most sense for you to learn.

Chapter 9: Industry Trends   The 3D animation industry is changing constantly, so it's important to be aware of what is on the cutting edge and what is on the horizon. Techniques and methods such as real-time rendering, motion capture, stereoscopic 3D, and point cloud data are integral to the future of the industry.

Appendix A: Answers to Review Questions   This appendix presents the answers to the review questions found at the end of each chapter.

Appendix B: Gaining Insight into 3D Animation Education   This appendix brings you interviews with experts in the 3D animation education field so you can glimpse some of the differences within the formal 3D animation educational system. The appendix includes interviews with the following professionals:

▶ Linda Sellheim, academic segment manager for primary and secondary education at Autodesk

▶ Larry Richman, dean of academic affairs at the Art Institute of California–Sacramento

▶ Steve Kolbe, assistant professor at the University of Nebraska–Lincoln

Appendix C: Learning from Industry Pros   This appendix presents interviews with professionals in the 3D animation industry. Some of the differences between the hiring methods of different 3D animation fields come to light in interviews with the following people:

▶ Brian Phillips, executive creative director at The Basement Design + Motion

▶ Jim Rivers, hiring manager at Obsidian Entertainment

▶ Rosie Server, senior recruiter at Sony Pictures Imageworks

Sybex strives to keep you supplied with the latest tools and information you need for your work. Please check its website at www.sybex.com/go/3danimationessentials, where we'll post additional content and updates that supplement this book if the need arises.

CHAPTER 1

3D Animation Overview

3D animation has become a mainstay in film, television, and video games, and is becoming an integral part of other industries that may not have found it all that useful at first. Fields such as medicine, architecture, law, and even forensics now use 3D animation. To really understand 3D animation, you must look at its short history, which is tied directly to the history of the computer. Computer graphics, one of the fastest growing industries today, drives the technology and determines what computers are going to be able to do tomorrow. In this chapter, you will look at present-day 3D animation and then look back at how the past has shaped what we do today.

▶ **Defining 3D animation**

▶ **Exploring the 3D animation industry**

▶ **Delving into the history of 3D animation**

Defining 3D Animation

3D animation, which falls into the larger field of 3D computer graphics, is a general term describing an entire industry that utilizes 3D animation computer software and hardware in many types of productions. This book uses the term *3D animation* to refer to a wide range of 3D graphics, including static images or even real solid models printed with a 3D printer called a rapid prototyper. But animation and movement is the primary function of the 3D animation industry. 3D animation is used in three primary industries:

> ▶ Entertainment
>
> ▶ Scientific
>
> ▶ Other

Each of these industries uses 3D animation in completely different ways and for different final output, including film, video, visualizations, rapid prototyping, and many others. The term *3D animation* is still evolving, and we have not yet seen everything that it will encompass.

A 3D artist is anyone who works in the production stage of 3D animation: modeler, rigger, texturer, animator, visual effects technician, lighter, or renderer. Each of these job titles falls under the umbrella term *3D artist*, and so each job can also be referred to more specifically: 3D modeler, 3D texture artist, 3D lighter, 3D animator, and so forth. These jobs are discussed in more detail throughout this book, to give you a good idea of the role of each on a day-to-day basis.

Exploring the 3D Animation Industry

Let's take a closer look at the three primary industries using 3D animation. This section details the various opportunities of each so you can see what a person wanting to get into 3D animation could do today.

Entertainment

The entertainment industry is the most widely recognized of the three primary 3D animation industries and includes film, television, video games, and advertising—each of which has subfields within it. The entertainment industry is dedicated to creating and selling entertainment to an audience.

Film

Two primary types of films are created in the 3D animation realm: fully animated films and visual effects films. In fully animated films, all the visual elements onscreen are created in 3D animation software and rendered. Examples include *Toy Story*, *Monsters vs. Aliens*, and *Shrek*. Visual effects films are typically shot with real actors, but the backgrounds or other effects are computer generated. *Jurassic Park*, *Sky Captain and the World of Tomorrow*, and *Tron* are examples of visual effects films.

The film industry is one of the largest industries using 3D animation. These films typically take about six months to four years to complete, depending on the scale of the project. The production crew can range from 3 people to 300, again depending on the scale of the overall film.

Fully animated full-length films can take two to four years to create and have a very large crew of hundreds of employees. One studio usually completes the whole film internally. Short films (those shorter than 40 minutes) often are created by individuals or small studios. These short films are usually done on the side or after hours as personal projects. Large studios might create a short film to test a new technique or production pipeline. These films can be completed in a few months with a large crew or may take years depending on the artists' work schedules.

Visual effects films are different from fully animated feature films in that they are shot by a regular movie crew. A visual effects supervisor helps with camera work and with collecting any other data needed for the addition of the visual effects. Then the completed shots are sent to visual effects studios to complete parts or the whole sequence of effects as needed. Today most visual effects–heavy films use one or two primary studios for most of the work to keep the effects looking consistent, but then farm out smaller shots or sequences to other studios to save time. Visual effects studios can be very large to very small, depending on the type of work they are expected to complete.

Television

3D animation is still trying to make its mark in the television industry. Creating a single 3D animated television show is quite expensive and time-consuming. Still, several of today's shows are being created with 3D software, including *South Park*, *Mickey Mouse Clubhouse*, and *Star Wars: The Clone Wars*.

A more common usage of 3D animation in television is the addition of 3D visualizations to regular shows on networks such as the Discovery Health Channel, History Channel, and Science Channel. These visualizations typically are used in educational shows to help the audience understand certain topics.

The television industry doesn't have the film industry's luxury of lots of time and lots of money. Television shows need to be made in months, not years. The budgets are tremendously smaller, and more content needs to be created in a single season. 3D animation in television shows usually does not have the overall quality of that in film, but can still be very good if a stylized final look is used in the project.

Video Games

The video game industry enables artists to use 3D software to create virtual worlds and characters that will be played in a video game engine. This industry is massively popular and is at least as profitable as the film industry. There are two primary fields in the video game industry: in-game 3D animation, which creates the actual game world that players are immersed in while playing the video game, and game cinematics, which are cinematically created cut scenes of a video game that help drive the story forward in between levels.

Video game cinematics are like mini movies between levels that allow the game developer to control the storyline of a game while the player progresses.

►

Low-resolution polygon modeling is covered further in Chapter 5, "Understanding Modeling and Texturing."

The in-game side of this industry is closely tied to the computer programming that makes playing the video game possible. The creation of in-game art is limited by the hardware and software that is used to play video games in real time. For example, a game destined for a console such as the Xbox 360 or PlayStation 3 requires low-resolution models in order to allow numerous characters to appear in the game at once, along with the background elements and all the props and effects. To allow for real-time rendering and game play, the modeling artist must stay within a specific polygon count for these low-resolution models. Once the 3D animation assets are created, the video game programmers will create a system enabling the asset to be placed into the game to be played.

Most game cinematics, like film, are limited today only by the budget and time needed to create the 3D animation assets and to render the final frames to be played in video. Game cinematic artists are similar to film 3D animators. They do similar work but typically in a faster timeline (although not as fast as television). Many game cinematic trailers and in-game cinematic scenes are of a very high caliber that can rival film.

►

Triple-A video game titles are games that are expected to do well commercially and typically take longer to develop.

Video games created for smart phones and tablets typically take a few months to develop. A large triple-A title such as *Gears of War* or *Crysis* might take 2 to 4 years to create. It is not unheard of for a game-development cycle to last 10 years, however.)

Advertising

The advertising industry is all about very short animations. Typically, only 10 seconds to 4 or 5 minutes is needed to show or describe a product or service. These short animations must be able to provide a great deal of information in this brief time span. Like film and television, 3D advertising animation can utilize an all–3D animated form or incorporate mixed-media visual effects for the final overall look.

Typical projects in this industry are television commercials, web commercials which can include print ads, and still imagery. A lesser-known side of advertising is product visualization (discussed in detail in the next section), in which the artist creates a 3D model to serve as a prototype of an actual product to show to an investor to create an interest in that product.

Advertising can have a very high level of quality but is created in a very short amount of time. Studios specializing in advertising animation are medium sized and follow a solid workflow in order to provide the fast turnaround needed for this type of animation.

Scientific

The scientific industries utilizing 3D animation include medicine, law, architecture, and product visualization. The use of 3D in these industries is not well known, however, because the final products are aimed at a specific audience and rarely are seen by the general public.

Medicine

The medical industry uses 3D animation in many ways, from creating a visualization of a specific medical event to depicting a biological reaction. For example, you can demonstrate what happens when plaque will build up in your arteries and will block blood flow to the heart, causing a heart attack. Art has been a part of the medical industry since the beginning of modern medical practices. Many of Leonardo Da Vinci's sketchbooks, for instance, focused on human anatomy and medical processes. These drawings, shown in Figure 1.1, were used by doctors to better understand early medicine. Even today you can see posters of human anatomy on the walls of doctors' offices. So it only makes sense that the medical field would take advantage of the new art form of 3D animation.

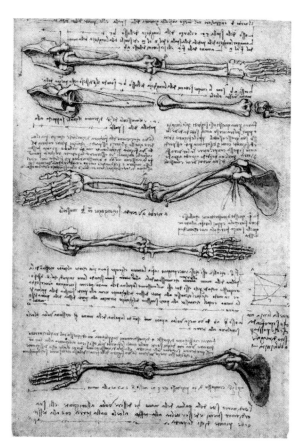

FIGURE 1.1 Da Vinci's study of the arm

The most popular medical 3D animation type is medical visualization used for education or marketing. This animation is used to educate the public and medical staff on new techniques or drugs. It is also used in marketing new medical products to investors or medical professionals, as shown in Figure 1.2. 3D animation can create a vastly rich visual guide to human and biological systems and can provide a great amount of information in a short amount of time.

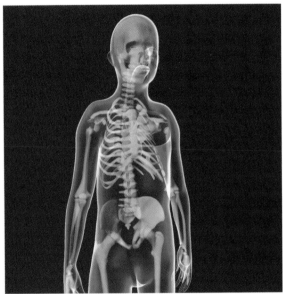

Image courtesy of and © Zachary Craw

FIGURE 1.2 Example of a medical rendering

Motion capture, a system of tracking human movement that can be used for medical research and the entertainment industry, is covered further in Chapter 9, "Industry Trends."

3D animation can be used in simulations to help medical researchers predict the spread of a disease or understand which body part will fail first under great strain without actually putting a person at risk. By using motion capture, researchers can create a library of movements and then study the effects of various stresses on the human form. New probe-like technology enables researchers to track muscle strain as they watch which muscles are working the hardest during a specific movement or series of movements. The U.S. Department of Defense and professional sports have an interest in this type of data because it can help indicate how a new piece of protective equipment might be working or hindering.

One other form of medical 3D animation is tied to the video game industry. Ongoing studies are looking at how video games might be used to help heal brain injuries. These video games stimulate different areas of the brain, potentially helping the regrowth of brain tissue. These studies are very new but are showing good results, which means that more of these types of games could be created for other healing applications.

3D animation in the medical sector is a vastly growing market that can be lucrative to an individual artist or small studio of professionals. The biggest drawback to this industry is that most people training today in 3D animation would rather work in video games or film and not for a drug company or university research project.

Law

Law animation falls into two fields: forensics and accident reconstruction and simulation. This type of animation is created to prove, disprove, or elaborate on facts in a court case, to help either the defense or prosecution. It can include pure computer physics simulations or just a hand-keyed animation of the crime scene to enable the judge or jury to move around or study the crime scene if needed. It can be used, for example, to prove that a gunman could or could not have shot someone from a specific location (see Figure 1.3) or to demonstrate a car accident scenario. These types of animations are often not allowed to be used as pure evidence but can be used to demonstrate a theory that the prosecution or defense may have on a specific case.

Forensics is a field that utilizes many different sciences to prove or disprove questions in the legal system.

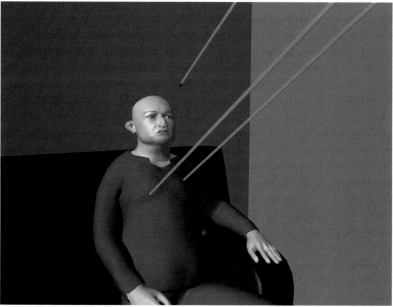

Image courtesy of and © Pat Howk

FIGURE 1.3 Forensics animation showing gunshot trajectory

Another aspect of this 3D animation field is the use of 3D laser scanning of a crime scene. This 3D laser scanning can create a perfect replica of a crime scene to be used as a reference when needed. This 3D scan can be accurate to within millimeters and therefore can be crucial to a court case or an investigation.

Architecture

Architects have been using computer-aided design (CAD) software since the 1980s to help them create better and more stable designs. Today architects use 3D software in conjunction with CAD programs not only to create models, but to test and visualize those models to see what structures would look like photorealistically before they are actually created. Software such as Autodesk AutoCAD and Autodesk Revit enable architects to test the stability of designs under certain conditions, to see whether they can withstand a specific type of natural environment or disaster. These CAD files can be converted and then rendered in software such as Autodesk 3ds Max and Autodesk Maya to enable investors and clients to see what a structure could look like from the outside and inside. This type of work is becoming more and more popular and can be a very cost-effective way to test certain material looks of a building before actually building it. You can see an example of interior and exterior architecture rendering in Figure 1.4.

Images courtesy of
© Justin Canul and Zachary Craw

FIGURE 1.4 Example of indoor and outdoor rendering for architecture

Product Visualization

One last scientific area is product design and product rendering visualization. This is similar to architectural rendering in that products can be designed and tested in 3D software and then rendered to show investors. After the design is drawn up, a 3D artist will create a 3D model of the product in 3D design software to test its construction. Then a visualization animation will be created to show how the product will work and how it is assembled if needed. This type of visualization helps investors have a better grasp of what they may be investing in and can be used for commercial purposes as well, for presales.

Other

The 3D animation industry is in its infancy, and the technology that is driving this art form is changing on a yearly basis. This rapid pace of change necessitates the "other" category because some fields are so new that they do not fit into established mainstream categories. A trio of these new 3D animation fields are art, augmented reality, and projection mapping.

Using 3D animation in *art* is just what it sounds like: the creation of 3D elements incorporated in a final product to be shown in a gallery or other art-exhibition venue. This could include still imagery to be framed and posted on the gallery walls or a 3D statue created in 3D software and then rapid-prototyped and placed into the gallery as sculpture. Typically today 3D art animation is video installations that will use animated forms in a non-story-based structure. Sculpture might utilize moving 3D animations to enhance the piece. These types of 3D animations are typically not character- or story-based, but simply moving forms projected onto the sculptures.

Augmented reality might be considered by some as an advertising form of 3D animation, but because it is so new, it is premature to lump it into a certain field. In augmented reality, a user looks at the real world and sees 3D elements added to it. Typically, we would look through a webcam and use a *marker* (usually an image) to lock the position of the 3D elements though the camera as seen in Figure 1.5. Other viewing devices today are head-mounted with a see-through visor that add the 3D elements to the visual real world. There are also handheld augmented-reality devices and tracking with the use of GPS to add visuals to this reality.

FIGURE 1.5 Example of augmented reality through a webcam. The paper the boy is holding has a marker that will allow the software to know where to place the image.

Projection mapping is a new technique that can make any surface, typically large buildings, into a video display. This technique uses projectors to project onto a building a 3D animation displaying new and exciting effects such as destruction of the building or lighting on that surface. This technique has been used to create many interesting effects, and it should become a mainstay in 3D animation in the future.

The History of 3D Animation

It is exciting to be part of the 3D animation industry today. Unlike drawing, painting, and other traditional art forms that have been practiced for centuries, 3D animation is still in its infancy. New ideas and techniques are created every year. To really understand the history of the art form, you must look at the technology behind it. 3D animation would not exist without computers, and many of the breakthroughs in computers have been directly driven by the 3D animation industry.

Early Computers

Some believe the first mechanical computer was the Z1, designed by Konrad Zuse in 1938. Figure 1.6 shows a replica in the German Museum of Technology. The other computer that is often said to be the first is the Colossus in 1943. Shown in Figure 1.7, this computer was used to help British code breakers decipher German messages. Neither of these resembles today's computers in appearance or behavior, but they put in perspective how young the 3D animation industry is, given that the tool required for this art form was invented only about 70 years ago.

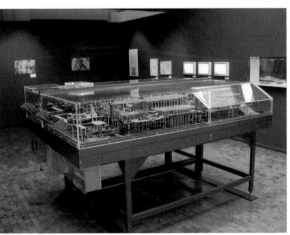

Image © ComputerGeek, from Wikipedia

FIGURE 1.6 Replica of the Z1 computer in the German Museum of Technology

FIGURE 1.7 Colossus computer used to break coded messages in WWII

Not until the late 1950s did John Whitney Sr. use a computer to create art and the opening title sequence of the Alfred Hitchcock film *Vertigo*. Whitney used a handwriting recognition tablet (created by Tom Dimond) in collaboration with Saul Bass.

1960s: The Dawn of Computer Animation

The 1960s is when the beginnings of computer graphics and computer animation were created. This decade is when we saw the computer evolve from a strictly calculating device into a tool that allowed for creation and change. This is in the idea of hardware with user interaction devices and software that allowed for changes in real time.

William Fetter is credited with creating the term *computer graphics (CG)* in 1960. He is often thought of as the father of 3D animation because of his work at Boeing, where he used computers to create 3D models of objects and even of a human body that came to be known as the Boeing Man.

In 1962, computer programmer Steve Russell and a team from the Massachusetts Institute of Technology (MIT) created one of the first video games, *Spacewar*. In this two-player game, two spaceships try to destroy each other while also trying to not collide with a sun.

The amazing part of these first achievements in CG is that these computers had no graphical user interface, which is something we take for granted today. Instead, users would face only a blank screen and a blinking cursor and would have to understand the system and memory to access any information.

In 1963, Ivan Sutherland created a computer drawing program called Sketchpad that employed a light pen to draw simple shapes. This system paved the way for many of today's drawing and painting programs to be perfected as drawing constraints enabled the creation of straight lines and perfect circles. The light pen used for Sutherland's system was one of the first human input devices into computers beyond that of a keyboard, switches, and dials. This system is also considered the first graphic interface for computers.

The computer mouse is one of the tools we all take for granted, but it was not invented until 1963. The original mouse, invented by Douglas Engelbart, was a block of wood with two wheels on the bottom, one facing vertically and one horizontally. The turning of the wheels controlled a pointer onscreen. Think about how you would have to interface with a computer today without a mouse.

1970s: The Building Blocks of 3D Animation

In the 1970s we saw the computer become smaller and faster, and the idea of 3D virtual surfaces was also being invented. Many of the basics of 3D animation we still use today like shaders and rendering were invented at this time. Also the first glimpse of 3D animation in film was witnessed.

In 1971, the microprocessor was developed, which allowed for the electronics of a computer to be miniaturized down to a single chip. Many of the building blocks of basic 3D animation were invented during this decade.

Researchers at the University of Utah created an algorithm enabling hidden surfaces to be rendered as 3D surfaces onscreen. Up to this point, the only thing a technician could do was draw wireframe lines, resulting in flat shading of polygons that made an object look faceted and blocky. But in 1971 Henri Gouraud created *Gouraud shading*, which allowed for the faceted polygon surface to render and look smooth. Figure 1.8 shows a comparison of flat shading and Gouraud shading.

Ed Catmull, while finishing his time at the University of Utah, created texture mapping in 1974 that allowed these early 3D graphics to achieve realism not seen to date. Catmull went on to create advancements in anti-aliasing and z-buffering and become the president of Pixar Animation Studios and Walt Disney Animation Studio.

In 1975, Martin Newell created the Utah teapot, or Newell teapot, to test rendering algorithms. That model is still used today, and some software programs have a Create Teapot button in honor of Newell and as an inside joke about the shape and its effect on the industry. The teapot was considered ideal at the time to test rendering because it has a round shape, a handle, and a spout to cast a shadow on itself (see Figure 1.9).

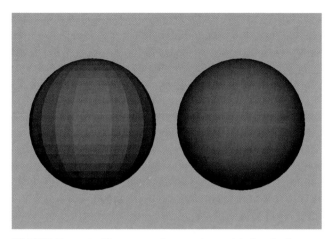

FIGURE 1.8 The same polygon sphere with flat shading on the left and Gouraud shading on the right

In 1978, James "Jim" Blinn introduced bump-mapping texturing techniques that can make a surface look as if it has bumps, bulges, and dents. This technique enables 3D models to look more realistic. He also created a texture mapping of surfaces called environment mapping to allow an object to look as if it is reflecting the world or environment around it. This was first demonstrated on the Utah teapot. At the same time, Bui Tuong Phong created a shading model to produce highlights on shiny objects, called the Phong reflection model. Later Blinn would modify the Phong shader to provide a softening effect on the highlights.

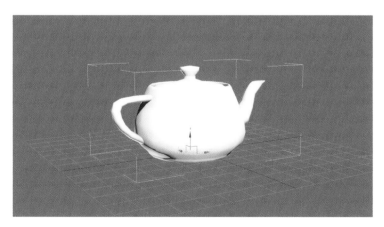

FIGURE 1.9 The Utah teapot in 3ds Max

Also in the 1970s, the first 3D animation studios were created, including Information International Incorporated (now known as Triple-I), Robert Abel and Associates, Digital Effects, and Lucasfilm. Lucasfilm also created a computer graphics division called Graphics Group, which eventually became Pixar.

In the mid to late 1970s, we began to see the first images of 3D animation in film, with a wireframe hand and face that Catmull and Frederic Parke created for the 1976 film *Futureworld*. In 1977, the Academy Awards introduced a new category of Best Visual Effects. Two years later, the movie *Alien* used a 3D animation sequence for the onboard computers screens to show a ship's landing sequence to help the film achieve a futuristic feel. In 1979, the Disney film *The Black Hole* used 3D computer graphics for its opening title screen.

The video game Pong, shown in Figure 1.10, was created in 1972 by Nolan Bushnell for Atari. One of the first video games developed, Pong is considered the impetus for today's commercial industry. Pong was a 2D game, but it laid the groundwork for the modern 3D games we see today.

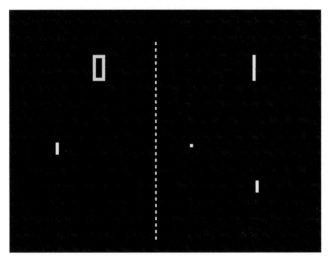

FIGURE 1.10 Screenshot of Pong

1980s: The Foundations of Modern Computing

To this point, computers were not readily available to people in their homes. Instead, computers were typically seen in university and government settings. Becoming an active user of these computers required a lot of knowledge. In 1975, Bill Gates created Microsoft. In 1980, IBM approached Microsoft to create an operating system for the company's first personal computer. At the same time that Microsoft was being born, Steve Jobs and Steve Wozniak were creating a personal computer and began Apple in 1976. These personal computers had an interface that people with little to no computer training could use in their homes.

In the 1980s, many of the basic techniques were now developed and were making 3D animation a viable commercial industry. Turner Whitted introduced raytracing in 1980, in a paper titled "An Improved Illumination Model for Shaded Display." Raytracing is still used today as a render technique for creating realistic reflections on surfaces, and many of the latest techniques are based on this algorithm.

In 1982, Silicon Graphics (SGI) was created and began focusing on making faster, more-efficient computers for 3D animation. These SGI computers remained a mainstay in almost the entire industry for two decades.

Also in 1982, Autodesk was created, and the company released AutoCAD for personal computers. Autodesk is now the world's largest company for CAD and 3D animation software. Autodesk played a large role in the move from specialized computers to the use of personal computers for computer graphics.

In 1984, a company named Wavefront Technologies created the first commercially available off-the-shelf 3D animation software. Previously, each company had to write their own software to create 3D graphics and animation. Although some studios still use proprietary software, most now use commercially available programs. In addition, Photoshop was released in 1988 to small markets (Photoshop 1.0 was released in 1990 for the Mac). This program would become the foundation of all 2D and photo-manipulation software used today.

In 1984, Apple released the first Macintosh personal computer, which was the first widely distributed computer to use a graphical user interface. The Macintosh, shown in Figure 1.11, became the largest non-IBM computer option ever seen.

Image © www.allaboutapple.com, from Wikipedia

FIGURE 1.11 Original Macintosh computer with a graphical user interface

▶

Virtual reality uses computer-generated environments to simulate a 3D experience in a certain place, world, or event. At the time of its invention, people predicted that VR would replace many different technologies like computer screens and televisions and that almost all training for military and vehicle operation would happen in a VR world. The commercial application of VR has never really fully developed, however.

In 1983, as researchers were working on new ways to interact and communicate with the computer, the *data glove* was invented. It allowed users to manipulate 3D objects in 3D space, which led to some of the first commercially available virtual reality (VR) systems.

Many animation studios were created in the 1980s including Triple-I, Digital Productions, Lucasfilm, Industrial Light & Magic, Pixar, and Pacific Data Images (PDI). Some of these studios lasted; some did not. With this industry being so new and small many of the artists and computer scientists all worked together at one time or another.

LONG LASTING STUDIOS

Many of the studios that are still in production today were created in the 1980s—for example, Lucasfilm, Industrial Light & Magic (ILM), Pixar, and Pacific Data Images (now PDI/Dreamworks).

Tron in 1982 had just over 20 minutes of 3D animated graphics including the bits, speed cycles, tanks, and game grid created by Triple-I. This 3D animation was extremely hard for the artists and researchers to complete, and *Tron* did not do that well in the box office. As a result, Hollywood at the time did not respect 3D animation's potential. Also in 1982, ILM created a few 3D animation sequences of a planet (during the Genesis Effect) in *Star Trek II: The Wrath of Khan*. ILM also created the digital Death Star projection in 1983's *Star Wars: Return of the Jedi*.

Lucasfilm created *The Adventures of Andre and Wally B.*, a short animated film all in 3D, in 1984. This short film was the first to incorporate complex backgrounds, squash and stretch animation, lighting with purpose, and motion blur. Although this film was not officially a Pixar project, many believe that it was the starting point for Pixar's later films, and it is on the DVD *Pixar Short Films Collection*.

In 1984, *The Last Starfighter* was the next Hollywood film to try large-scale 3D animation after the mediocre reception of *Tron*. Digital Productions created about 25 minutes of animation for the film, but it did not do well at the box office, and again Hollywood did not get excited about 3D animation.

In 1986, Disney again tried 3D animation in the film *The Great Mouse Detective*. At that time, Disney—which had a monopoly on the traditional animation market and was considered the best at animation—was pushing 3D animation forward. They also looked at expanding 3D animation for their next films.

In 1986 and 1988, Pixar (which was not then part of Disney) released two new short films, *Luxo Jr.* and *Tin Toy. Luxo Jr.* was the first film under the studio name Pixar. Created by Catmull and directed by John Lasseter, this short film showed people that 3D computer animation could create a worthwhile character performance and was not just a tool for coloring and backgrounds. *Tin Toy* was Pixar's second film, again with Lasseter directing. It was the first computer-generated short film to win an Oscar.

In 1989, ILM created a water creature for the film *The Abyss* that would move like a snake made of water though the underwater vessel to investigate the people aboard. No one had seen an effect like this with photorealistic rendering and movement; the water snake also interacted with the live actors and even mimicked them in the performance.

1990s: 3D Animation Achieves Commercial Success

In the 1990s, 3D animation really began picking up commercial steam in film and even in video games. *Terminator 2* was released in 1991, showcasing a liquid-metal terminator who looked like the actor Robert Patrick but had morphing abilities. New advances in digital compositing also enabled background elements to change seamlessly. Hollywood began to pay attention to what 3D animation could do for film. That same year, Disney released *Beauty and the Beast* with a large sequence of the ballroom dance utilizing 3D animation to create the camera movements and all of the background. The film's success reinforced Hollywood's decision to pay more attention to 3D animation as a new technique for filmmaking.

Two years later, *Jurassic Park* was released with photorealistic dinosaurs composited in with live-action environments and actors. The animated dinosaurs were able to interact with these live-action elements. At first the studio did not think computer-generated 3D creatures could achieve the look and believability needed to pull off a movie of the scope of *Jurassic Park*. The studio and director considered stop-motion animation for the dinosaurs, but ILM created a test that proved they could create the realism needed for these creatures. This film went on to win the Academy Award for Best Visual Effects.

In 1994, the first all-3D television series *ReBoot* was aired. This show was the first of its kind. No one to this point wanted to create a 3D animation show under the constraints of tight television timelines. *ReBoot* survived four seasons, and some efforts have been made to re-create the show.

In 1995, Pixar released the first fully 3D animated feature film *Toy Story* to great success critically and commercially. This film paved the way for more feature-length 3D animated films, 1998's *Antz* and *A Bug's Life*, and 1999's *Toy Story 2*.

In 1999, *Star Wars Episode 1: The Phantom Menace*, created by George Lucas and ILM, was released and was a huge success at the box office. *Star Wars Episode 1* had a main character that was fully 3D—a first—and 90 percent or more of the visual elements of the film were enhanced by 3D animation for computer graphics. Also that year *The Matrix* was released with the use of 3D animation helping in the Bullet Time effects that this film is known for. Also released in the 1990s were other films that utilized the advances in 3D animation, such as *Total Recall* (1990); *The Mask* (1994); *DragonHeart, Independence Day, Stuart Little, Twister* (1996); *Starship Troopers, The Fifth Element, Titanic, The Lost World: Jurassic Park* (1997); *Armageddon*, and *What Dreams May Come* (1998).

In the video game realm, in 1994 the Sony PlayStation home console system was released and was one of the first home console systems to be able to handle 3D graphics with hardware accelerations. Games like *GoldenEye 007*, released in 1997 on the Nintendo 64, included free-roaming 3D levels and paved the way for more-complex gaming experiences compared the to the 2D side-scrolling games created before. Other games with this free-roaming 3D gameplay were *The Legend of Zelda: Ocarina of Time* (1998), *Shenmue* (1999), and *Driver* (1999).

Changes in hardware also had a big impact on video games. In the 1990s, 3D graphic accelerators such as the 3dfx Interactive Voodoo Graphics chip and NVIDIA's TNT2 processor became standards in gaming on a personal computer. NVIDIA also released the first consumer-level graphics processing unit, the GeForce 256. These accelerators were needed because the gaming industry was using new 3D gaming engines such as Quake that needed all the horsepower possible to play the games at full quality.

▶

A *graphics accelerator* is a video adapter that has its own processor to help the computer render graphics.

2000s: The Refining of 3D Animation

In the 2000s, more technology was being created to support the growing 3D animation industry, and there seemed to be a race every year between what the industry wanted and how the technology would dictate the industry's advancement. In the early 2000s, personal workstations could handle most commercial 3D software so that very expensive graphic workstations were no longer needed. 3D video games were taking over the video game industry. NVIDIA took over the game graphics card industry and became a standard in home computers. New video game consoles were released with more-accelerated hardware to make video game play more immersive and with better graphics and better frame rates.

The film industry was trying to outdo the last CG/3D film released with better graphics and visuals. Pixar's *Monsters Inc.* (2001) showed that 3D fur could be accomplished with good effect. *A.I.* (2001) pushed boundaries in 3D animation techniques in visual effects. *The Lord of the Rings: The Fellowship of the Ring* (2001) pushed new techniques with crowd simulations. *Final Fantasy: The Spirits Within* (2001) attempted to create photorealistic humans for the full 3D animated film. (This film did not do well critically but did push the 3D animation industry into trying to create more-believable human characters.) *The Lord of the Rings: The Return of the King* (2003) made great advances in 3D animation with the motion-captured 3D-animated Gollum character.

By the 2000s, people had become accustomed to seeing high-quality 3D animation and visual effects work. Almost all films were being touched up in one way or another. Even the advertising industry began using 3D animation, and most people did not even notice it. Car commercials, for instance, began using 3D models of cars, rarely using the real car.

The future of 3D animation is wide open today (Chapter 9 takes a look at today's cutting-edge trends). With so many new techniques, hardware, and software coming out every year, no one can say for sure what is going to happen. But an exciting factor of this industry is that because it is less than 50 years old, many of its pioneers are still alive today and are still creating. You can meet them online or at conferences around the world. This is like meeting Leonardo Da Vinci or Rembrandt and asking them for help or for their thoughts about their art. There has never been an industry or art form offering such access to the masters with the knowledge that they are the ones creating the new art. This is truly an exciting industry and will be for the foreseeable future.

THE ESSENTIALS AND BEYOND

The 3D animation industry has grown so much and so fast in the last few decades that other fields are still figuring out how the potential of 3D animation may help them. And the hardware and software industry is driving and being driven by the 3D animation industry. Each of these industries will become stronger because of the other. 3D animation pushes the computer industry to create faster and smaller processors, and the 3D art field is pushed by the computer industry to come up with new techniques and software to match the hardware of today. The industry is truly alive and exciting to work in. 3D animation is constantly changing and evolving, and with the culture of today will become only larger and in more demand.

(Continues)

THE ESSENTIALS AND BEYOND *(Continued)*

REVIEW QUESTIONS

1. Which of the following is not considered a field within the entertainment industry?

   A. Film

   B. Product visualization

   C. Video games

   D. Advertising

2. True or false: 3D animation always means motion.

3. What are the two 3D animation fields within the video game industry?

   A. In-game animation

   B. Game publishing

   C. Cinematic animation

   D. Game programming

4. True or false: Forensic animation is used today to aid in court cases, but is not to be used as pure fact.

5. True or false: Architectural animation can be a time-saver by enabling architects to test a design under stress.

6. Why is the history of 3D animation so closely tied to computer technology?

   A. Because computers are the primary tool used to create 3D animation

   B. Because the computer art field has pushed computer technology forward

   C. Because both industries are being driven forward as each pushes the limits of what can be done each year

   D. All of the above

7. True or false: In the late 1980s and the 1990s, computer animation and visual effects really took off as an industry.

8. The computer mouse was invented in what year?

   A. 1955

   B. 1963

   C. 1968

   D. 1971

9. What year was the first commercial 3D animation software available?

   A. 1963

   B. 1978

   C. 1979

   D. 1984

10. What year was the first fully 3D animated film created?

    A. 1963

    B. 1988

    C. 1999

    D. 1995

CHAPTER 2

Getting to Know the Production Pipeline

You can picture the 3D animation production pipeline as a car assembly line. Each person does a job in a sequential order to create the entire car in an efficient, affordable, and timely way. The result is an effective manufacturing process and a lower cost of the final product. The same is true today with the 3D animation production pipeline, which can consist of 400+ people or as few as 2. Every artist working on a 3D animation production pipeline will eventually have to hand off work to a different artist to work on.

So as a 3D artist, it is fundamental that you understand how the work you do will affect the next few steps in the production pipeline. This chapter starts by describing the stages of the assembly line and how they are linked to one another. Then you will see a more detailed explanation of the particular production stages. Finally, you will see some of the tools that keep the entire production team on the same page.

▶ **Understanding the production pipeline's components**

▶ **Working in preproduction**

▶ **Working in production**

▶ **Working in postproduction**

▶ **Using production tools**

Understanding the Production Pipeline's Components

A 3D animation *production pipeline* is a group of people, hardware, and software aligned to work in a specific sequential order to create a 3D animation product or asset. The final product could be a traditional one such as a feature film, short film, television show, or video game, or it could be something totally different. For example, a startup company looking to fund its new idea or product may hire a 3D product visualization studio to model and then rapid-prototype a final product model for investors. The specific hardware and software used may differ between project types, but the fundamental stages of the 3D animation pipeline are the same throughout. The three main stages of the production pipeline are as follows:

- ▶ Preproduction
- ▶ Production
- ▶ Postproduction

Each segment of the 3D animation industry uses the three main stages of the production pipeline slightly differently. The entertainment industries of film, TV, video games, advertising, and visual effects utilize the three stages in a similar fashion. The preproduction team will take its time to make sure to tell an engaging story with interesting characters. The production team, if the preproduction plans are laid out correctly, will then create the project. The postproduction team will make the project that looked acceptable in the production stage look fantastic by adding 2D visual effects and color corrections.

In the scientific industries of medical animation, architecture, product visualization, and law, artists spend almost the entire production timeline in the preproduction stage. The final products or assets created in these industries must be represented realistically and factually, and rarely (if at all) be embellished. These industries invest a lot of time in the preproduction stage, in the research and development of exactly what it is they are trying to represent or create. The scientific industries employ not only 3D artists, but also many scientific professionals who are consulting on these projects. In the production stage, the 3D artists create the product or asset. Postproduction results in the output of the project or asset in its final form.

Before looking at the individual components of the preproduction stage of a 3D animation project, you should see the entire 3D animation production pipeline (see Figure 2.1).

Working in 3D Animation Preproduction

Preproduction is the planning, designing, and research phase of the entire 3D project. This is an indispensable stage because it is where the great ideas are generated and production plans are created that will help you understand how to manage the project. A good idea with a solid production plan has a much better chance of being completed than a great idea with no plan.

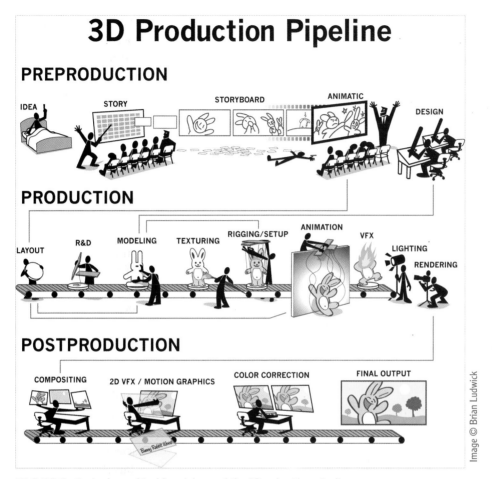

FIGURE 2.1 A graphical breakdown of the 3D animation pipeline

The preproduction stage is split between two teams: artists and management. The artists create the ideas, story, and designs. The management team creates the production plan. To further break it down, there is a creative management team, also known as the *creative leads*, who work directly with the artists. The management team generally is in charge of shopping the project to investors (though sometimes that role is handled by an amateur filmmaker trying to get his or her movie out there).

The various entertainment industries all treat the preproduction stage very much the same. The artists devote this stage to coming up with good ideas, writing those ideas into an engaging story, and then deciding how to visually tell that story. These industries spend up to half of their entire production time-line in the preproduction stage.

After watching a movie adaptation of a best-selling book, you have probably heard or even said, "The book was way better than the movie." That is because there is a big dissimilarity between the storytelling of a written story, which is meant to be read, and the storytelling of a visual story, which is meant to be seen. To make a story read well onscreen, the entire production team must take different aspects into consideration: How to stage the camera angles to best tell the audience what is going to happen? What colors should be included in the project to lead the audience in mood and feeling? What music, sound, or silence should be used along with the story to push mood?

The medical-animation industry spends preproduction time in research and development on the type of animation they are going to produce. Artists need to know what type of medical technique or organic system they are going to visually describe in their project. During this time, the artists participate in extensive research and use expert consultants to validate that their visualizations are factually correct. Like their counterparts in the entertainment industries, these artists also have to understand how to best show what they are trying to explain or describe; they must consider matters ranging from correct staging of cameras to overall pacing of the animation and final edit of the project.

Architecture 3D artists, like those in the medical-animation industry, spend most of their production time in the preproduction stage. Design and functionality are the primary goals of these artists. If the architecture project is fully approved, the end product is a structure to be created in the real world, where people are going to work, live, and play. There can really be no cutting corners in this phase.

Artists working in product visualization, much like those in architecture, spend a lot of time in this preproduction phase to make sure their product design and functionality is just the way they want it. The final product may be a rapid prototype of the final model, so the product can be seen in the physical world before putting it into production. *Rapid prototyping* is physically creating a virtual object in the real world by using an additive construction technology. Most rapid-prototype machines today work like a 3D laser printer. A strong laser fuses small particles of plastic together, one layer at a time, to create a larger object. These machines can also use an ink-jet head that places thin layers of plastic material on top of one another until the larger object is created.

The legal industry is one that may not spend much time in the preproduction stage. Teams in this industry might reenact a crime with a computer simulation to prove it could or could not happen. As another example, a forensics team might use a 3D scanner to collect data from a crime scene, for a investigator or attorney to be able to go back into the crime scene "virtually" much later after the crime or in a courtroom setting. Artists in this industry have to research techniques of how to correctly show the event they are representing, or research technologies that will aid in their work, but the designs of objects are not very important. The more basic and generic the designs of objects, the better in this industry, because inaccurate detail could mislead the judge and jury in their decision-making process. However, the final staging and camera are important to show the deciding parties what they must see to make correct judgments.

Today we can make almost anything look visually stunning in 3D. But without a good solid concept, you have nothing more than a series of pretty pictures that will be forgotten as soon as your audience is finished viewing it. In 3D animation, the final product *always* must tell a *story*, no matter what segment of the industry you are working in.

In almost all animation industries, it is fairly easy to understand the central role that a story plays in a project. The entertainment industries are generally creating linear visual stories for a general or specific audience. Even in product visualization and architecture, where the 3D animators' job is to create a design or realistic rendering of an object or building that has not been produced in the real world, you must still tell a story. Whether using still imagery or moving video, you must express the story of that product or building in a way that is captivating enough to attract investors to your product or project. Even in 3D animation industries that at first do not seem to fit this production model, making certain your preproduction is in order will make your project stand out in a world of overstimulation.

A *linear story* has a definitive beginning, middle, and end.

The preproduction stage is divided into five components and, depending on the type of project you are working on, you may use all of them or only some of them. The components of the preproduction stage can also be completed in a different order or can be completed all at once to aid the overall creative process. The typical order of these components is as follows:

- ▶ Idea/story
- ▶ Script/screenplay
- ▶ Storyboards
- ▶ Animatic/pre-visualization
- ▶ Design

Idea/Story

The idea for a project can come from just about anywhere and from almost anything. An idea can be sparked by a single word, a sentence, a color, a smell, a sound, passing conversations with a stranger, or eavesdropping on someone else's conversation. That spark just needs to be enough to ignite a dialogue within yourself or with others to want to work out that idea.

Ideas should be something fun and simple, and not something you settle in on yet. I tell my students in my classes, "You must be willing to kill your babies at any time." I know it sounds horrifying and disturbing, but this phrase expresses that you should never get so attached to one idea that you would not be willing to kill it if it is not good enough. Attachment to a bad idea can get you stuck in a proverbial corner that you may not be able to get out of.

IMPROV AS AN IDEA-GENERATION AID

Idea generation is not the easiest thing to be good at as a beginner; it does take a lot of practice. You must be able as an idea person to generate ideas quickly and intelligently. One way to help practice good idea generation is to participate in an improvisational acting class. I know, it sounds strange to take an acting class to come up with good ideas, but improvisational acting is the art of spontaneous action and reaction. It will train your brain to think quickly and to generate quality ideas instantaneously, and it will help you purge all your basic or trite ideas. It was once said to me that all of us have hundreds of bad ideas that we must be able to purge from our systems before we can have good idea flow. An improvisational acting class can help give you an outlet to cleanse those bad ideas out of your system.

After you work out the basic premise of a good idea that you think is worth pursuing, it is time to turn it into a narrative form. This loose story at this point is not a formal short story, script, or screenplay, it is just a basic idea of the total story arc. A better way of thinking of this story is as an outline or written abstract of your idea. This is also the time to draft the basic details that you will want to include in the project, such as who the characters are, or to create some of the big story moments. The following are some questions to ask yourself during this idea/story component:

- ► Who are the characters?
- ► What is this project for?
- ► Who is your audience?
- ► What is the conflict?

- ▶ What is the final product?

- ▶ Who will want to use my idea?

- ▶ Who will want to buy my idea?

- ▶ What is the payoff for my audience?

If you can answer these questions, you are ready to move a step forward in the production pipeline.

Script/Screenplay

The *script* or *screenplay* is the formal written form of the final story. It has written within it the basic character movements, environment, time, actions, and dialogue. This literary form is intended for the preproduction and production team to create a visual idea of the overall story. Many people on the preproduction and production teams will look at the script and will need to be able to gather information from it quickly.

3D animation final products are usually stories you are showing—not telling—the audience. Therefore, a script is not typically the final product for an audience to sit and read. Most people who do not work in a visual storytelling industry would not understand why some descriptions are included in a script or left out of a script. The script must describe what will be seen and heard onscreen for different production teams to know what will be created. The script format is a specific one, and knowing what should and should not be described in a good script or screenplay takes practice.

The final script is the written backbone structure for the rest of the production. The typical format for a written script usually equals about 1 minute of screen time per page. This format is fairly standard among the 3D animation and film industries.

Many script-writing software packages are available on the market today. These software packages help a scriptwriter focus on only the content of the story and not the final script formatting.

The typical length of a script depends on the type of project. A feature-film script is about 100 to 120 pages in length. A 30-minute TV-episode script is about 15 to 22 pages. But wait, you say, a 30-minute TV episode should be about 30 pages in length if a page of a script equals about a minute of screen time. But you have to remember that a 30-minute TV episode is usually about only 22 minutes long, because there are about 8 minutes worth of commercials to fill the 30 minutes. Figure 2.2 shows the typical written format for a script.

```
FADE IN:

1    INT. ANIMATED FOREST - DAY (CGI-CREATED FANTASY WORLD)

     A clearing in a creepy animated forest.  Leafless trees.  An
     ill wind. The SNAP of branches. Something approaches.  An
     Orc-ish warrior (CARL) in a green hat bursts into the
     clearing.  He's carrying a battle axe, running zig-zag.

                         CARL
              Serpentine, Brent!  Serpentine!

     He races across, plunges into the trees on the far side.

     A sickly Elf (BRENT) stumbles into the clearing.  Pauses,
     glances around, terrified, then runs into the forest beyond.

     Silence.  Then a young, tom-boyish Sorceress (SHAUNA)
     strides into the clearing.  She stops, surveys the
     situation.

     RUSTLING from the far side of the clearing as Carl and Brent
     part the branches and peek from a bush at Shauna.

                         SHAUNA
              Quit screwing around.  Get over
              here.

     Shauna scans the surrounding forest as the two approach.

                         BRENT
              Maybe there was a mutiny and Alex
              got himself killed.

                         CARL
              Yeah, fragged by his own troops.

     A weird noise in the distance.

                         SHAUNA
              (No, he's too devious for
              that.  I've got a feeling he's
              still out there.
                   (To Brent)
              Get the spyglass and see if
              anyone's around.

     Brent removes a small, hand held telescope from his shoulder
     bag.  He puts it to his eye, peers into the woods.


                                               (CONTINUED)
```

Image © Matt Mullins and Rich Swingley

FIGURE 2.2 This example of a film script shows basic written formatting.

Storyboard

The *storyboard* is the visual story form of the script/screenplay. You can think of it as a comic book of your script. A storyboard is also the first visual representation of your entire story. It includes early ideas of camera staging, early representations of possible visual effects, and some key character poses or scene events that will be in the project. Each image in a storyboard visually depicts a story beat, or moment, from the script. Figure 2.3 shows an example of a storyboard.

Image © Brian Ludwick and The Basement Design + Motion

FIGURE 2.3 A small snippet of a storyboard from a short animated film

Storyboards are also another way to come up with and write a story. Many animators skip the script/screenplay stage because of their lack of training in formal writing and use the storyboard as the script. For a visual artist, this can be the fastest and most effective way to work through a story. There is a saying that *a picture is worth a thousand words,* and after you see a story, you will see opportunities to make that story better. A storyboard shows gaps and continuity holes in the story that will need to be tidied up.

Storyboards can be anything from quick thumbnail sketches on the back of a napkin to a fully developed idea created by a team of story artists, using the latest and greatest software and digital art tools. But in the end, a storyboard is what is used for the whole production team to visually understand what is going on in the project. So if your team is composed of 2 friends, the bar napkin will probably be enough. But if your team includes 200 or more artists, you will need to have a fully developed final storyboard.

It is, in my opinion, worth the time and effort to create a fully realized and developed version of your storyboard. The storyboard is the glue that will tie together all of the next production steps. More and more animation industries are taking the time to storyboard their projects. Industries such as product visualization and architecture use storyboards to indicate the way that a product should break apart to best describe the product or the best way to have a camera fly through the building to show all the amenities.

Animatic/Pre-visualization

An *animatic* is a moving form of the storyboard. If you think of a storyboard as a comic book, an animatic is a limited animation of your entire story. The animatic can be created in just about any way you create a simple movie on the computer. It is, in its most simple form, just the storyboard images timed out to temporary dialogue and simple sound effects, to show the sequence pacing of the project. The preproduction team will go back and forth between the storyboards and animatic to create the final edit of the entire project.

The animatic allows the director and editor to create the editing style and pacing for the entire project. It is easy to look at individual shots of 3D animation by themselves and think they are complete, but when you put many of the shots together, they may not flow visually. Directors of live-action films and TV can shoot from multiple angles, and all those different camera angles provide many options for editing the footage in postproduction. 3D animation does not allow for cutting in the postproduction stage; cutting animation shots or sequences in postproduction is entirely too expensive unless absolutely necessary. Thus, one of the major differences between animated films and television compared to live-action film and television is that the final edit for an animated project is in the preproduction stage, not the postproduction stage. An example of an animatic video can be viewed from the book's companion files, available at www.sybex.com/go/3danimationessentials.

The *pre-visualization*, or *pre-vis*, is typically utilized for visual effects in live-action films. Because the amount of 3D animation or 3D visual effects that go into these types of films and television shows is expensive, producers of these projects like to know what all of the shots will look like before they are shot. This can be helpful to the director and director of photography in knowing what type of camera angles to shoot on set to match the visual effects. It also can help the actors understand what kind of big scary monster is about to eat them or throw them through a building. A lot of live-action directors have a hard time at first making the jump into animation and visual effects–heavy films because of the complexity of these projects in the preproduction stage.

Design

In the *design* component, the final look of the project is decided. For the entertainment industries, this includes the character design, prop design, costumes, and environment designs. Preproduction designers or concept artists use just about any medium to create their conceptual art—from pen, pencil, charcoal, pastels, or traditional paints to computer software such as Adobe Photoshop or Corel Painter. Figure 2.4, Figure 2.5, Figure 2.6, and Figure 2.7 show examples of concept art.

It does not matter what is used to create the art, just that the concept and design is fully conveyed. The final look of the art often reflects the artist creating it. But the most important aspect is that the mood and concept must be fully realized. The reason for the design component being in the preproduction stage is that a concept artist can quickly draw many options for a character design in a day and then finalize a design to a director's liking. In contrast, a professional 3D modeler can take up to a week to create a final model, and the director would not want to wait that long to then change the concept of what that model should look like.

Image © The Basement Design + Motion

FIGURE 2.4 A simple character in the default-modeling pose

Image © Kelli Davis

FIGURE 2.5 Character concept sketches

Image © Dan Baldwin

FIGURE 2.6 An environment design

Image © Kelli Davis

FIGURE 2.7 An environment sketch

Working in 3D Animation Production

The budgets have been made, the plans have been created, and 3D production artists have been hired. Now the *production* stage can start. At this stage, all of your planning and decision making from the preproduction stage pays off. All of the preproduction material and designs are handed off to the appropriate artist to be brought to fruition. This stage is where all of the final visual elements of a 3D animation project are created. This is when the assembly-line concept truly comes into play. Each artist is responsible for a small part of the project and then must hand it off for the next artist's contribution.

If the preproduction stage is done well, the production stage becomes much easier. The goal of the preproduction stage is to foresee as many problems and make as many design decisions as you can. You do not want your production artists having to guess at what they are supposed to be creating. For instance, your modeling team having to design the characters, environment, and props while they are actually modeling will take too long, and you do not want to be making story arc changes after the animators have already animated sequences in the animation stage. The production stage is time-consuming enough to create all that is needed in the tight deadlines given in today's market without having to worry about design principles, or even worse, having to re-create an asset after it has been made. I am not going to say that spontaneous design changes do not happen in the production stage, but usually these are add-ons to the components and not total design changes.

The production stage includes the following components:

- ▶ Layout
- ▶ Research and development (R&D)
- ▶ Modeling
- ▶ Texturing
- ▶ Rigging/setup
- ▶ Animation
- ▶ 3D visual effects (VFX)
- ▶ Lighting/rendering

Figure 2.8 shows a humorous way of thinking about the production line in 3D animation.

PRODUCTION

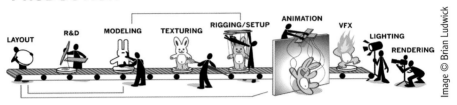

Image © Brian Ludwick

FIGURE 2.8 A way to envision the assembly line of the 3D-animation production stage

Layout

In the 3D *layout* stage, you create a 3D version of the animatic. This component is vital because in the 2D animatic, you can often cheat in terms of factors such as perspective angles, scale of characters to camera, or the distance objects are from one another—but in 3D, it is sometimes difficult to cheat these things. A 3D layout artist starts with the 2D animatic and begins matching the different shots with a 3D camera, 3D characters, and a 3D environment. The 3D layout becomes the new blueprint guide for the rest of the 3D animation production team. An added bonus to this 3D layout stage is that the director can now work out any complex camera moves that you just cannot draw out easily in a traditional storyboard and 2D animatic.

The 3D layout is one of the stages that can begin in the preproduction stage and move into the postproduction stage. 3D layout should begin as soon as you have created *proxy geometry*—low-resolution representations of your final models. These include the scale and basic shape of the object. You can see the difference between a proxy model and a final model in Figure 2.9.

A layout artist takes basic information such as the characters' size, shape, and environment and begins simple animation of the characters and the cameras. For the 3D layout, the proxy models do not need extra attributes such as a face or even fingers to describe the visual story. Basic animation transformation information—indicating, for example, a character moving from point A to point B, or the direction that the character is facing to the camera—is all that is needed. The characters or moving props usually just float from one area to another. But this basic animation allows the director to really start designing the composition of each shot from the camera's point of view.

Layout today can be very sophisticated, enabling the director to have a clear vision of what a sequence will look like. The layout can include lighting and even visual effects.

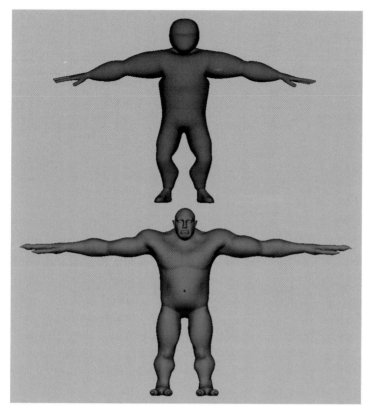

FIGURE 2.9 A proxy representation (top) and the final model (bottom)

The 3D layout edit file will also grow with the rest of production as the production moves forward. The edit files are typically created in an Avid system or in video-editing software packages such as Adobe Premiere or Apple's Final Cut Pro. The production team can add the final voice-over work from the actors, begin composing the final musical score, and add *foley* (live recording of sound effects synced to the film) to the project after the 3D layout is completed. You can now easily insert your rough and final animation takes into the 3D layout to see how they are reading next to one another in the final edit. Directors and animators can make sure that the camera moves and the continuity of the whole project holds up after the animation is added.

The 3D layout stage also allows many other components of the production stage to begin working sooner than they usually would in the pipeline. Later in the production cycle, the layout artist will begin *set dressing* (adding all the major and minor final props to the environments) the sets for final animation checks and preparing for the lighting component. Figure 2.10 shows the basic look of a 3D layout.

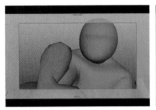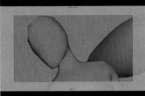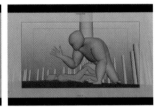

FIGURE 2.10 Images from a 3D layout in sequential order to demonstrate the basic look of the images

Research and Development

Technical director (TD) is a very broad job title in the 3D animation industry. It can mean just about anything, depending on which studio you are at.

Research and development (also known as *R&D*) is a component that also spans the entire 3D animation pipeline, from preproduction to postproduction. In R&D, a team of artists from many different components work with technical directors on upcoming technical challenges in the project. For example, in Pixar's *Finding Nemo*, the R&D team had to figure out how to create the look of water, including the little floaty things in the water. At the time of that film's production, with a release date of 2003, no 3D animated film had depicted water, because it was considered too difficult to control and render efficiently. Yet *Finding Nemo* had water elements in almost every shot. So getting the look and movement of water was very important to master during the production. In the 2010 release of *Tangled* by Walt Disney Animation Studios, the R&D team had to create a way for the animators to control Rapunzel's hair but still get it to flow and move like real hair. This one task took the R&D team several years to complete. In DreamWorks Animation's *Monsters vs. Aliens*, released in 2009, the R&D team had to create a system enabling the animators to control B.O.B., the blue gelatinous blob character. The R&D team's challenge was to make a character that had no real shape but that could be animated with a shape when needed.

Many studios are now doing their R&D on creating a workflow for *stereoscopy* (stereoscopic 3D), to work with 3D animated characters in a live-action background plate. A shot is filmed with a stereoscopic camera that stages the composition in a way that enables a 3D character to be placed into it later. R&D teams are always working on the next best thing and are more than likely creating an effect we have not yet seen.

Modeling

Everything that needs to be seen onscreen or rapid-prototyped has to be modeled. A *model* is a geometric surface representation of an object that can be rotated and viewed in a 3D-animation software package.

There are many techniques for creating 3D models. You can create them from scratch in a 3D-animation software package such as Autodesk's Maya, 3ds Max, or Softimage. You can use laser scanner technology to scan a real object and create a digital 3D representation of that object. You can digitally sculpt your object as if it were clay in software packages such as Autodesk's Mudbox or Pixologic's ZBrush. Models can be created procedurally, which means that mathematical algorithm input is used to create an organic 3D pattern or full 3D model. Software packages such as e-on software's Vue enable you to model realistic and stylistic natural environments. You can even use dynamic simulations to create your models or use them to add destruction to a current model.

There are different types of modeling software in the 3D animation industries, and all of them have specific purposes. The entertainment industries typically use Autodesk's Maya, 3ds Max, or Softimage; Luxology's modo; or Side Effects Software's Houdini. These software packages can do more than just modeling—including animation, physical dynamic simulation, texturing, lighting, rendering, and compositing. The modeling processes that these software packages support are polygonal modeling (polys), nonuniform rational basis spline (NURBS), and subdivisional surfaces (subD).

The architecture and product-visualization industries usually model in software packages including Autodesk's AutoCAD, the Robert McNeel & Associates Rhinoceros and Dassault Systemes SolidWorks products, and Google SketchUp Pro. These software packages do not provide as much in terms of an all-encompassing usage with animation, dynamics, and rendering, but do an excellent job of exact-scale production modeling. These types of software primarily use parametric solid modeling techniques, which means they allow the user to draw curves or outlines of objects, and the software fills in the surfaces.

Law and medical industries will use any of the preceding software, depending on their needs for a specific project. These industries will use any of the listed model types to accomplish their project goals as well.

After the models are fully approved, they can go into three different components of production at once. The models can go back to 3D layout to allow the layout artist to use the final models to better align the cameras and set dressing.

The models can go to the texture artist to be painted and shaded. And finally, the models can go to the rigging/setup artist to have the control systems placed in them for animation. Examples of different modeling techniques can be seen in Figure 2.11, Figure 2.12, and Figure 2.13.

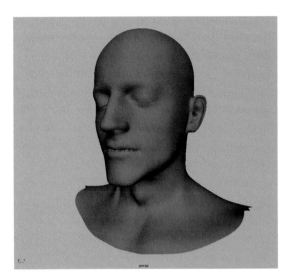

FIGURE 2.11 A head modeled by hand in Autodesk Maya with polygons

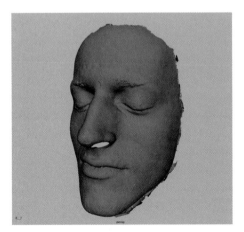

FIGURE 2.12 A raw laser scan of a head by a NextEngine desktop 3D scanner that was then converted into polygon geometry and viewed in Autodesk Maya

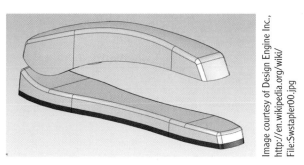

Image courtesy of Design Engine Inc., http://en.wikipedia.org/wiki/File:Swstapler00.jpg

FIGURE 2.13 A parametric model made using SolidWorks

Texturing

In the *texturing* component, texture artists apply color and surface properties to the geometric models. The models generally come to the texture artist in a program's default shaded flat color. The texture artist's job is to make the model's surface look like it does in the concept art or to match its real-world counterpart. If the model is to be a wood table, for example, the texturing artist will make sure that the tabletop when rendered looks like the wood it would be made of. Or if the director changes his or her mind, as directors often do, and now wants that tabletop to be metal, the texture artist must make it look like metal.

Texture artists use various software packages and techniques to complete this task. The artist might hand-paint the textures or use photographs to piece together the texture in Adobe Photoshop, for instance. Texture artists can now paint directly on the 3D object in real time in software packages such as Autodesk's Mudbox, Maxon's BodyPaint 3D, or Pixologic's ZBrush. Figure 2.14 shows a model before texturing in the default gray color, and the same model after textures are painted.

Images © After Hours Animation

FIGURE 2.14 Final model before textures have been applied (left) and the same model after the textures have been applied (right)

Rigging/Setup

Rigging is the component of the production pipeline during which a control rig is put into a geometric object so the animators can move that object. It is the rigger's job to aid the animators by creating a system of controls that allow the animators to work as quickly and efficiently as possible. Every object that moves in any 3D animation project will have some kind of system to control it.

This control system can range from a simple parent/child hierarchy to a very complex character rig including joints, controllers, skinning/enveloping, a muscle system, and a floating GUI (graphical user interface) in the work view to aid the animator's selections and keyframing. If you have no idea about the meaning of any of the terms in the preceding sentence, do not worry. I explain it all in the next few chapters.

This component is quite technical and requires an artist with good problem-solving skills. The rigging artist often works closely with or on the R&D team. Figure 2.15 shows a final character model with its control rig—the curves the animators can select to assist moving the object.

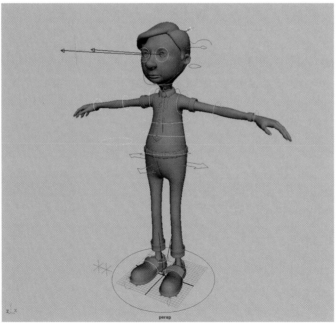

Image © After Hours Animation

FIGURE 2.15 Final model with its control rig turned on

Animation

In the *animation* component, the movement of objects or characters is created. The animators take the layout file as a starting point to get the characters, set, and camera into a scene and then add the final performance or movement.

In the entertainment industries, the animator crafts the performance of the characters. Character animators are typically thought of as the actors in the animated projects. The animators must make the audience believe that what they are seeing onscreen is real and alive. Character animators must understand weight and timing but also be able to provide a physical acting performance that creates a personality for that character that can be understood onscreen.

The types of animation that can be used are hand-keyframed animation (in which an animator creates each pose and sets keyframes for them), motion capture (in which an animator transfers the motion captured from an actor to a control rig and cleans up the motion), and procedural animation (in which a programmer creates a set of rules and the character moves according to those rules). This is a simple explanation of character animation. A more in-depth explanation is presented in Chapter 6, "Animation and Rigging." In most entertainment industries' production pipelines, the animation stage is the most time-consuming component of the production stage.

The scientific industries do not need the same type of animation as the entertainment industry. The scientific industries rely on spinning objects, breakaway animation of products or organic systems, camera fly-throughs of buildings, and organic motions of natural occurrences. This type of animation relies heavily on procedural animations and some hand-keyed motion.

Animation is a skill that not every 3D artist is good at, and poor animation can kill any 3D project. Even if the models are perfect and the lighting is great, unrealistic or distracting motion will pull your audience out of watching your project; instead they'll be noticing the bad movement. Therefore, it is important to have talented animators on your production team.

3D Visual Effects

The 3D *visual effects (VFX)* artist animates everything but the characters or props the characters interact with—for example, fur, hair, cloth, fire, water, and dust, to name just a few. This component, like rigging/setup, is a technical job that also needs an artistic eye. Most 3D visual effects are based on a dynamic physics engine within software that uses natural physics such as air, gravity, and drag to manipulate these systems. So a basic understanding of physics and math is an absolute must. But a 3D VFX artist must also have a subtle artist's touch.

The types of effects a 3D VFX artist works on are often called *invisible effects*, because the goal of these effects is to enhance the shots they are in, not to overshadow them. The 3D VFX artist's job is to have the audience not even notice that the effects are there, unless you are, let's say, blowing up an entire planet and want everyone to see it.

Lighting/Rendering

Lighting is the painting component of the production stage. The lighting artists look at the color guides from the preproduction stage and create the lighting and mood for a scene or sequence. Lighting in a 3D application is similar to the real-world lighting of film or photography. 3D lighters have access to multiple light types that mimic lights in the real world—for example spotlights, lightbulbs, and sunlight.

After setting up all the lights, the lighter will break the scene into *render passes*, which are individual parts of the rendering process. In these render passes, you can render out parts of the whole scene, such as individual objects, shadows, highlights, color, and much more. These passes are put back together again in the compositing component of the postproduction stage. Chapter 7, "Lighting, Rendering, and Visual Effects," contains a more in-depth explanation of render passes and compositing. In Figure 2.16, you can see a final rendered and composited still from an animated short film. This image was composed from 16 render passes.

FIGURE 2.16 Image of a still from a short animated film

Working in 3D Animation Postproduction

Postproduction is the completion and output stage of a 3D animation project, but again this can mean different outcomes for different industries. The entertainment industries use this stage to really make a project stand out through visual effects and color corrections. This is the icing on the cake that makes a project look polished and professional. The scientific industries use this stage to double-check the accuracy of projects and to output projects to their chosen media.

Outputs in the scientific industries could be rapid prototypes, video fly-throughs, video demonstrations, or raw point-cloud data. (Point-cloud data is covered in depth in Chapter 9, "Industry Trends.")

You may have heard the saying *fix it in post*, and as much as I hate to admit it as a 3D artist who would like to have the production stage be perfect every time, sometimes fixing things in postproduction is more cost-effective than committing hours of rendering time to fix a shot. The postproduction stage is where you can make a project that once looked amateurish look professional instead. Postproduction artists have access to many tools that can make or break the final look of a project—tools such as compositing software, motion graphics software, editing software, color correction software, and final output options.

Postproduction can be a simple and fast process if the preproduction and production teams planned for issues that may arise in postproduction. But having proper planning is not always enough to ensure a smooth postproduction. Clients often change their minds mid-project, and a production that is in progress cannot just start over. So it will usually come down to the postproduction artist to have to make these fixes at the end of a production. For instance, many feature films do not start out as 3D stereoscopic films, but become 3D stereo films because the production companies think that type of film will make more money. Starting with a nonstereoscopic film and adding the 3D stereo effect can be difficult and time-consuming. The postproduction team must be able to troubleshoot a solution to meet just about any want or need of the client, as long as the client is willing to pay extra for it.

The postproduction stage includes the following components:

- ► Compositing
- ► 2D visual effects (VFX)/motion graphics
- ► Color correction
- ► Final output

Compositing

In *compositing*, the postproduction artist can layer all of the imagery created and filmed to make a final output image. This layering can be a simple task with only a few layers to manage, or it can become a complex task with hundreds of layers matched together. The imagery can be all 3D generated images; 3D and 2D graphics mixed; or 3D, 2D, and live-action film plates.

2D Visual Effects/Motion Graphics

2D visual effects and *motion graphics* are often mixed into the compositing stage. The compositor and 2D visual effects artists can be the same artist, but at some studios they are not. The lighting artist may complete the initial composite for a shot and then pass the pre-comp on to the 2D visual effects artist to work on and finalize. The 2D visual effects artist will add effects that are much simpler to achieve at the end of a project in a 2D application than in a 3D application. The following are examples of such effects:

This list of 2D effects just scratches the surface of those that can be completed in postproduction.

▶ Sparks

▶ Pixie dust

▶ Dust

▶ Rain drops

▶ Background replacements

▶ Camera shake

▶ Green-screen removal

▶ Rotoscoping

Rotoscoping **is the act of tracing an object in film or video to be able to add or remove that object.**

A motion-graphics artist uses the same techniques as a 2D visual artist, and again may be the same artist as the 2D visual effects artist. But the motion-graphics artist's job is to create the graphical design elements of a shot if needed. This type of work can be seen in film title sequences and in television station bumpers.

Color Correction

Bumpers **are the 2- to 10-second station logos that are animated between shows.**

Color correction, also known as *color timing* or *color grading*, is when the entire project is adjusted to make sure all imagery color is consistent and matches the final output source. All 3D animation projects are worked on as individual shots, and then looked at in sequences and finally as a whole project. A *shot* is created every time the camera changes, and there are thousands of shots in a feature film. Each shot needs to be corrected to achieve the look of the film. Color correction can be very artistic and highly technical at the same time. It takes an expert eye and lots of practice to become good at color correction. Figure 2.17 shows a before-and-after example of color correction.

FIGURE 2.17 A shot before (left) and after (right) color correction

Final Output

The final output of 3D animation can come in many different forms: film, video, Internet, rapid prototyping, 3D stereoscopic film and print media. Each of these output types have different workflows and technical limitations that are beyond the scope of this book. But the most common output type is digital video that can be played on the computer or Internet. The largest technical limitation to this type is color correction because not everyone's computer and monitor is calibrated and will look different. More on this topic in Chapter 3, "Digital Imaging and Video."

Using Production Tools

In a 3D animation production pipeline, a domino effect can easily happen if one of the stages or components is not completed fully or correctly and the project moves forward in the pipeline. This mistake will cause a huge blockage in the pipeline, and fixing that blockage can mean having to backtrack a few steps in the production. Having to backtrack or stop production is a significant problem because time is money in the animation industry.

The goal of a production pipeline is to minimize that domino effect. The 3D animation industry is collaborative. At times, such as in the film industry, hundreds of people will work on one single project. A well-thought-out and planned production pipeline is the most efficient way to keep everyone working toward one goal and keep all artists on the same page, even if they are not in the same room, the same building, the same city, the same state, or the same country.

Let's return to the car assembly-line analogy from the start of the chapter. In a car assembly line, each stage of that assembly line must be physically close to one another. Cars are big and heavy objects and cannot be moved around freely until they're fully assembled. But in 3D animation, the only thing that gets moved around are computer files. As computers have become more powerful, more affordable, and smaller, it is no longer a necessity for everyone working on a 3D animation project to be in the same place. More and more 3D animation artists are working from home and can work at the level of quality needed on a home computer workstation. Working from home is not always the best case on medium to large productions, because it limits the spontaneity of sharing ideas and critiques with other creative people in the studio environment. However, it does allow independent film or video game producers to recruit higher-caliber talent from around the world if needed.

So how do you keep everyone involved in a 3D animation project efficiently informed and up-to-date even if they are not in the same building or country as you? There are some basic tools you can use to make sure everyone is in the know.

Production Bible

A *production bible* is collection of forms and documents—such as production timelines and asset-tracking sheets—of an entire 3D animation project to allow management and artists to know what has been completed in the pipeline and what is still a work in progress. This production bible used to be a physical three-ring binder that the management team would all have to keep updated on a day-to-day basis. Many studios have made the production bible digital for faster updates and universal access by all involved. A great way of putting all of these documents in a central digital place without having your own team of computer scientists involved is Google Docs. Having all of these documents on Google Docs allows multiple users to look at and update the documents at the same time.

A *production timeline* is an estimated schedule of all of the stages of production. How are the estimated times calculated? Well, having a general sense of the time it takes to complete each production stage requires a lot of experience. The project's producer creates a large timeline of the entire project and then looks at the amount of work each stage of the production pipeline should take.

A producer also uses the *production triangle* (Figure 2.18) to help decide the goals of a project.

FIGURE 2.18 The production triangle

This production triangle illustrates the basic types of choices a producer must make when organizing a project and creating a timeline. In the production triangle, you can choose only two of the three corners. Your project can be fast and cheap, but the overall quality of the project will be lacking. Your project can be cheap and good, but it will take much longer to complete than normal. Or your project can be good and fast, but it will cost you a lot more than normal projects. A production timeline can look like just about anything, as long as it makes sense to the people it affects. Typical types of production timelines are as follows:

Gantt Charts These bar charts display start and finish dates for different stages of a production and indicate how long they should take to complete (see Figure 2.19).

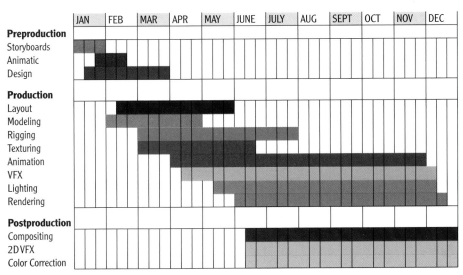

FIGURE 2.19 An example of a Gantt chart for animation

PERT   The Program Evaluation and Review Technique (PERT) was designed by the U.S. Navy to analyze and represent tasks required to complete a project. Milestones that must be completed are indicated by numbers typically enclosed within a circle or rectangle. The lines show the paths to each milestone, which is dependent on the milestone before it. The *t* stands for the expected time of completion; the *o* and the *m* stand for optimistic time and most likely time, respectively (see Figure 2.20).

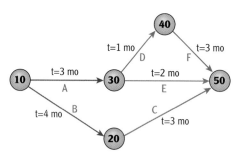

FIGURE 2.20 A PERT chart

Calendars   Sometimes just a basic calendar is used, with colorized individual start and finish dates of the production components, and an outline to highlight the production milestones needed to complete the project.

Production Boards   A production board is simply a board or a wall on which pieces of colored paper are placed. Project milestones are written on the papers and placed in the order they will be completed. This is not at all a high-tech method but a useful one in a small- to medium-sized studio, where all the artists are in the same room and can always see the board.

In addition, production software can be purchased to create these types of charts automatically, to help you create a timeline. Examples include Jungle Software's Gorilla, Entertainment Partners' Movie Magic Scheduling (formerly EP Scheduling), and Progeny Software's Timeline Maker. The prices of these software options range from $100 to $400.

Anything you see in a 3D animation project must be created by an artist, and everyone else on the project must know of that asset and of its current status—from characters, to props, products, buildings, roads, trash, individual leaves on trees, and even blades of grass. *Asset-tracking sheets* are documents that allow artists and management to know who is working on what, and the current status of each project asset. The basic types of sheets are as follows:

Shot Sheet   The director and producers use shot sheets to keep track of each shot in a project. With projects such as film that have thousands of shots, it can become difficult to know what every shot is at any moment. A shot sheet has the name of the project at the top, the shot name, the frame count or time code for the shot, a description of the shot, and if possible, an image from the shot from the animatic or layout for quick shot recognition. Shot sheets are updated frequently during a production to make sure all shots and any changes are up-to-date. Figure 2.21 shows a sample shot sheet.

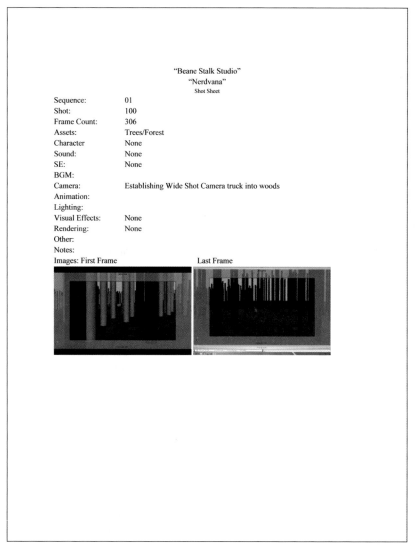

FIGURE 2.21 Sample shot sheet from a short film

Model-Tracking Sheet   Within the model-tracking sheet is the name of every model in the production, the name of the artist asked to complete the model, the anticipated date for that model's completion, and then the date of its actual completion. These sheets usually include the assignments of texturing and rigging artists as well. Table 2.1 is a template for a model-tracking sheet.

TABLE 2.1   Template for a Model-Tracking Sheet

Asset Name	Dept.	Artist	Date Assigned	Model Completed	Texture Completed	Rig Completed	Final Completed
	Model						
	Texture						
	Rig						
	Final						
	Model						
	Texture						
	Rig						
	Final						
	Model						
	Texture						
	Rig						
	Final						

Animation-Tracking Sheet   Much as model-tracking sheets track individual assets, animation-tracking sheets track the individual animation and layout shots. In the entertainment industries, the animation stage is typically the longest component to complete and has the most artists. So keeping track of all the shots is important. The animation-tracking sheet lists each shot, the animator assigned to the shot, and due dates for that shot. Table 2.2 shows a template.

Lighting/Rendering–Tracking Sheet Lighting- and rendering-tracking sheets track the progress of the final phases of the production stage. This sheet enables producers and lighting artists to know where they are in the lighting and rendering process. As on other tracking sheets, the shots are listed with artists assigned to them, due dates, and completion dates. Figure 2.22 shows part of a lighting- and rendering-tracking sheet in use.

TABLE 2.2 Template for an Animation-Tracking Sheet

Shot Name	Layout	Rough Animation	Final Animation
Name of shot	*Name of artist/date*	*Name of artist/date*	*Name of artist/date*

Shot	Animation	Basic Lighting	DOF Rendered	Amboc Rendered	Beauty Rendered	Pre Comp	Notes	Extra Lights	Extra Lights Rendered	Additive Notes	Final Comp	Things to Fix
Seq 1												
100	Done	Done	Done	Done	Done	Done	Done	9/12/2010	9/13/2010		9/14/2010	
110	Done	Done	Done	Done	Done	Done	Done	9/12/2010	9/13/2010		9/14/2010	
120	Done	Done	Done	Done	Done	Done	Done	9/12/2010	9/13/2010		40438	Re-Rendered Comp 1-1-11
130	Done	Done	Done	Done	Done	Done	Done	9/12/2010	9/13/2010		40438	
140	Done	Done	Done	Done	Done	Done	Done	9/22/2010	Done	Needs hair on male worker, and bald female worker		
150	Done	Done	Done	Done	Done	Done		9/23/2010	Done			
155	Done	Done	Done	Done	Done	Done		10/6/2010	Done			
160	Done	Done	Done	Done	Done	Done	Done	9/22/2010	Done			
170	Done	Done	Done	Done	Done	Done	Done	9/27/2010render	1/14/2011			
180	Done	Done	Done	Done	Done	Done	Done	10/18/2010Rendering	1/14/2011			
190	Done	Done	Done	Done	Done	Done	Done	10/18/2010Rendering	1/14/2011			
200	Done	Done	Done	Done	Done	Done	Done	10/19/2010Rendering	1/18/2011			
210	Done	Done	Done	Done	Done	Done	Done	10/21/2010Rendering	11/17/2011			
220	Done	Done	Done	Done	Done	Done	Done	1/3/2011Rendering	1/17/2001			
230	Done	DoneTest	Done	Done	Done	Done	Done	1/4/2011Rendering	1/17/2011			Made new scene
240	Done	Done	Done	Done	Done	Done	Done	1/4/2011Rendering	1/17/2011			
250	Done	Done	Done	Done	Done	Done	Done	1/22/2011	new precomp			Put in Key and Fill. Started the render.
260_270	Done	Done	Dan	Dan	Dan/ can't move forward until characters are fixed (no movement)	Dan	Done	N/A				
280	CUT	CUT	CUT	CUT	CUT		CUT	CUT	CUT		CUT	
290	APPROVED		Adam	Adam (Redo)	Adam (Redo	Andy	Done	Liz. Running out of memory, won't render		needs AO inside		
CUT295	Kristen Done	Done	wong	Wong	Wong	Wong						
300	Done	Done	Done	Done	Done	Done	Done	N/A				
310	Done	Done	Done	Done	Done	Done	Done	1/3/2011	Done			
320	Done	Done	Done	Done	Done	Done	Done	1/3/2011	Done			
335 Is this the right shot	Kristen Redo Matt and Molly animation????????	Done/No Time Warp	Not Needed	Done	Store rendered, Characters not	rendering	Done	1/3/2011	Done	need inside light rendered		need the inside sun light
340	Done	Done	Done	Done	Done	Done	Done	1/3/2011	1/4/2011			Ready for the SUN & Moon animation
295 1	Done	Andy	Andy	Andy	Andy	Andy		Done	Done			Shots are in the Animation folder
297	Clock shot CU	Done	Done	Done	Done	Andy						
298	M Clock	Done	Done	Done	Done	Andy						
300	Push In	Done	Done	Done	Done	Andy						
305	Push Out	Done	Done	Done	Done	Andy						
Seq 2												
100	Done	Done	Done	Done	Done	Done	Done	N/A				
110	Jordan	Re-Done	Done	Done	**Finished**	Done	Done	N/A				
120_140	Done	Done	Done	Done	Done	Done	Done	N/A				
130	Done	Done	Done	Done	Done	Done	Done	N/A				
140	CUT	CUT	CUT	CUT	CUT		CUT	CUT	CUT		CUT	CUT
150	Done	Re-Done	Done	Done	Done	Done	Done	N/A				
160_170	Done	Done	Done	Done	Done	Done	Done	1/5/2011Rendering	1/17/2011			
180	Done	Done	Done	Done	Done	Done	Done	N/A				
190	Kristen/DONE	Kinda done		Done	Done	Done	Done	1/5/2011Rendering				
210	Chris DONE	Done	Done	Done	Done	Done	Done	1/5/2011Rendering	1/17/2011	Not sure what happened		
220	Kristen	Done	Done	Done	Done	Done	Done	1/6/2011Rendering	1/17/2011			
230	Done	Done	Done	Done	Done	Done	Done	N/A				
240	CUT	CUT	CUT	CUT	CUT		CUT	CUT	CUT		CUT	CUT
250	Done	Done	Done	Done	Done	Done	Done	1/6/2011Rendering	1/17/2011			
260	Done	Done	Done	Done	Done	Done	Done	N/A				
270	Done	Done	Done	Done	Done	Done	Done	N/A				

FIGURE 2.22 A lighting- and rendering-tracking sheet in use

Folder Management and Naming Conventions

Folder management and naming conventions are one of the invisible tools of a production pipeline that a lot of people may take for granted until someone does not use them correctly. With so many people working on a project, there must be a unified naming convention for file and folder management. A production cannot afford the lost time searching for a misnamed or misplaced file. I know it sounds silly, but with projects having thousands of files and hundreds of folders, files can and will become lost. Folder names and filenames can be anything as long as they are unified and consistent. Typically, short and descriptive names are best, but again the names can be anything.

THE ESSENTIALS AND BEYOND

Because most 3D animators specialize in one or two different jobs and may not ever work in any other jobs, it is vital that beginning 3D artists understand the entire 3D pipeline, and how their work will affect the next stages in a production. You now understand how the entire 3D animation production pipeline works, from the basic three stages of a production—preproduction, production, and postproduction—to the individual components of those stages. With so many components to complete, it is easy to see that missing a step in the 3D animation production pipeline can cause many problems. But getting all of the stages and components correct can make for a fun and efficient workplace.

REVIEW QUESTIONS

1. Preproduction includes which component?

    A. Storyboards   C. Modeling

    B. Animation   D. Lighting

2. True or false: A 3D animation production pipeline is similar to a car assembly line.

3. Which of these is not one of the three main stages of a production pipeline?

    A. Postproduction   C. Visual effects

    B. Preproduction   D. Production

4. What is typically the longest stage to complete in the production pipeline?

    A. Animation   C. Postproduction

    B. Preproduction   D. Modeling

(Continues)

THE ESSENTIALS AND BEYOND *(Continued)*

5. What tool might a concept artist use to create art?

    A. Pencil   **C.** Computer

    B. Paint   **D.** All of the above

6. Which stage of the production pipeline is the most important?

    A. Preproduction   **C.** Postproduction

    B. Production   **D.** Rigging

7. The _____ component of the preproduction and production stages will create a 3D animatic.

    A. Animation   **C.** Layout

    B. Storyboard   **D.** Character design

8. Why are asset-tracking sheets so important?

    A. To give interns something to do   **C.** To show the project investors all of the work you are doing

    B. To keep everyone involved on the same page   **D.** All of the above

9. Name two of the of production timeline chart types.

    A. Gantt   **C.** Production board

    B. NotePad   **D.** Back of a napkin

10. One page of a script usually equals about how much onscreen time?

    A. 1 minute   **C.** 5 minutes

    B. 2 minutes   **D.** 10 minutes

CHAPTER 3

Understanding Digital Imaging and Video

Because 3D animation is integrally tied to the computer, it is vital that you learn as much about computer graphics as possible. That doesn't mean you need to learn how to write code and begin creating your own image formats and codecs, but a good grasp of how the computer displays your images will help you tremendously in your day-to-day work. This understanding will enable you to create better imagery and make you a more employable 3D artist. This chapter provides an overview of digital imaging and video to give you a broad base to build your foundation of knowledge and create great 3D.

▶ **Understanding digital imaging**

▶ **Understanding digital video**

Understanding Digital Imaging

Digital imaging is the creation of digital images. These digital images can be created by tools such as digital cameras, digital video cameras, 3D animation software, digital painting programs, digital sculpting programs, and scanners. All of these tools operate under the same fundamental rules and principles of the digital world that determine how an image is displayed with what quality level and physical size of the file. This section presents a few of the larger principles so you can better understand the images you are going to create.

Pixels

What is a pixel? You might say, "I know what a pixel is: a box or rectangle of light that makes up a monitor or television set so we can see images." But it's not quite that simple.

Let's first look at how humans see. In the real world, we see images through our eyes with smooth, continuous color and tone. However, to display these images digitally onscreen, we have to break all the information down into a simpler format that a television or computer can understand.

A *pixel* is a sampling of an image at a certain location. Therefore, pixels do not have any true size or shape. Pixels are the smallest visible units of a digital image on a displayable screen. On a monitor, they are tiny dots or rectangles of red, green, and blue that are grouped together to create a color sample. These groups are typically thought of as being laid out in a perfect two-dimensional grid, as shown in Figure 3.1. But in the real world, there are different types of grid layouts and different shapes of pixels. For instance, a television Cathode Ray Tube or CRT has a striped pattern, a PC CRT has a diagonal pattern, and some laptop Liquid Crystal Display or LCD monitors have a triangular pattern. You can see four versions of these grids in Figure 3.2.

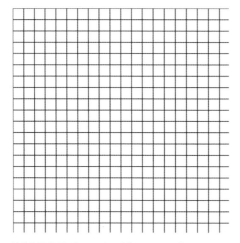

FIGURE 3.1 A grid pattern: the most common misconception of pixel layout

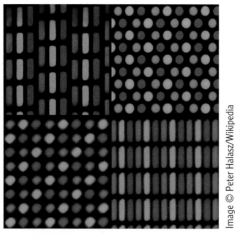

Image © Peter Halasz/Wikipedia

FIGURE 3.2 Examples of pixel geometry on four different monitors

Because a pixel is just a point sample, the more pixels you have, the sharper your digital images become (see Figure 3.3). But the more pixels you have, the more information it takes to display that image. A typical computer monitor displays thousands to millions of these pixels in both directions to depict the images you see onscreen. A standard National Televsion System Committee or NTSC television displays 720 vertical pixels and 480 horizontal pixels, for a total of 345,600 pixels. A 1080 HD television has 1,920 vertical pixels and 1,080 horizontal pixels, or a total of 2,073,600.

FIGURE 3.3 An image displayed at 1280×720 (top), 320×180 (middle), and 80×45 (bottom)

The word *pixel* is also used in other contexts. For example, in the print world, a pixel is known as a *dot*. You may have heard of pixels per inch (ppi) and dots per inch (dpi). Both terms refer to the number of dots per inch that a printer will put down to create an image. As with pixel resolution on a monitor, the more dots you have, the better the representation of the original image. Most monitors today have between 72 and 96 pixels per inch. But for print, that spacing is just not enough. Typically, you need 150 to 300 dpi to get a quality print from today's printers.

So what does knowing what a pixel is have to do with you as a new 3D artist in the 3D animation world? You need to know this background in order to understand display aspect ratio and pixel aspect ratio, presented later in this chapter. In addition, nearly all of your work will be displayed on a monitor or television, so understanding the most basic, visible part of that work is necessary in order to achieve the highest-quality imagery.

Raster Graphics vs. Vector Graphics

All digital images are either raster graphics or vector graphics. This section details both categories.

Raster graphics are built around a data structure that represents your image with points or pixels that are typically viewed on a monitor. In fact, a raster image is the typical image you will see on a computer. Raster graphics are also resolution dependent, which means that at the correct viewing percentage, they will look sharp and clear, but if you zoom in, they will pixelate and lose their overall quality.

Vector graphics are composed of geometrical math-based primitives of lines, points, curves, and polygons. Vector graphics are not resolution dependent and can be scaled to any size without losing any quality.

Figure 3.4 shows a vector graphic and a raster graphic magnified 2,400 times. The vector image is still clean and crisp, but the raster image is pixelated.

Raster graphics are typically viewed and manipulated in programs such as Adobe Photoshop and Corel Painter. These programs have many tools (for example, the Brush, Clone Stamp, Blur, Dodge, Smudge, and Eraser tools) that enable digital artists to change and manipulate images on a pixel level as they see fit. In addition, mid-level and high-end image manipulation software can create custom effects and filters (such as Blur, Pixelate, and Mosaic) that will change the look of your image.

Vector graphics are used in programs such as Adobe Illustrator and Adobe Flash. These programs have detailed tools for drawing lines and points, including the Pen tool, Pencil tool, Shape Builder tool, Line Segment tool, and Type tool. These tools enable artists to create vector shapes and fill them in with color and gradients. You can also add effects to vector graphics, but these effects and filters are much more limited because of the nature of vector art. These effects include drop shadows, inner and outer glows, and pathfinders.

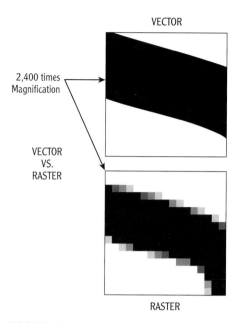

FIGURE 3.4 A raster image and a
vector image magnified 2,400 times

So which is better? There is no real right or wrong answer; it really depends
on the final output and project you are working on. If you are creating a logo,
package design, or other graphic design, vector graphics are preferred. If you are
texture painting, concept painting, or doing other photo-based image manipu-
lations, raster graphics are preferred. But an understanding of both is a good
idea in 3D animation. Many CAD-like programs produce vector-based outputs
or plans to work from. Also, a design company may give you vector graphics to
convert and place on a 3D object as a texture. In 3D animation, the preferred
output methods take all vector graphics and convert them to raster images for
final output to screen and print.

Anti-Aliasing

Have you ever looked at a computer screen and noticed that the edges of some
images look very jagged and others look very smooth? *Anti-aliasing* fixed the
jagged edges of the smooth-looking images.

Figure 3.5 illustrates anti-aliasing. The word on top does not have anti-aliasing
applied, and the word on the bottom does. If you look closely, you will see that
the top word looks jagged along the edges, and the bottom word looks cleaner

and has smoother edges. The zoomed-in letter *A* of both words is magnified 500 percent to emphasize the difference between the two words on a pixel level.

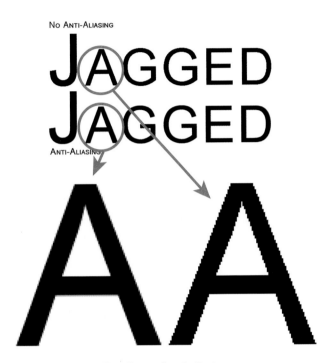

FIGURE 3.5 The effects of anti-aliasing

By default, computer graphics use *point sampling*—a sample of a single point within each pixel—to judge the color of those pixels. The color at the sample point is assumed to be the one and only color of that pixel. (A pixel can be only a single color.) However, simple point sampling is not always accurate, depending on the resolution of the monitor you are using. Figure 3.6 shows a simplified display of red dots that represent the point sample for each pixel. The color of each pixel will be determined by the color under each red dot (in this case, white or black). This will cause stair-stepping in the image, because the pixels split by the diagonal line are not being sampled fully.

Anti-aliasing is a subsampling of pixels that helps determine what color they should truly be. Figure 3.7 shows an example of a computer sampling image data into pixels and then correcting it with anti-aliasing. The image on the left in Figure 3.7 is the original smooth-edged line; the grid on the images represents the resolution of pixels onscreen. If the sample points of the pixels along the edge of the line fall on the black area and make the entire pixel black, you'll get a result like the center image—a stair-stepping effect. But if you add anti-aliasing to the image, more samples will be taken per pixel, and the computer will have a better understanding of what color the pixels should be, resulting in the image on the right.

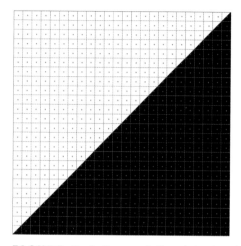

FIGURE 3.6 Representation of simple point sampling

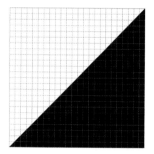 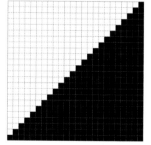 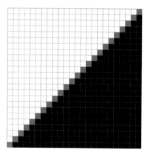

FIGURE 3.7 The original image with a pixel grid overlaid onto it (left), a representation of the simple sampling of pixels to create the image (center), and the image with anti-aliasing applied to create a more accurate image (right)

You can add anti-aliasing (subsampling) to each pixel, as seen in Figure 3.8. The blue dots represent these subsamples, which will help accurately determine what color each pixel should really be.

> **Figure 3.7 is not an accurate representation (as you learned earlier, pixels do not really form a grid pattern), but it's a good way to illustrate anti-aliasing.**

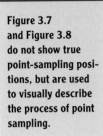

Figure 3.7 and Figure 3.8 do not show true point-sampling positions, but are used to visually describe the process of point sampling.

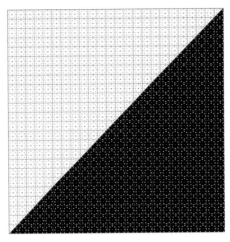

FIGURE 3.8 Representation of anti-aliasing sampling

Why not use anti-aliasing in all of your imagery? There are a few reasons:

A color index is used within image file types to store a set number of colors that the image can display.

▶ Anti-aliasing requires extra computer power. This is no big deal for still images, but for video games that have to run in real time, this extra processing power can be a challenge.

▶ Anti-aliasing can wash out small text so much that it becomes unreadable on a digital display or in print.

▶ Depending on the file type, color bit depth (discussed later in this chapter), and color index you use, anti-aliasing could cause you to overcalculate your color index with too many colors, which can lead to large file sizes or lack of color when needed.

Anti-aliasing within render engines is discussed further in Chapter 7, "Lighting, Rendering, and Visual Effects."

Anti-aliasing affects the quality of the final rendered image. So understanding this will help tremendously in creating a proper quality level in your images. Also anti-aliasing is involved in texture mapping and contrast values as well as in 3D render engines such as mental ray and V-Ray.

Basic Graphic-File Formats

File formats are particular ways of coding information for storage into a computer file. Each format allows specific types of information to be communicated, and each has its own limitations and features, such as compression type, maximum file size, and bit depth. There are many graphic-file types out there today. Some have specific purposes, and others are general in their usage.

In addition, some file formats are proprietary and therefore can be used only for specific purposes within specific software. Others are open formats in which the code is published to the world and can be used by anyone. Here is a list of graphic-file formats and their basic usages, divided into categories of raster and vector image formats:

Raster File Formats

JPG or JPEG (Joint Photographic Experts Group)   Primarily used in the creation and manipulation of photographs, this file format provides smooth transitions in color and tone for color and black-and-white images. This file format is widely used in digital photography and general printing. The format uses lossy compression, meaning that multiple saves can degrade the image, but lossy compression will greatly reduce the total file size to easily be transferred and posted to the Web.

TIFF (Tagged Image File Format)   This file format is widely used among graphic artists, photographers, and the publishing industry. This format can use lossy or lossless compression or no compression at all, which makes it useful in image manipulation over time, as you can avoid degrading the overall image quality. This file type can carry an alpha channel, which is useful in compositing multiple images together.

TGA (Truevision TGA or Targa)   This is used by animation and television artists because it matches NTSC and Phase Alternating Line or PAL video formats. It is a lossless image format that can carry an alpha channel. This file format is more widely used for final outputs to monitors and televisions than for print because of its color depth for high-end printing.

GIF (Graphics Interchange Format)   Because this file format allows only 256 total colors in an image, it is used on the Web for basic lines and color graphics. This file format allows for lossless compression for sharp and crisp lines, and for animation and low-resolution video to be displayed within the image.

PNG (Portable Network Graphics)   This format was created to replace the GIF format. A PNG file provides a greater range of color options than GIF, as it's not limited to only 256 colors and will carry an alpha channel for transparencies. This file format does not allow animations as well.

PSD (Adobe Photoshop Document)   This proprietary file format for Adobe Photoshop is excellent for any digital image that Photoshop supports. This file type can carry alpha channels and image layer options. It uses lossless compression, so no data or quality will be lost.

PDF (Portable Document Format)   This open file format can represent flat documents including text, graphics, fonts, vector lines, and any other information needed to display the image. This image type is used by many industries as a final output option to show work; typically, it is not the file type people natively work in.

EXR (OpenEXR)   Created by Industrial Light & Magic, this high dynamic range imaging (HDRI) file type is used in 3D animation rendering. This file type allows for 16-bits-per-channel floating-point information in a lossy or lossless compression type. This file type also allows for multichannel outputs for 3D rendering in not only RGB (red, green, and blue) channels but also RGBA (red, green, blue, alpha) channels for compositing purposes, such as rendering diffuse, specularity, transparency, and shadow render passes.

Vector File Formats

EPS (Encapsulated PostScript)   This reasonably predictable PostScript file describes the image or text within it to be printed. A PostScript file is full of commands on how to lay out a printed page, not individual pixel information. PostScript files work well with vector graphics, because vectors are based on math and information for curves and points.

AI (Adobe Illustrator)   This proprietary file format is used with Adobe Illustrator. It is specific to vector art and can be opened in other image manipulation programs including Adobe Photoshop, Adobe After Effects, and Corel Paint.

FLA (Adobe Flash File)   This proprietary file format is used in Adobe Flash, vector-type animation software that can be used for traditional animation, web design, and video games.

SWF (ShockWave Flash)   This proprietary file type is linked with Adobe Flash, and can be a self-contained video player and interactive game player. This is a popular file type for games and videos run in web browsers.

Channels

You may be asking yourself "What are these channels we are talking about?" *Channels* are representations of the individual red, green, and blue (RGB, monitor display) or cyan, magenta, yellow, and black (CMYK, print) information of a digital image. A channel, typically seen as a grayscale image by the user, represents the value of one of the specific primary colors included in the final image. Because a channel is grayscale, it symbolizes the 256 tones of the bit depth for the color it represents (RGB) in a 24-bit image. Extra channels can be added for effects and different uses such as transparency and z-depth. These extra channels are not normally used in simple image manipulation but can be helpful in layering multiple images to create a final image composition. Figure 3.9 shows the grayscale representations of an image in Adobe Photoshop's channels.

Alpha channels are the most commonly used extra channels added to the channel mix. The alpha channel is a black-to-white channel that allows for image transparency. White represents opaque, and black is completely transparent. Alpha channels are useful to a 3D animator when rendering in multiple passes in order to layer the passes together in compositing software such as Adobe After Effects. Figure 3.10 shows an example of using an alpha channel to work with two flat color layers. The alpha channel is used to cut the text out of the top layer and display the bottom layer.

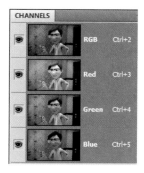

FIGURE 3.9 Screen capture of an image in Adobe Photoshop with the RGB channels open

FIGURE 3.10 The blue solid layer is on top of the green layer, but adding an alpha layer enables the green in the text to show through.

One issue that can come up in 3D rendering is pre-multiplying the RGB channels with the alpha channel. In a *pre-multiplied image*, the edges of the image around the alpha channel are softened to provide a clean cut between the rendered object and the background. But the RBG and the alpha will multiply the softened edges, and the color will begin to darken around the softened edges of the image. This will cause a ring around your object in the compositing stage, as seen in Figure 3.11. Most compositing software can compensate for pre-multiplication, but you should still be aware of the issue.

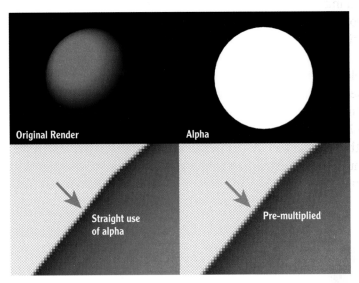

FIGURE 3.11 The original render (top left) and the alpha channel for that render (top right). In compositing software, a straight alpha creates a darkening along this magnified edge (bottom left), but the pre-multiplied option compensates and provides correct color.

Color Depth or Bit Depth

Color depth, or *bit depth*, indicates the number of bits used to represent a single pixel in a raster image. The higher the color depth, the smoother the transition of color and tone between pixels. So what is a bit? The mathematical computer language is called the *binary language* or *binary code*, and is represented with two numbers: 0 and 1. So bit depth is the number of bits of memory allowed per pixel. Because the only possible alternatives per bit are 0 and 1, the bit depth in color will be 2 to the power of x, where x is the allowable bit depth per file type to see how many variations of color a pixel can have. So an 8-bit image can have 256 colors available per pixel ($2^8 = 256$).

Color depth can also be represented in RGB color space with bits per channel. An 8-bit-per-channel or 24-bit image can have 256 colors per red, 256 colors per green, and 256 colors per blue channel, with a total of 16,777,216 colors available (256^3 or $256 \times 256 \times 256$). This 24-bit image type is suitable for displaying most digital images because the human eye can (arguably) see only about 10 million colors. So 16 million–plus colors should be more than enough to create a convincing image. In 3D animation, many people are now using 16-bit-per-channel images, for a total of 281 trillion colors. If we can see only 10 million or so colors, why is this necessary? Well, it comes in handy in image manipulation. When crunching levels on an image and performing color correction, you can get color or tonal banding with 8-bit-per-channel images. There is just not enough information after you begin narrowing the amount of color information with these tools. With the use of a 16-, 24-, or 32-bit-per-channel image, you have much more information to discard during the image manipulation stage without creating the banding effect and other unwanted image issues. Figure 3.12 shows an example of an 8-bit image before and after level manipulation.

▶

Binary code is based on two numbers—0 and 1—and is used like an on/off switch. 0 is off, and 1 is on.

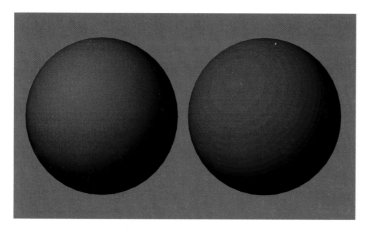

FIGURE 3.12 The original render (left) and the render after a few extreme level changes (right). Notice the banding along the surface of the ball on the right.

Color Calibration

Have you noticed that all computer monitors and televisions look a little different from one another? You may have noticed this if you have looked at a digital picture at home and then had your friends or family open the picture on a different computer, and the image looks too dark or too bright. Or maybe you have gone to a large television store and seen all the televisions side by side, showing the same images, but they all look different in color and brightness. This is because the screens are not calibrated for accurate and consistent color display.

Color calibration provides a way to make all your monitors have the same color profile and color response, to match the input and output devices. Color calibration is necessary, because you do not want to complete work for a client and have it look just the way you want it to, only to discover that the project looks terrible in color and brightness on the client's computer.

Color calibration requires more than just a few button pushes of the brightness, gamma, and hue controls. You must understand what is going on with hardware, software, lighting conditions, and color space. Not all of the monitors you see and work on need to be calibrated, but the monitors you work on just before final output should be, to ensure correct levels for final viewing.

Mac and PC computers showing the same image on the same type of monitor will display the images differently.

The best thing you can do as a 3D artist is to work in a color-managed environment to ensure the best input and output. A color-managed environment is color corrected to ensure that all monitors are the same. This requires two extra devices—a colorimeter and a spectrophotometer—but they are worth the cost. A *colorimeter,* which sits on the monitor and connects to the computer, runs through a series of tests to determine the color gamut of the monitor and creates a custom color profile for it. A colorimeter can also look at multiple monitors and create a central color profile to allow the displays to match. A *spectrophotometer* analyzes the colors of a print from a printer, so you can then use a colorimeter to create a color profile of the monitor that matches the colors from the printer.

The biggest problem is that not everyone who uses a television or computer is going to color-calibrate their devices. In the end, the best thing you can do is to create an image that will work for the majority of people in the digital world. You can compensate for differences right before the final image creation. If you are on a PC and the image looks correct, you can darken the midtones to compensate for viewing on a Mac. If you are working on a Mac, you can lighten the midtones to look better on a PC. There are always going to be discrepancies, so you can make minor adjustments for good viewing on all monitors.

Another factor that must be investigated in color calibration is the color mode you are going to work in. A *color mode* is the specific type of color option you are going to be working in for the final output. For work on a computer or television screen, RGB color mode is best. For print, you would want to work in CMYK color mode. There are HSV and YUV color modes as well. It is possible to work input and output into different color modes, but you should do this at an early opportune time of image editing to account for any color loss early on. The process of changing an image created in one color mode to a different mode can cause color loss, because the new mode may not have all the colors available in the original palette.

ADDITIVE AND SUBTRACTIVE COLOR MODELS

Additive and subtractive color models are based on color mixing between mediums like paint or printing and light. Subtractive color mixing will darken the overall color to black as more colors are added. Additive color mixing will lighten the overall color to white as more color is added. This topic will be discussed further in Chapter 4.

RGB Color Mode   *RGB* stands for *red, green, and blue*. In RGB mode, these colors are mixed in an additive manner to create the colors seen on a monitor or television. This color mode is based on the human perception of color. Humans see wavelengths of light in the range of 400 to 700 nanometers (nm). This range enables us to see from violet to red in a continuous rainbow. In our eyes, receptors called cones are sensitive to red, green, and blue light.

CMYK Color Mode   *CMYK* stands for *cyan, magenta, yellow, and black*. In CMYK mode, these colors are mixed in a subtractive form specifically for print. This subtractive model is not a native format for a computer because the screens are created in a additive color mode with light.

HSV Color Mode   *HSV* stands for *hue, saturation, and value*. This color mode is also known as HSB (hue, saturation, and brightness) and HSL (hue, saturation, and lightness). This color mode is actually a transformation of RGB mode, which means that it is a color picker model to allow for easy color selection.

YUV Color Mode   YUV color mode uses luma (Y) and two chrominance (UV) components. Luma is the brightness of the image and chrominance is the color. This color mode is used to interface between analog and digital equipment like digitizing old VHS tape. This format is used to compress data into the MPEG and JPEG file formats.

COLOR PICKER

Color picker is a tool in all graphics software to allow for quick selection of a color. These color pickers come in many different forms from a palette of different colors, dialing in the RGB color directly to a complex form of controls to dial in hue, saturation and value.

CIE stands for the *International Commission on Illumination*. The acronym comes from its French name, Commission Internationale de l'Éclairage.

The next option to consider in color calibration is the color gamut. *Color gamut* is the range of visible colors the device you are working with can capture and output or represent in the color mode you are working in. The CIE XYZ color gamut is the standard to which all other color modes and color spaces are compared because it provides the full color gamut of the human eye. The RGB and CMYK color modes can work only in a range within the CIE XYZ color gamut because of their inability to display all of the colors available to the human eye. This limitation is caused by today's technology; with each advancement, we come closer to making all colors available. Figure 3.13 shows the CIE XYZ color gamut with a triangle inside of it indicating the RGB color mode within it. As you can see, there are still many colors not available in the RGB color gamut (shown outside the triangle).

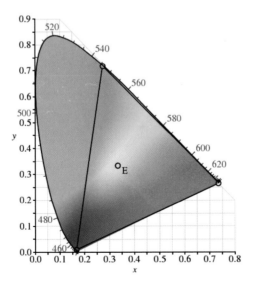

FIGURE 3.13 CIE XYZ color space with the RGB color mode represented within the triangle

When working in RGB and then switching to CMYK, you will have trouble achieving the colors you want. For example, you will not be able to achieve a pure red in CMYK as you can in RGB. So how do you know if you are out of the range you can work in? Fortunately, most imaging software today will warn you that you are out of range for a specific color mode.

The next option in color calibration is the white point for your device or image. The *white point* is the reference point for all white to mimic in the image or device. You may have noticed that photographs taken indoors look more yellow than photos taken outdoors. This is because of the light source: indoor lighting is typically made of incandescent lights, whereas outdoor light is sunlight. Incandescent lights emit a much more yellow light than the sun. The white point of your image taken inside can be shifted to make the white in the image look more white to the viewer. This shifting of the white point is called *chromatic adaptation transform* or *white balancing*. These shifts in white will shift the entire color space to match the look of the image. You can also set the white point on a monitor or television. This option is available in the advanced controls of the monitor or TV's display options. Typically, you can make your screen more white, blue, or yellow.

One of the biggest problems in color calibration is *gamma correction*, the non-linear operation to code luminance values for an image or device. Gamma correction is supposed to help digital images better represent the way the human eye would truly see an image in the real world. What it will do for you as a 3D animator is overdarken or overlighten the midtones of an image to flatten the overall look. There are two ways to apply gamma correction. Software can apply gamma correction to allow for a more dynamic image, and the display device can also apply gamma correction into the viewing properties of that device, which can double the amount of gamma correction, resulting in an overcorrection. What you can do as a 3D digital artist to combat gamma correction is to understand what gamma correction is and then how to best compensate for it in postproduction for final output.

Understanding Digital Video

In *digital video*, many digital images are played sequentially to create a moving image—unlike digital imaging, which typically creates still images. Digital video has a few of its own specific rules and principles with regard to the standard display devices the videos are played on and the way the devices handle the many images to create video. The capture of digital video is similar to that of digital still images, but for video the capture devices must be able to capture many sequential images at a steady rate defined by the user.

Resolution, Device Aspect Ratio, and Pixel Aspect Ratio

Resolution is the number of pixels on a digital monitor or television screen. *Device aspect ratio* is the height-to-width ratio of the physical screen you are using. *Pixel aspect ratio* is the height-to-width ratio of pixels on that screen.

Since the beginning of television, screens around the world have had different pixel aspect ratios that have been more rectangular in shape. Today computer monitors and HD televisions have standard pixel aspect ratios equaling square pixels. So when looking at an image on a computer screen and then transferring that image to a television screen, the image will look squashed or stretched. This problem of a nonuniversal pixel shape is becoming easier to deal with because HD televisions have square pixels, but we are still a long way off from not having to worry about this problem anymore. So let's break down each of these pixel aspect ratio options so you can better understand the issue of distortion.

Resolution is the easy part; 1080 HD televisions are set to a resolution of 1920×1080, so there are 1,920 pixels going horizontally and 1,080 pixels going vertically across the screen. To get the total number of pixels, you multiply the number of pixels in the width by the number in the height—in this case, $1,920 \times 1,080 = 2,073,600$ total pixels. 720 HD is set to 1280×720, the standard NTSC American television resolution is set to 720×486, and European PAL television resolution is set to 720×576.

NTSC and PAL are both considered to have a device aspect ratio of 1.33 or 4:3. To get the device aspect ratio of a screen, you divide the number of pixels in the width by the number of pixels in the height. However, doing that in this instance gives the following results:

NTSC $720 \div 486 = 1.48$

PAL $720 \div 576 = 1.25$

So how are these two television formats considered to have a device aspect ratio of 1.33 or 4:3? Well, we will need to factor in the pixel aspect ratio of these television types. Pixels are not the same shape from one standard to another. NTSC has a pixel aspect ratio of 0.9, and that means that the pixels are not square; they are vertical rectangles. PAL pixels have a ratio of 1.066 (sometimes referred to as 1.1), which makes them horizontal rectangles. You can see the shapes of the different pixels in Figure 3.14.

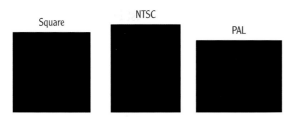

FIGURE 3.14 Square, NTSC, and PAL pixel shapes

To get the aspect ratio for these two television standards to 1.33, you multiply the pixel aspect ratio by the resolution:

$$\text{NTSC } 720 \div 486 \times 0.9 = 1.33$$

$$\text{PAL } 720 \div 576 \times 1.066 = 1.33$$

Okay, the math works, but what does this mean to you as a 3D artist? It means that you will need to plan ahead to be able to work in any format. If you take an image of a perfect sphere in a 3D application and render it to square pixels of a computer monitor, for example, the sphere will look perfectly round. However, if you then look at the same image on a NTSC television, it will look stretched vertically, as shown in Figure 3.15.

So how do you fix this distortion? You plan ahead and compensate for the distortion. You will first always need to know your final output medium. Let's say you know your project is going straight to DVD in the United States, so it will be at NTSC standards. You will work on a computer screen with square pixels, and everything will look just fine. But in the rendering, you will need to squash your final image by 0.9 to compensate for the vertical stretch of NTSC pixels. If you compensate correctly, you will not see any distortion on the final image. Figure 3.16 illustrates the compensation.

Monitor

NTSC

FIGURE 3.15 A 3D rendered sphere on a square-pixel monitor and an NTSC television

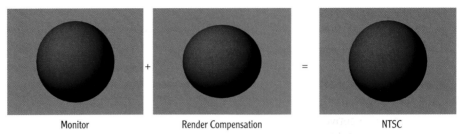

Monitor   Render Compensation   NTSC

FIGURE 3.16 A sphere rendered out squashed in the square-pixel display to look correct on an NTSC television

HD television with square pixels is becoming universal across the world, so this distortion problem will eventually go away.

But sometimes your project will have a worldwide distribution across different platforms. The only options are to render slightly larger than needed to be able to scale it to fit the different platforms or to render multiple versions of your project. Both will add time to the final output of the project.

Safe Areas

Safe area is a term used by the television industry to describe the area onscreen that is guaranteed to be seen by the audience and therefore safe to contain images and text. Older televisions could not guarantee that every pixel of the screen would be seen, because of the bezel the screen would sit in, overlapping the screen (see Figure 3.17). Safe zones are becoming an issue of the past because of the existence of flat-screen televisions and because many videos and movies are being viewed on computer screens. But an understanding of these zones is important. I still see local, cheaply produced commercials with the text too far to the side or too far down to be readable. So this safe zone is still something to keep in mind while creating the composition of your projects.

Image © woodleywonderworks/Flickr

FIGURE 3.17 An extreme example of a very limited (and round!) safe area on an old TV

There are two types of safe areas: a title safe zone and an action safe zone, which you can see in Figure 3.18. The *title safe zone* is the area of the screen in which the editor can be very sure that any text will be seen by the audience. This area starts about 20 percent in from the outer edges of the screen. Old televisions would cover up part of the visible pixels, and an editor could not be sure every television would be the same. Leaving a 20 percent margin of error was safe. Old CRT televisions also had a convex screen shape, so a viewer sitting by the side of the television might not be able to see the text.

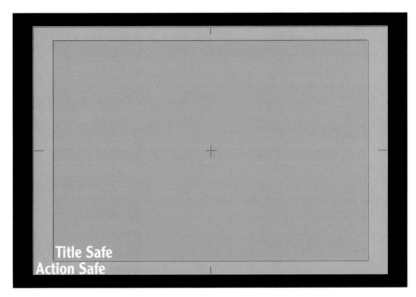

FIGURE 3.18 A 4:3 television with the title safe zone in blue, the action safe zone in yellow, and the full screen resolution in black.

The *safe action zone* is the area in which an editor can feel assured that any action will be seen by the audience. This safe action area starts about 10 percent in from the outer edges of the screen and is not as compacted as the title safe zone because otherwise the actions would be too tightly centered onscreen and not have room to move within the composition.

Interlaced and Progressive Scanning

This section describes how a computer screen and television display images. Computer screens and televisions do not flash the entire image up at one time, over and over and over. Instead, they vertically scan the images you see in small

Persistence of Vision is a theory that states the human eye will carry an afterimage for about one-twentieth of a second.

Hz stands for *Hertz* and is a unit of frequency defined as the number of cycles.

lines, the size of a pixel. There are two types of scanning for computer monitors or televisions: progressive scanning and interlacing scanning.

Progressive scanning draws a whole image, like a photograph, from top to bottom until the image is completed. This progressive vertical scanning occurs at a very high rate, and the Persistence of Vision theory indicates that we will never perceive the scanning on the monitor. The speed at which this scanning happens is called the *refresh rate*. You may have witnessed a flickering on your computer monitor that typically means the refresh rate of the monitor needs to be adjusted for smooth movement. Most LCD screens today refresh at about 60 to 72 Hz.

Interlacing was created because old television sets could not hold an image on the screen through the phosphors long enough before the scan could complete, so the image would fade away before the next cycle. So the lines were broken into alternating even and odd lines, enabling the television to draw the image faster. These alternating lines are called *fields*. The actual images would be captured in *subframes* at twice the usual display frame rate. These images are captured at 60 subframes a second, to be combined at 30 whole frames for final display for example. These subframes would only have to capture half the lines of total resolution. These two captured subrames are scanned one after the other on the screen to create the final image. Figure 3.19 is a representation of these fields. A quick way to see whether video is interlaced is to look for stair-stepping in fast-moving video, as shown in Figure 3.20. This stair-stepping is not really noticeable in real time but on a paused frame can be seen very easily.

Beyond the simple reality of the television not being able to hold the image onscreen long enough, interlacing allows each scan to happen faster because only half the pixels of the screen need to be scanned. This allows for a smaller analog bandwidth and read and write speeds that are able to show smooth video. The analog bandwidth is not a digital bandwidth like with the Internet but rather is analog coaxial cable bandwidth. Even today, HD televisions come in both 1080i (interlaced) and 1080p (progressive) options. When HD first came onto the scene, the technology had not yet become available to be able push out 1,080 lines using progressive scan refresh rates needed to get smooth motion. Today you still sometimes see an interlacing television sold, but most cable, satellite television, DVD, and Blu-ray players can now easily handle progressive scanning data rates.

Line 1	Odd
Line 2	Even
Line 3	Odd
Line 4	Even
Line 5	Odd
Line 6	Even
Line 7	Odd
Line 8	Even
Line 9	Odd
Line 10	Even
Line 11	Odd
Line 12	Even
Line 13	Odd
Line 14	Even
Line 15	Odd
Line 16	Even
Line 17	Odd
Line 18	Even
Line 19	Odd
Line 20	Even

FIGURE 3.19 A representation of the fields of interlacing video

FIGURE 3.20 Notice the stair-stepping lines in this still image of interlaced video

Compression

Compression is the reduction or reordering of data in your file to make that file smaller so it can be more easily distributed and viewed. However, the way you compress images and video can greatly change the quality and usability of those files.

The compression of video and image files has two basic parts: compressing and decompressing. The act of compressing and decompressing always comes as a duo, and a codec is used to start and complete this process. *Codec*, short for *compression/decompression*, is a program that allows the ease of viewing or editing video or images. The primary idea of compressing a file is to use only what information is needed and to lose data that is not as important, to shrink the file size.

WHICH CODEC TO USE?

If you have ever compressed a file, you probably have seen a lot of codec choices. Honestly, most of these are outdated and not used, but are kept for legacy and compatibility reasons. Most people will use only one or two options at a time, until a newer and better version is released and typically well distributed among users. I use the QuickTime H.264 codec for all my video compression. So as a 3D artist, you will need to find one or two codecs that work for you and is compatible with today's video players. And the only way to do that is a little research that includes trying them out.

As covered briefly in Chapter 2, "The Production Pipeline," there are two basic types of image compression: lossy and lossless.

Lossy compression allows for the loss of some data to shrink the final file size. Human observation of visual data is taken into account when the codec is discarding data to give a good representation of the original image. But the bottom line of lossy compression is that you are losing image quality in exchange for a faster playback and smaller file size—and after that information is lost, it cannot be brought back.

Lossless compression does not allow for a loss of quality. This type of compression typically does not create as small of a file size as a lossy compression, but the final quality is the most important aspect of lossless compression.

Additionally, video can use either spatial or temporal compression. Both types use the fact that many of the same colors and shapes are used in the span of a video. *Spatial compression* looks at each frame individually, picks out the differences, and changes only the information that is different from frame to frame. *Temporal compression*, instead of looking at the differences of every frame, chooses certain frames called *keyframes* in which to write all the pixel information. Then for all other frames between the keyframes, the codec writes only the pixel information indicating differences from these keyframes. The frames between the keyframes are called *delta frames*.

You can see a representation of temporal compression in Figure 3.21. The first and the seventh frame are the keyframes, and frames 2, 3, 4, 5, and 6 are the delta frames. Because the white background of the example never changes, the codec does not need to keep that information on the delta frames. Only the major differences of the red ball between the two keyframes are noted. In this process of temporal compression, you will get a lot of image distortion if your original imagery is fast moving or flashing. But you can get some very good results with smooth-motion video.

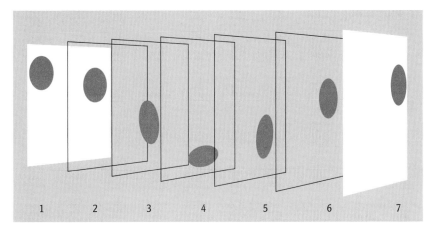

FIGURE 3.21 A visual representation of temporal compression

Frame Rate and Timecode

Frame rate is the number of times each frame is displayed onscreen for each second in video, film, or video games. Frame rate is also known as *frames per second (fps)*. The basic frame rates that artists use today are as follows:

► 24 fps is the frame rate for film.

► 25 fps is the frame rate for PAL television.

▶ 29.97 fps is the frame rate for NTCS television.

▶ 30 fps is the frame rate for progressive video.

▶ 6 fps to 100+ fps is the frame rate for video games.

These basic rates have been in use for some time, but some of the general frame rates are changing because of technology enhancements. There are reports that film may begin using 48 fps or higher to allow for smoother motion onscreen. Film and animation have used a rate of 24 fps since the 1920s, and some people think that it is time to upgrade.

Timecode is a method of allowing synchronization and identifying recorded data in video material. This method associates a number with each frame so we can sync audio and other video to and make notes about the footage. The most common form of timecode for video is SMPTE. This SMPTE timecode carries binary code for time that looks like this: 01:35:12:15. From left to right, this timecode indicates *hours:minutes:seconds:frames* (HH:MM:SS:FF). Using SMPTE timecode, we can dial in the hour, minute, second, and frame of a video clip.

However, the SMPTE timecode doesn't work well with the NTSC standard frame rate of 29.97 fps, because SMPTE does not have any storage for decimals. So the smart people in the video-editing world created a timecode called *drop-frame timecode*. It does not actually drop frames from your video, but renumbers the timecode to represent the actual time more accurately. Over the course of a 24-hour day, the SMPTE timecode math running at 29.97 fps would be ahead of the real-world clock by almost a minute and a half. Using the drop-frame timecode will match the time to about a millisecond by dropping the 0 and 1 of the first second of every minute, except for the minutes that are divisible by 10. This allows for the decimal point from the NTSC frame rate. Thankfully, video-editing software includes an option that takes care of syncing frames for you. You can tell that you are working in drop-frame timecode because a semicolon (;) will be used between the numbers, not a colon (:) as in the SMPTE timecode.

▶

SMPTE stands for *Society of Motion Picture and Television Engineers*.

Digital Image Capture

You can use various tools to capture photo-like digital images: scanners, cameras, and video cameras. Although these tools are different from one another and perform different functions, they have similar capturing options.

Scanners allow you to place an image or object on a glass flatbed to be optically scanned, similar to a copy machine. Scanners use a bright light under the glass flatbed with sensors attached to vertically scan the image or object and collect the visual information. Most people today take this common technology for granted.

Digital cameras have come a long way in a short amount of time. These capturing devices can now capture very high-definition images with the aid of a lens at an incredible rate. There are different types of digital cameras on the market today. The point-and-shoot digital camera is the least expensive and smallest type, and many people have one today. They are easy to use with automatic settings for taking a good overall picture. Digital single-lens reflex (DSLR) cameras are more expensive but enable you to have greater control and to attach various lenses and accessories.

Digital video cameras enable video to be recorded at various frame rates. There are a variety of video cameras available. Professional video cameras capture video at a much greater resolution than other varieties and allow different lenses to be mounted. As of this writing, they can capture up to a 4K resolution (4096×2304). HD camcorders are the most popular consumer-level video cameras that will shoot different resolutions and at different frame rates. These video cameras are affordable for the general public. Some people use webcams, but these typically have to be attached to a computer and capture images at a limited resolution.

Each type of device captures images at different resolutions. Scanners offer the highest resolution but also take the longest to capture an image. Digital SLR cameras can capture a very high resolution image (some up to 5616 × 3744 pixels which is 3 times the size of HD 1080 resolution) but can capture only a few frames per second. These DSLR cameras are now being equipped to capture video from 24 to 60 fps at HD 720 and HD 1080 resolutions. And video cameras can capture a high number of frames per second but do not provide a very high-resolution setting like a scanner or camera.

THE ESSENTIALS AND BEYOND

This chapter has presented some of the computer graphics basics used in 3D animation. As the 3D animation art form grows and matures, the technology that drives it will as well. Having a good foundation in the computer graphics basics of today will enable you to grow with the technology and industry. You still have many other computer graphic basics to learn later in this book, but understanding them will be easier now that you've read this chapter.

You looked at the smallest visible form on a monitor, the pixel. You now know how those pixels subsample themselves to better represent an image. You've looked at different image file formats and ways to compress those files to a smaller size. I explained why your images look different on different monitors and computers, and presented a few concepts of digital video and how video compares to still digital images.

(Continues)

THE ESSENTIALS AND BEYOND *(Continued)*

REVIEW QUESTIONS

1. Which of these is not correct?

   A. A pixel is always a square.

   B. Pixels are laid out in a perfect grid pattern.

   C. A pixel is the smallest visible form of a screen.

   D. The more pixels you have, the better the resolution.

2. True or false: You can see all the colors of a 16-bit-per-channel image.

3. True or false: The frame rate for NTSC television is 30 fps.

4. Color calibration will use which of these concepts?

   A. White point

   B. Gamma correction

   C. Color mode

   D. All of the above

5. True or false: Raster graphics are resolution dependent.

6. True or false: The resolution of a monitor has a direct effect on the device aspect ratio.

7. How many colors can an 8-bit image display?

   A. 512

   B. 256

   C. 262,144

   D. 65,536

8. Most LCD monitors refresh between what Hz rates?

   A. 60 to 72 Hz

   B. 120 to 240 Hz

   C. 24 to 60 Hz

   D. 800 to 1,000 Hz

9. What are vector graphics typically used for?

   A. Photos

   B. Line and color graphics

   C. Digital painting

   D. All of the above

10. What does the drop-frame timecode do?

    A. Drops frames from video to make the timecode closely match the real-world clock for the NTSC frame rate

    B. Drops frame numbers to keep video numbers running on whole numbers at a frame rate with a decimal point in it

    C. Drops the timecode off the video file

    D. Drops frames of animation off a video

CHAPTER 4

Exploring Animation, Story, and Pre-visualization

3D animation has borrowed concepts from many other fields. You must be willing to study these principles from other disciplines to become a well-rounded 3D artist. Traditional animation techniques, story creation, and pre-visualization still resound in today's digital world, and you need to have a good grasp of those ideas to succeed.

This chapter presents an overview of some of the most important concepts in your journey of 3D animation. (The next three chapters cover modeling, texturing, rigging, animation, visual effects, lighting, and rendering in more detail.) You'll begin with some specific animation concepts. Then you will look at story creation, because as a 3D animation artist—even as an architectural-rendering artist—you are always trying to tell a story. Finally, you will examine pre-visualization practices that will help you tell your story through the camera lens. But don't think you are finished learning these concepts after reading this chapter. You will be learning new ones for the rest of your career.

▶ **Using principles of fine art and traditional animation**

▶ **Building a good story**

▶ **Using pre-visualization techniques**

Using Principles of Fine Art and Traditional Animation

Animation is an extremely diverse field that pulls core concepts from other fields, such as film, television, and the visual arts to help give artists boundaries to work within. Techniques such as *really seeing* what is in front of you, using basic lighting, and employing color theory are there to give artists a solid foundation to start from. When 3D animators have a basic understanding of these boundaries, they can then break the rules as they see fit. This section covers the following topics:

▶ Modeling

▶ Texturing/lighting

▶ Character animation

▶ Visual effects

Modeling

3D digital modelers need to use a few basic techniques related to traditional sculpting in order to optimize the work they can produce. Although these concepts are not all that technical, they take a lot of time to learn and master. These basic modeling practices are as follows:

▶ Learning to really see

▶ Using references

▶ Understanding anatomy

▶ Working with the uncanny valley

Learning to Really See

As a visual artist, it is critical to learn how to *really see* what is in front of you, and not to assume that you already know what something looks like. You must see the detail in your surroundings and pay close attention to minutiae. A still-life painting would be just a picture of a vase and some fruit if the artist didn't focus on the details of these everyday objects.

We see the human form every day, for instance, and take for granted that we know what it looks like. But many artists have a difficult time drawing the human body because they use their assumptions to draw the figure without looking at its details. Bodies drawn this way will not be in correct proportion, and the true shape of the body will not be reflected.

Learning to really see is just as important in 3D modeling as it is in drawing. I have seen many beginning 3D artists try to model a human being without using any references to guide them. Usually the result looks more like a strange, deformed alien than a human. These students then ask, "Why does the model not look correct?" I ask whether they have studied to obtain a mastery of the human form. No, they say. Then I ask whether they looked at any references of the human form before modeling. No, they say again. And those are the reasons for the incorrect models: you have to see the object and know what it looks like before you can re-create it. This holds true for cars, boats, guns, swords, animals, and every other object you will model.

Using Reference Images

As a 3D modeler, you do not usually have the luxury of modeling an object while looking at its real-life counterpart in front of you. Let's say you need to model a tiger. Taking your desktop computer to the zoo and setting up in front of the tiger exhibit is not really practical. Of course, you could take your sketchbook with you to the zoo and sketch a tiger—and this is a good way to get reference—but this would be time-consuming. You could also take a camera to the zoo and take pictures, which would save you some time, but you'd still have to factor in the travel.

As an alternative, the Internet is a great place to find images that you can use for references. It's fast, and you don't have to leave your studio. In addition, you can use books for their pictures and explanations. As a 3D artist, you should begin collecting a personal library of books related to your field. If you are modeling a building or a car, you can look at blueprints to get a core understanding of the shape and construction.

It might seem as if you can never have too many reference materials. However, be sure not to miss deadlines while you are searching for more references as a safety net! I have seen this happen.

Understanding Anatomy

Having true knowledge of the underlying structure of the human body helps artists understand what needs to be shown in a model. This understanding enables artists to correctly depict what is on top of the structure as well—for instance, showing how skin moves over bone and muscle.

As a 3D modeler—and especially in character modeling—this understanding of anatomy is key to creating models that look authentic. Knowing the way the skin stretches over the elbow or flows over the shoulder to the bicep and tricep muscles, for example, will make your models look real and not so computer-generated. Modelers rarely have to model the actual muscles and skeleton of a character, but attempting to create them a few times will help you as an artist understand the structure under the flesh. This knowledge will come in handy if you need to depict an emaciated person or an animal, for instance. If you are creating an alien or fantasy creature, having an understanding of real animal and human anatomy will help you create a skeletal and muscular structure that the audience will find plausible.

Working with the Uncanny Valley

The *uncanny valley* theory is credited to the field of robotics. It states that as a robot begins to look and act more like a human, it becomes unappealing if it is not perfect. Figure 4.1 is a graph of this phenomenon; the dip in the chart indicates the uncanny valley.

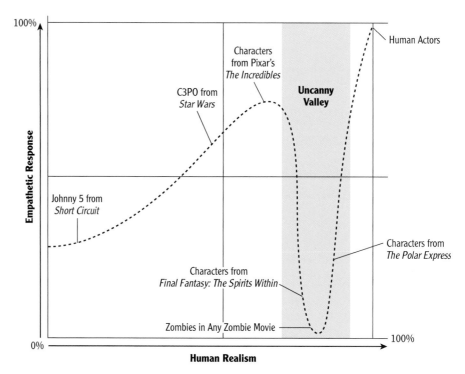

FIGURE 4.1 The uncanny valley

This same theory can be applied to 3D animation. As we get closer to being able to make completely photorealistic human characters, any mistakes we make cause the audience to feel uneasy and to find the characters unappealing.

As seen in Figure 4.1 the characters on the left side moving up the hill are more appealing to the audience up to The Incredibles with their stylistic human design. But as we dip into the uncanny valley characters like zombies will make the audience uneasy because they are dead creatures that are moving. But 3D characters considered more photorealistic from a design standpoint, like *The Polar Express*, will become very unappealing due to the little nuances of the animation of the faces, and body movements, which will make the audience, not connect with these characters, which is not the response for this type of film.

This phenomenon is a problem because one of the Twelve Basic Principles of Animation, which you'll learn about later in this chapter, is appeal. You want to stay on either side of the uncanny valley. So you have a choice to make: you can make characters stylistic to allow the audience to accept them as humanlike, or you can attempt to break beyond the uncanny valley and make 3D characters so believable that the audience will not find them creepy.

Texturing/Lighting

Texturing and *lighting* are grouped together here because they are based on similar concepts. Texturing adds color to the surface of an object, and lighting adds illumination and mood to a scene. To perform either job well, you should have an understanding of the other. Both texturing and lighting use principles originating from the traditional visual arts. Both try to tell a story without words, depend on basic lighting of a subject, and require you to build up a shot with layers.

Telling the Story without Saying a Word

Both texturing and lighting must tell an object's story without saying a word. Texture and lighting artists must put the implied words into the picture. Each object that is to be textured has a story to tell, and the texture artist must bring it out by creating the object's surface properties and color. The lighting artist then looks at the environment and adds ambience to the scene with light or the absence of light.

Texture artists should start each assignment by "interviewing" the object to get to know it before they start. Ask the following questions:

▶ What are you?

▶ Where do you live?

▶ How old are you?

- ▶ Who or what lives with you?

- ▶ What are you made of?

- ▶ What is the most important feature about you?

The answers to these questions will tell you how to texture the object. You will know whether the object is made of wood, metal, or plastic; whether it lives underwater, in the desert, in a city, or in a rural area; and other important factors that make up every object's surface and color. Texture artists should study painting, photography, and digital painting with software such as Adobe Photoshop or Corel Painter.

Lighting artists take a slightly different approach when starting to work on a scene. They begin by trying to understand what the atmosphere or mood should be for the shot. Then they determine the most important objects or theme to illuminate. Is this a standard light setup to show off the object, as for product visualization, or is the goal to light a scene to elicit a feeling from the audience, as in movies, television, or games? Lighting artists should study photography lighting, film lighting, and painting to see how artists use light to create a mood. Just as in texturing, the lighting artist is looking to tell a story with just lighting and color.

Using Basic Light Setups

The most basic type of lighting setup is the *three-point light set*. It consists of three lights:

- ▶ Key light

- ▶ Fill light

- ▶ Rim/kicker light(s)

Figure 4.2 illustrates the three-point light setup. The *key light* is placed to one side of the camera and above the subject. This is the strongest light in the setup and casts the majority of the light. The *fill light* is set up opposite the key light and is at the same level or slightly lower than the subject. The fill light has half of the light intensity of the key light and is there to prevent the shadows of the subject from dropping down to pure black. The rim/kicker light is behind and above the subject to add a rim to the outline of the subject, to separate it from the background. The rim light's intensity varies for each setup; it can be brighter or lower than the key light if need be.

FIGURE 4.2 An example of a three-point light setup in a 3D application (left) and the final rendered still of that setup (right)

This setup can be applied to most shots as a starting place for 3D lighting, even natural lighting used in architectural rendering. The key light would be the sunlight, the fill light would be bounce light from other objects and the sky, and then the lighting artist would add rim/kicker light as needed for artistic effect. Figure 4.3 shows an example. This shot has only one light source, the light through the window, but the scene still has three-point lighting. The direct light from the sun is the key light. The light that bounces off the floor and walls is the fill light, and the sky's ambient light is the rim light on the back of the skeleton's head.

 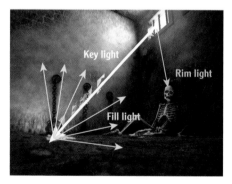

FIGURE 4.3 Example of natural three-point lighting (left) and the three-point light directions (right)

Employing Color Theory

There are two main approaches to mixing colors: an additive color model and a subtractive color model.

The *additive model* uses light in an additive manner to achieve white. It states that if you mix red, green, and blue (RGB) light, you will create white light. This model is the primary use for computer monitors today. Figure 4.4 shows this additive light behavior.

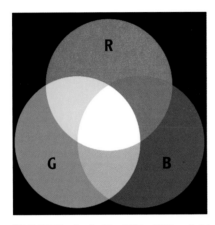

FIGURE 4.4 The RGB additive-light model

The *subtractive model* is based on a pigment or dye mixture. When using this model, mixing red, yellow, and blue (RYB) in painting or cyan, magenta, and yellow (CMYK) in printing creates black. Figure 4.5 shows these subtractive models.

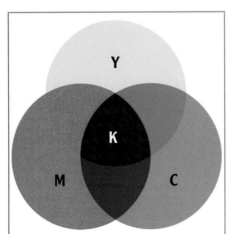 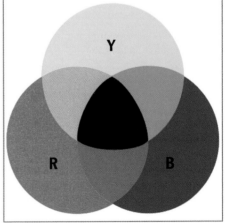

FIGURE 4.5 Example of the CMYK and RYB subtractive color models

Both of these color models are the primary standards for mixing color today with light used in monitors or inks used in printing. However, one challenge is that these models do not incorporate concepts such as hue, saturation, or value, which is an easier way that a user can select color in the digital realm.

Hue indicates the primary color selection, *saturation* is the amount of pure color saturation of the hue selection and *value* is how much of the hue's color selection is displayed in an additive light model, such as that used on a computer screen as seen in Figure 4.6. Saturation is determined by the amount of light to color and is represented by a slider from white to the hue color, and value is the brightness perception of a color, which will be represented by a slider between black and the hue color. Figure 4.6 shows an example of a color selection picker. Notice the sliders at the bottom of the image; these sliders are the hue, saturation and value sliders that can allow a digital artist easy selection of color.

F I G U R E 4 . 6 A color picker
with hue, saturation, and value

Another option to think about as a texture and lighting artist is color schemes and how to best utilize them in your work. The first one to look at is the *complementary color scheme*, which on a color wheel uses the colors opposite each other—for example, red and green, yellow and purple, and blue and orange. Figure 4.7 shows a color wheel indicating complementary colors. This type of color scheme is often used to design graphics and logos that stand out because they have a lot of visual energy.

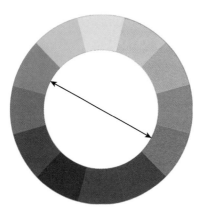

FIGURE 4.7 An example of complementary colors on a color wheel

The *analogous color scheme* (Figure 4.8), often seen in nature, is usually a color scheme that is easy to look at. This scheme typically uses two to three colors that are beside each other on the color wheel, such as green and yellow-green or red-orange, orange, and yellow-orange.

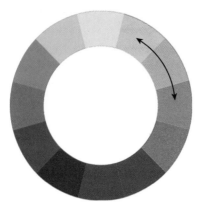

FIGURE 4.8 An example of three analogous colors on a color wheel

A *split-complementary color scheme* (Figure 4.9) is composed of a main color and the two colors beside its complementary color. One example is green, red-orange, and red-violet. Like the complementary color scheme, this scheme has energy but is easier to look at for extended periods of time. This color scheme is usually good for websites and presentations.

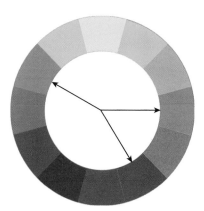

FIGURE 4.9 An example of split-complementary colors on a color wheel

Using Layers

The 3D images you see on the Internet, television, and film are not created in an animation program and rendered in one glorious shot. Creating that great imagery requires many layers built on top of one another. In texturing, for example, it is common practice to use numerous layers in Adobe Photoshop to create the various color maps for your object.

Never flatten your layers, even when you think you are finished. You never know when your client or director might want to change the look of an object, and if you still have the layers, fixing the file is easy.

The same concept holds true for lighting: you will never render just one image from your 3D application and say it is perfect. Many layers are needed to complete a shot that would be too difficult to complete in one layer. In addition, when showing a client a final render, it is easier to fix the image in the compositing software in real time than to re-render an entire 3D scene.

Character Animation

Any animator in any medium must understand the *Twelve Basic Principles of Animation*, which were created by the legendary Nine Old Men at Walt Disney Animation Studios. The original purpose of this rule set was to create a common language in this very new field so that animators would have a shared understanding of how to design realistic animations that followed the basic laws of physics.

The Twelve Basic Principles of Animation are as follows:

- ▶ Squash and stretch
- ▶ Anticipation
- ▶ Staging
- ▶ Straight-ahead action and pose-to-pose
- ▶ Follow-through and overlapping action
- ▶ Slow-in and slow-out
- ▶ Arcs
- ▶ Secondary action
- ▶ Timing
- ▶ Exaggeration
- ▶ Solid drawing
- ▶ Appeal

Squash and Stretch

An object in motion will *squash and stretch* to display weight and flexibility. The most basic demonstration of this principle is a deformation of a bouncing ball. As the ball drops to the ground, it stretches until it hits the ground, at which point it squashes. The ball then stretches out again as it bounces off the ground, as seen in Figure 4.10.

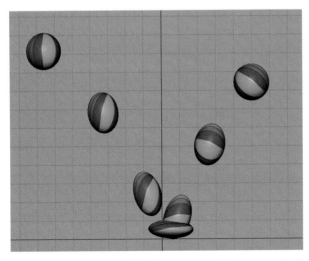

FIGURE 4.10 A bouncing ball at different stages of animation

The squash and stretch principle applies everywhere within animation, from the smallest to the largest movements. When applied to a character, squash and stretch can mean a deformation or a pose change. For instance, the deformation of squash and stretch can be seen in a character's eye blink. Figure 4.11 shows a close-up of the eye in the main key poses of a blink. These poses are as follows:

1. The eye is in the default basic position.

2. The eye is squashed in the down position.

3. The eye is stretched in the surprised position.

4. The eye settles back to the default position and shape.

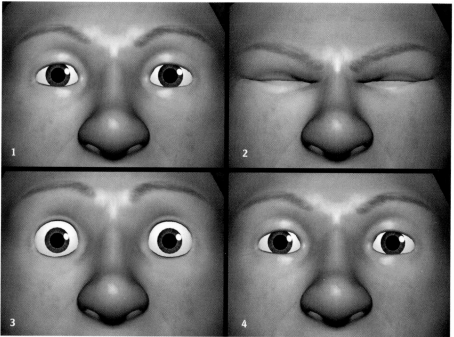

Models and character rig © After Hours Animation

FIGURE 4.11 Four key poses of an eye blink

In large-scale motions (such as a person leaping), it is not the character geometry squashing and stretching, but the entire character pose, silhouette, and outline that squash and stretch. Figure 4.12 illustrates a leaping character moving through these poses:

1. The character starts in a standing position.

2. He squats to start the jump (squash).

3. He jumps forward, extending his arms and legs (stretch).

4. He squashes again, with his legs extending past the torso.

5. The character stretches out once again to anticipate the landing.

6. He squashes again in the landing of the jump.

7. He settles back into the standing position.

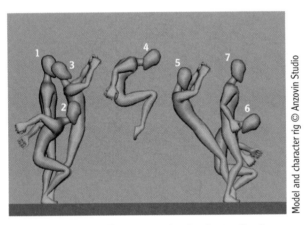

FIGURE 4.12 Main poses of a simple standing leap

Anticipation

Anticipation is a principle indicating that the audience should see or understand what is going to happen before it happens. Viewers who are not given proper cues might miss what is happening onscreen, and you do not want the audience to miss anything.

As an example, imagine an animated image of a boxer. In the animation world, we want the audience to know when the big knockout punch is about to happen. To accomplish this, you have the character move into a big windup pose, and if possible, hold for a beat before the punch happens. Figure 4.12 shows this pose. Of course, in the real world, a boxer who did this would be knocked down instantly by his opponent. When we watch boxing, we miss half the fight because the fighters are moving so quickly and are trying to *not* allow the opponent to anticipate any moves.

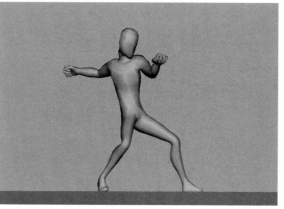

Model and character rig © Anzovin Studio

FIGURE 4.13 Large windup for a boxing punch

Under the principle of anticipation, generally an action is depicted as moving in the opposite direction first. Notice in Figure 4.13 that the boxer winds up right to punch left. If you watch any Chuck Jones *Looney Tunes* animations, you will notice that before characters run offscreen, they pose in the opposite direction that they are about to run in.

Anticipation is not always so apparent, though. It helps subtle realistic animation as well. Stand up with your feet shoulder-width apart and then step forward with your right foot. Did you notice that to complete this right-foot step, you first had to shift your weight to your left leg for balance? You have to first move left to move right, and vice versa. Figure 4.14 illustrates this example.

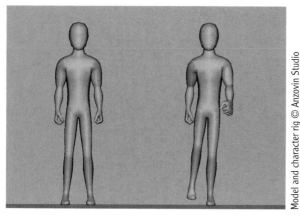

Model and character rig © Anzovin Studio

FIGURE 4.14 A figure standing in a neutral pose and then shifting weight to his left to step with his right foot

Staging

Staging is the way you will fill your screen with the motion of animation and the placement of objects to allow the audience to best understand what is happening. Through staging, you compose the frame in the most clear and concise way possible to communicate the action. For example, if two characters are talking to one another, to best stage this idea, you want them close together and facing each other. However, for film and television, you also need them to face the camera. So you have to stage the characters facing the camera *and* each other. Figure 4.15 shows examples of good camera placement for staging a two-person shot.

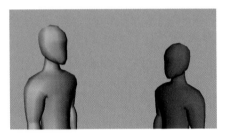 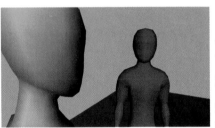

Models and character rig © Anzovin Studio

FIGURE 4.15 A typical shot that crops the characters at the waist (left) and an over-the-shoulder shot of two people talking (right)

Figure 4.16 shows an incorrect way to stage the same two people talking. By using an overhead shot, the audience can't see any of the facial expressions or reactions of the characters.

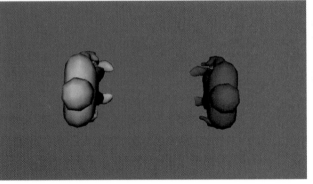

Models and character rig © Anzovin Studio

FIGURE 4.16 An overhead shot is not a good way to show two people talking.

Another component of the staging principle is the set dressing that an animator uses. *Set dressing* is the stage where an artist will assemble the digital 3D set from many different models. Someone has to place the props into the scene and arrange them to look natural. The distance between objects greatly changes how a character gets from point A to point B. For instance, imagine that a character walks into a room and wants to sit at a desk. The location of the chair in the room dictates how that person will sit down. If the chair is a few feet from the door, the character might take one large step and jump to sit in the chair and ride and spin to the desk. But if the chair is under the desk, the person will have to walk to the chair and pull it out to sit in it.

Straight-Ahead Action and Pose-to-Pose

Straight-ahead action and *pose-to-pose* are two techniques used in traditional animation that help the animator in knowing how to approach a shot.

Straight-ahead action entails drawing each frame in sequential order. *Pose-to-pose* is a technique of drawing out the key poses of an action first and then *in-betweening* the action between the key poses. The following list shows the main pros and cons of each technique.

Straight-Ahead Pros and Cons

> ▶ Spontaneous actions can develop in animation created in sequential order either by allowing for mistakes that may add personality to the animation that would be easily planned out or by allowing for a flow of creativity in the process of animation that may aid the animator.

> ▶ You can easily create fluid motion.

> ▶ It is difficult to show a lead animator or director your progress in the animation. This is difficult because the lead or director can only see what you have completed at any time without seeing the animation in its entirety, and without the entire story of animation will not be able to give a complete critique.

> ▶ If you need to change the animation, you may have to start over from scratch.

> ▶ The animation can run too long or too short for a sequence because of a lack of planning the exact number of frames per shot.

Pose-to-Pose Pros and Cons

> ▶ Animation can be planned out to the frame to allow for exact timing in a longer sequence of animation shots.

> ▶ Often motion is not fluid; the animation may look like a character moving from pose to pose.

In addition to straight-ahead action and pose-to-pose, 3D computer animation uses additional character animation techniques, such as hierarchy and hybrid approaches. Hierarchy is breaking the character into separate parts and animating them in order of importance of motion, like the lower body first, then upper body and then the arms in a walk cycle animation. Hybrid is a cross blend between pose-to-pose and straight-ahead and is a very popular technique used to day in performance animation. These techniques are explained in Chapter 6, "Rigging and Animation."

In-betweening is interpolating the motion between two key poses by adding more key frames.

▶ Animation can be checked on in an early blocking stage without requiring major updates because few keys are needed for blocking. Blocking is the term given to the animation stage of creating the key poses of a shot or sequence that will be used to show the animator's idea of the performance.

Follow-Through and Overlapping Action

Follow-through enables animators to show that parts of an object may continue moving even after the whole object has stopped. For instance, when a character who has long hair has stopped walking, the hair will overshoot the body/head and then settle to a stop. *Overlapping action* applies to a character's body parts, which move at different rates of speed while the entire body is moving. This can be seen in a fat character's belly jiggle, for example, which may move faster or slower than the character as a whole.

Figure 4.17 shows an example of a tail following an object. The follow-through and overlapping actions can be described as follows:

1. The large ball is resting. The large ball has a tail attached to a small ball.

2. The large ball moves up, and the small ball follows behind.

3. The large ball moves down, and the small ball moves to try to catch up to the large ball.

4. The large ball comes to a rest again, and the small ball is following the larger ball's motion.

5. The small ball passes by the large ball with an overshoot.

6. The small ball settles to a stop.

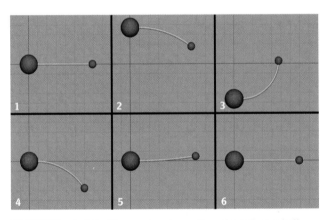

FIGURE 4.17 The overlapping action of a tail on a ball

Slow-In and Slow-Out

Slow-in and slow-out (also known as *ease-in and ease-out*) describes the acceleration and deceleration required when an object starts moving or comes to a stop. A good example of these principles is a car drag race. The race cars sit at a dead stop until the light turns green. Then the drivers punch the accelerator and take off down the track, but the cars do not instantly go from a dead stop to top speeds. Instead, they have to build up to those speeds; this is slow-in. Once across the finish line, the drivers hit the brakes, and the cars release a parachute to slow down over time. They do not come to an immediate standstill; this gradual deceleration is slow-out.

These principles are seen in all animation, from that of a bouncing ball to a piston. You can tell that a bouncing ball is accelerating during a drop based on the spacing of the ball positions. Figure 4.18 shows an example. At the beginning of the drop, the ball does not have much movement between frames. This makes the ball move slowly. Then as the ball is about to hit the ground, the frame spacing is father apart, which makes the ball move more quickly. Varying the distance between frames to change the speed of the ball works because the frame rate is always constant.

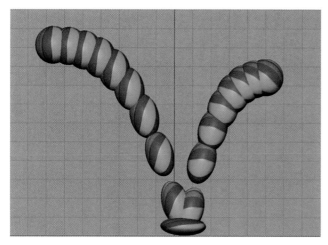

FIGURE 4.18 A bouncing-ball animation illustrating slow-in and slow-out

Arcs

Most objects move in *arcs*. Your arms and legs, for instance, rotate around their joints (these rotational points are called *pivot points* in 3D animation). When you throw a ball, gravity takes effect and pulls the ball down to the ground, which makes the flight path an arc motion as well. Very few things move in a linear (straight) motion, except some mechanical objects. Figure 4.19 shows an example of arc motion. As the character jumps, you can see that the arm swinging forward and back creates two arcs.

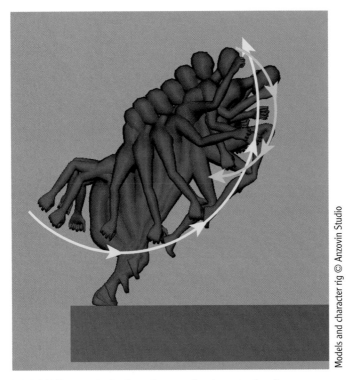

Models and character rig © Anzovin Studio

FIGURE 4.19 In these frames of a character leaping, you can see the arcing motion of the arm.

Secondary Action

Secondary action supports the primary action. For example, say that you are animating a woman crying to a friend and explaining that her significant other has just broken up with her. The primary action of this scene is the crying and explaining. You could add a secondary action—the woman wiping her nose or reaching into a bag to get a tissue to wipe her eyes—to support the primary action of the scene.

Secondary actions can be good way to add comedy to a scene, but you should be careful not to let them take over If our character tries to pull a tissue out of her bag but the tissue gets stuck, for example, or the character cannot find the tissue, that could add interest to the performance. However, if the character really struggles to find the tissue and then throws the bag because she cannot find the tissue, that secondary action takes over the primary action of the emotional crying. Take care to not allow this to happen!

Timing

Timing is how long it takes to do something. As an animator, you will be typically working in 24, 25, or 30 frames per second, depending on the format used for output. Consider how long it takes, for example, for a character to sit down. As a beginner animator, you should act out the motion with the aid of a stopwatch and see. Let's say it takes 1.5 seconds to sit down. At 24 frames per second, you will have to use 36 frames to complete the sitting action. This is timing. Some people have a natural instinct about how long it takes to complete a task, but most of us need practice and the use of video or in-person references and a stopwatch.

Exaggeration

Exaggeration is a tool to make animation more extreme. This technique must be used wisely to create the proper effect, but even realistic animation needs some exaggeration. For example, motion capture is used to record and translate the motion of a real person onto a 3D character. But straight motion capture typically does not feel like it has enough weight to the movement, even though it is from real life, so a touch of exaggeration is needed to achieve the desired result.

The animator spends time cleaning up the captured motion and then adds exaggeration to make it feel vibrant. For example, to create a character jumping in a basketball game, an animator would use motion capture to record a professional basketball player. Then the animator would exaggerate the squat before the jump and add a little height to the jump to make the overall animation more exciting.

Solid Drawing

Solid drawing (also now known as *knowledge of software*) is the understanding of basic and technical concepts to allow the artist to focus on the art and not the drawing or what buttons need pressed in the 3D animation software. In the early days of traditional animation, animators needed to be able to draw any object or character from any 3-dimensional angle, so solid traditional drawing skills were a must to the art form. This solid drawing was also important to traditional animators because it would allow them to animate quickly with a firm understanding of what they do.

But today in 3D animation, computers can render objects from all angles perfectly by default, so this principle has evolved into having a good understanding of the software you are using. With a solid understanding of software, animators don't need to spend any time looking for what button to press to achieve the look they want to create.

I am not saying that you do not need to know how to draw—because you do. I get this question from a lot of prospective students and parents: "Why do I need to draw if I am going to be on the computer all day?" And the answer to that question is that 3D animation is a type of visual communication, and the fastest way to visually communicate is to draw. 3D animation is a slow and tedious medium, so you do still need to be able to draw to be able to let someone know what it is you want to accomplish in 3D animation.

Appeal

Appeal is a principle indicating that the audience must connect to a character through its personality. A story's hero must be someone you want to root for throughout the entire tale. The bad guys need appeal as well. They need to be appealingly *bad*, though, so your audience won't like them more than the hero. Appeal is developed through the characters' visual design and personalities.

VFX

You have to be able to jump many technical hurdles in the visual effects (VFX) field. However, the basic VFX concept is very simple: VFX artists must be able to truly see the effect they need to create and then break down the process to allow for an easier creation of that effect.

Using Reference Images

As a VFX artist, you could be asked to create just about any natural effect seen in the world today, as well as effects that have never been seen before. Just like modelers, VFX artists must be able to find references for any effect they want to create (and then perhaps embellish it). For instance, if creating a lava river flowing down the side of a volcano, the VFX artist should first find a video of lava doing just that to use as a reference point for the effect. A VFX artist who skips that step might spend a massive amount of time creating the effect only to have the director say that the lava is moving like water, so do it again.

Breaking Down the Shot

VFX artists also have to do research on an effect in order to understand the effect well enough to break it down into its essential pieces. Breaking down the shot enables the artist to avoid having to fix everything if the director is unhappy with the effect. The artist can then also speed up the simulating process by working with smaller pieces.

This process is similar to the "learning to really see" concept in modeling. For example, a cannon firing is actually multiple tasks that happen at one time. The cannon ball fires out of the cannon. But before that ball comes out, fire and smoke precede and follow the cannon ball's exit. So as a VFX artist, it would be beneficial to first animate the ball moving and then simulate the fire just before the cannon ball's exit. You would finish with creating the smoke before and after the cannon ball firing and adding the sparks and such for effect.

Building a Good Story

Stories have been a part of human existence throughout history. As in millennia past, we live and breathe stories every day. For an audience to be truly entertained, stories must have interesting characters, obstacles to overcome, and satisfying conclusions. But building all of these dynamic elements from scratch and weaving them into an original story is time-consuming and difficult. This section covers some basic structures and concepts that will get you started in creating a story that holds an audience's interest, and that they might be willing to pay for.

Story Arc

Why do nearly all stories seem similar? Well, the same story structure has been in use since the beginning of storytelling.

The structure of a beginning, middle, and end is the first layer of this overall story framework. All stories must have a beginning, middle, and end. Otherwise, the story is incomplete. Have you ever heard a story without one of these pieces or a joke without a beginning, middle, or end? It is hard to understand what is happening without all three parts. But a story arc requires more than just these three simple elements.

The next layer of the story arc is the tension or excitement level. A film, for instance, typically starts with an exciting opening to get the audience's attention and to draw the audience into wanting to watch more of the film. Then the film has a small fall in tension that then builds up again in multiple crises, each one bigger than the last, until the final fight or confrontation. Finally, tension falls again to allow the audience to come down at the end.

This story arc is written into the script and sometimes has a formulaic property to it. For instance, pages 1–5 might present the hook that makes us interested in the story, by page 10 the first large event happens, by page 20 the dilemma occurs, and the story builds up to page 90, where the hero hits the low point. The hero will rise higher than ever by page 110 and then will come back down in the last pages of the script. This formula is an unwritten standard, and is why you can tell when something will happen just by the time in the story.

Character, Goal, and Conflict

A good story must have three basic elements:

  ► Characters

  ► A goal

  ► Conflict

Without all three elements, the story will not hold interest. A story could have all three elements and still be horrible, though, so practice with and a solid understanding of the elements are needed.

Characters

Characters are used to show who the story is about and whose eyes we see the story through. The main character drives all of the other elements that create the story. This person has to be interesting enough to hold the audience's attention for the entire story. But there are usually other characters who are involved with the main character and who serve a purpose as well.

Archetypes can be manifested in too many forms to mention in this book, but many characters fall into the following archetypes:

  ► The hero is the main character.

  ► The friend or sidekick is a support character for the main character to learn from or lean on.

  ► The villain is the opposite of the hero and is trying to stop or destroy the hero.

  ► The challenger is a person, creature, or event the hero must overcome.

▶ The trickster tries to trick or outwit the hero.

▶ The shape-shifter is not who he seems to be when first introduced.

These character archetypes must not be confused with stereotypes. You can think of these archetypes as attributes to be added to the characters to make them more interesting. Just because the main character must be the hero does not mean he will have stereotypical hero traits. The best heroes are the ones who do not know they are heroes until they have no choice but to be one. The same is true for the villain. The best villains are normal, everyday people who may even have many herolike attributes but whose view on life has been skewed by some event.

Table 4.1 presents a few movies and their hero and villain character traits. You will notice that these heroes are not infallible. They may have bad marriages, be poor fathers, or have no skills at first. Similarly, villains don't have to be terrible people—they might have debilitating diseases, be heartbroken, or be trying to protect the people they love, and these traits have given them a different perspective on life that can lead to terrible actions.

TABLE 4.1 Side-by-side hero and villain traits

Film	Hero Name & Traits	Villain Name & Traits
Unbreakable	David Dunn: Bad marriage Not a great family man Cannot hold down a job Denies his superhero abilities	Elijah Price: Rare disease of osteogenesis imperfecta (bones break easily) Because he spends much of his life reading comic books while waiting in hospitals, he wants to find his polar opposite—someone who does not break Causes horrific accidents to find someone who does not break
The Incredibles	Mr. Incredible: Loses his will to be happy after society takes away the opportunity to be a superhero Marriage suffers because of his lack of enthusiasm Not a present father to his children	Syndrome: Very intelligent Early in life wants to be a superhero like his hero Mr. Incredible in his prime Is told as a child that he cannot help by Mr. Incredible Decides that he will make trouble for the general public and then defeat that trouble to be seen as a hero

(Continues)

TABLE 4.1 *(Continued)*

Film	Hero Name & Traits	Villain Name & Traits
Star Wars: The Complete Saga	Luke Skywalker: Grows up as a farmer in the middle of nowhere Starts as a whiny teenager with no skills Is suddenly thrown into a war and must step up to the hero role	Anakin Skywalker/Darth Vader: Was pulled away from his mother to train with the Jedi Mother dies before he can save her Is promised that he could save the ones he loves if he studies the Dark Side Must destroy everything he knows to go to the Dark Side

Goal

The *goal* can be anything the main character wants and is willing to overcome obstacles for. The goal might be an object the main character wants to obtain, an event the main character wants to attend, or an accomplishment he's working toward.

The goal cannot be as simple as a character's desire for an ice cream cone, for example, if the character simply walks to the freezer, discovers she is out of ice cream, and walks back to the couch. But using the ice cream cone as a goal would work if upon finding the empty freezer, the character rushes out the door, drives to a store, finds that the store is out of ice cream, and so drives to another store on the other side of town, and on and on and on she goes to obtain the ice cream.

Consider the following examples of goals from movies:

▶ A car—*Dude, Where's My Car?*

▶ The princess—*The Princess Bride*

▶ To go to the party—*Superbad*

▶ To get new legs—*Avatar*

▶ A weekend at the boss's house—*Weekend at Bernie's*

▶ White Castle burgers—*Harold & Kumar Go to White Castle*

Conflict

There must be a *conflict* as the character pursues the goal, or it would not be an interesting story. If your main character wants to find the treasure from a map, and could just follow the map and dig up the treasure, that would be boring to watch. But if the hero had to outsmart traps, fight monsters, and almost die in the process, those conflicts make the story worth watching. All conflict adds drama and makes a better story.

There are many types of story conflicts. The following are the basic conflict types and some movie examples:

Man vs. Man—*Die Hard, Rocky, The Terminator, Sin City, Blood Work*

Man vs. Nature—*Jaws, Dante's Peak, The Day After Tomorrow, Twister, The Birds*

Man vs. Society—*V for Vendetta, Braveheart, Malcolm X, The Patriot, Falling Down, Fight Club*

Man vs. Himself—*Blade, American Psycho, Memento, RoboCop, The Dark Knight*

STICK TO YOUR CORE CONCEPT

All stories have a central concept, theme, or meaning. Making sure that you stick to that central concept is important. You can change characters, environments, and even the plot of your story, but you cannot change the concept. All aspects of your story are there to support the central concept but not to change it.

This sounds like a no-brainer, right? But once you get into creating characters and environments, you will sometimes find yourself wavering on the central concept to aid in that character creation. It is a good idea to write down your central concept and put it on the wall or somewhere you can see it often. This will remind you of what it is you are trying to say while you are immersed in your long 3D production.

Your central concept is a high-level theme, not the specific premise or plot of the story. Here are some central-concept examples:

▶ Change is never easy.

▶ Learn to let go.

▶ Never give up.

▶ Always shoot for the moon.

▶ Just show up.

▶ Small confined space, cannot get out with snakes.

▶ The day just keeps repeating.

(Continues)

STICK TO YOUR CORE CONCEPT *(Continued)*

This simple concept is what you must run all other ideas past to see whether they support that idea or conflict with it. Keeping this central concept short and sweet is what makes it ideal. The longer and more complicated the central concept becomes, the harder it is to check its status against all the elements.

The Hero's Journey

Have you ever noticed how all movies or television shows seem to follow the same pattern in storytelling? This is not a coincidence. Joseph Campbell, an American mythologist, writer, and lecturer, found after years of study in comparative mythology that throughout different cultures and different time periods, storytellers have used the same narrative structure. Campbell named this story structure a *monomyth*, or *the hero's journey*. This hero's journey has 17 stages from which the story emerges. Not all stories use all of the elements of the monomyth, and some even focus on just one, but these 17 stages in one form or another are found in all stories.

Call to Adventure   The hero is introduced to the audience in a mundane world doing normal things when something calls the hero to the unknown. This occurs in *The Lord of the Rings: Fellowship of the Ring*, when Frodo Baggins finds the ring and is called to meet Gandalf in another town.

Refusal of the Call   The hero refuses the call to action. For example, in *Star Wars*, Luke refuses to go with Obi-Wan to Alderaan because of a family obligation.

Supernatural Aid   After the hero has accepted the call, the hero's guide presents the hero with some sort of gift that will help later in the story. In *Mulan*, Mulan's ancestors send a guardian dragon to help her on her journey.

The Crossing of the First Threshold   The hero is now officially beginning their journey and has passed the threshold of their comfort zone, as in *The Lord of the Rings: Fellowship of the Ring* when Frodo crosses the Shire border.

Belly of the Whale   This is the point of the journey at which the hero becomes fully willing to change in order to become who she needs to be. In *Kill Bill: Vol. 2*, the bride is locked into a coffin and buried, and she must decide not to panic in order to get out of the situation alive.

The Road of Trials The hero is challenged on the journey and typically fails one or more of these challenges. An example of this occurs in *Shrek*, as the ogre is about to defend the princess from the merry men of Sherwood Forest and is shot in the rear end by an arrow.

The Meeting with the Goddess At this point, the hero meets someone who he will love completely. A good example occurs in *Cars*, when Lightning McQueen meets Sally for the first time.

Woman as Temptress The hero is tempted to stray from the journey. This temptation does not have to be a person. In *The Lord of the Rings: The Two Towers*, Frodo decides to keep the ring for himself rather than destroy it.

Atonement with the Father The hero must at this step confront her largest fears; again, this confrontation does not have to be with a person. This can be seen in *Alien*, when Ripley gets in the power loader suit and confronts the queen alien in the ship's docking area.

Apotheosis Someone on the journey dies to save the hero or to rest peacefully. In *Star Wars*, Obi-Wan is struck down by Darth Vader but does so willingly, knowing there is more waiting ahead of him.

The Ultimate Boon This is the culmination of the hero's journey. In *The Lion King*, Simba takes his place as the king and roars.

Refusal of the Return Having found the ultimate boon, the hero does not want to return to his ordinary world. In *Cars*, Lightning McQueen stays in Radiator Springs at the end of the movie instead of pursuing his dream of big sponsorship.

The Magic Flight At this stage, the epic escape occurs—with the boon if needed. This escape can be just as dangerous as the hero's main journey. In *Raiders of the Lost Ark*, Indiana Jones obtains the golden idol but must then race out of the cave to escape a large boulder trying to crush him.

Rescue from Without The hero typically needs help on the journey and needs a guide to return to normal, everyday life. In *The Lord of the Rings: The Two Towers*, Frodo destroys the ring but is too tired to escape, so his companion Sam helps him out of the volcano.

The Crossing of the Return Threshold The hero takes what was learned on the journey and tries to fit it back into everyday life after the journey. In *The Lord of the Rings: The Two Towers*, Sam decides to relearn how to live in the normal world and gets married and starts a family.

Master of Two Worlds   The hero learns to balance the old world and the new world seen after the journey. In *Star Wars: Return of the Jedi*, Luke becomes a Jedi and can now live in the Jedi world and the real world at the same time with no new trials.

Freedom to Live   The hero learns to not fear death or regret the past after the lessons of the journey have been mastered. In *The Lord of the Rings: The Two Towers*, Frodo decides to go to the sea with the elves and Gandalf to finish his life.

Other Storytelling Principles

A few more storytelling principles lend themselves nicely to basic storytelling and animation. They are empathy (not sympathy); the rule of three; and show, don't tell. These principles do not directly tie into each other but are used to help create better stories.

Use Empathy, Not Sympathy!   Empathy is the ability to understand another's feelings and to see yourself in that person's shoes. Sympathy, on the other hand, is the understanding of another person's feelings, but the viewer may not experience the feelings vicariously as with empathy. Empathy creates a much stronger connection to characters and enables the audience to be connected with your story rather than just understanding your story.

You should always try to create characters that the audience can relate to in some way. This does not mean that your characters have to be boring, normal people, but you must find a way to make them have traits all people can relate to. Your characters can be exceptional in all ways, but if you can find one trait the audience can relate to, that will allow the connection.

The Rule of Three   This concept—used in writing, film, animation, comedy, and advertising—states that words, things, or situations are funnier or remembered better if done in groups of threes. You can see this in many of the *Looney Tunes* or *Tom and Jerry* cartoons. Wile E. Coyote wants to get the Road Runner, and during the cartoon he will try three different ways, all of which fail by the end of the show. You will also see the rule of three in advertising, as it is thought that you must say the name of a product at least three times to make sure it sticks in the viewer's mind.

Show, Don't Tell   Whether you're writing a novel or a film script, you want to paint images in the audience's mind. You do not merely *tell* the audience what is going to happen or how a character is feeling; you want to *show* it to them. Use actions, thoughts, dialogue, and senses to lead the audience through the story. This concept is universal in storytelling, but can be quite literally interpreted in fields such as character animation and texturing. Use the visual medium to your advantage unless it's absolutely necessary to tell the audience something explicitly. (This principle relates directly to the next section, "Using Pre-visualization Techniques.")

VIDEO GAMES: PRESENT A LINEAR STORY OR LET PLAYERS DECIDE?

Most video games present a character that the player controls through a scripted, linear story. Although many of these games provide ways for the player to control the game—for instance, allowing the character to move freely through an environment—these games still require tasks to be completed in a certain order.

But today many gamers are looking for a way to make their own game content—not by writing game code or creating game platforms, but by controlling the content within a given world. In recent years, games such as *The Sims* and *Spore* have allowed gamers to control nearly everything about their worlds and the interaction between characters.

The Sims, first released in 2000, was one of the first games offering this type of game play. *The Sims* truly paved the way for games of this type and became one of the highest-selling PC games of all time. *Spore,* created by the same game designer of *The Sims*—Will Wright—allows players not only to control what happens in the game but also to create the characters and world elements. Players can model and texture the characters as they see fit, and then the game animates the characters for them.

Using Pre-visualization Techniques

Pre-visualization is a technique used in film and television that utilizes 3D animation to plan the pacing, cuts, and camera angles of a sequence. This pre-production method enables the director to know exactly what will be needed to create the actual shots.

Pre-visualization is typically a lower-quality 3D animation that gives all of the visual information needed to plan for certain shots. For example, a director considering a helicopter shot could use pre-visualization to decide in the preproduction stage whether this shot is really needed, without wasting the money during the production.

Pre-visualization practices have come from years of film and television training that have shown how to frame a shot, how to move the camera, and when to cut to a different shot. These concepts enable the art of visual storytelling—taking a written script and making it visually read onscreen. There are three main areas of pre-visualization techniques:

▶ Basic shot framing

▶ Camera movements

▶ Editing

Basic Shot Framing

The audience can see only what you show them. Therefore, shot framing is important because you do not want the audience to miss anything you are trying to show. By controlling what will be framed in a shot, you can lead viewers' eyes to see exactly what you want them to see.

If you don't understand how to frame a shot so that viewers can see what they need to see, the results can be catastrophic. You will spend so much time on 3D animation that having an audience miss something would be a shame. It would also be bad if you are trying to sell a new product or building, but the investors miss important details.

Consider the following when framing a shot:

▶ Aspect ratio

▶ Basic shot types

▶ Basic composition rules

▶ Directing the viewer's eye

Aspect Ratio

The *aspect ratio* is the height-to-width ratio of the screen size you are working with. This is an important detail to nail down before venturing any further with shot framing. (Aspect ratio is also discussed in Chapter 3, "Understanding

Digital Imaging and Video.") Just as an artist uses a certain size canvas or paper in traditional visual arts such as drawing and painting, a 3D animator must work with a certain screen size or composition size. You have to know the size of your canvas in order to plan the composition of the shot. The most common ratios used today are as follows:

- ▶ 4:3—the square television format
- ▶ 16:9 —the ratio for HD televisions
- ▶ 1.85:1—the standard for most US movies
- ▶ 2.39:1—the ratio of anamorphic widescreen theatrical movies

Figure 4.20 shows examples of these aspect ratios.

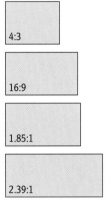

FIGURE 4.20
Aspect ratios for screen displays

Basic Shot Types

Basic shot types are the language of cinematographers in describing a shot before it is framed. These basic shot types are ways to describe what will be shown in the shot, with no thought about final frame composition. The basic shot types are as follows:

Extreme Wide Shot   Also known as an *establishing shot* (see Figure 4.21), this type of shot helps viewers know where they are and the positions of objects and figures. Seeing details is generally hard in an extreme wide shot, so it is used sparingly, and primarily to help the audience when the location has changed.

Model © After Hours Animation

FIGURE 4.21 An extreme wide shot

Wide Shot   Also known as a *long shot*, this type fills nearly the full vertical height of the screen with the subject. A wide shot also can be used as an establishing shot, to allow the audience to see the surrounding area. Figure 4.22 shows an example.

Model © After Hours Animation

FIGURE 4.22 A wide shot of a theater with a character standing in front of it and to the left

Medium Shot A *medium shot*, or *mid shot*, shows the main subject in more detail than the wide shot. If the subject is a character, the character is typically framed from the waist to the head (see Figure 4.23).

Model © After Hours Animation

FIGURE 4.23 A medium shot

Close-up In this shot, one subject takes up the entire frame. If a character is the subject and we are shooting a close-up of the character's head, the chin will be just above the bottom of the screen and the top of the head will be just below the top of the screen (see Figure 4.24).

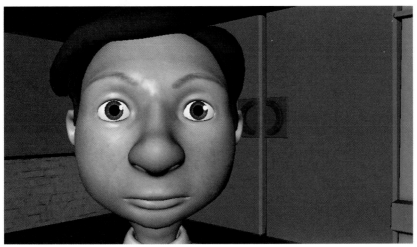

Model © After Hours Animation

FIGURE 4.24 A close-up shot

Extreme Close-up   This shot focuses on a small detail of the subject. For example, Figure 4.25 shows an extreme close-up of a character's eyes.

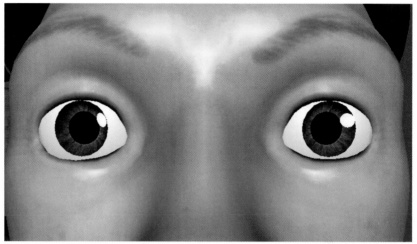

FIGURE 4.25 An extreme close-up shot

POV   A point-of-view (POV) shot illustrates a character's point of view. You can use any of the shot types already discussed, as long as the audience can clearly tell that the shot is coming from a certain character's point of view (see Figure 4.26).

FIGURE 4.26 A POV shot

Over the Shoulder This shot frames the back of one character's head on one side of the screen, and another character's face or the environment on the other side. This type of shot is used all the time in television, film, and even video games. Figure 4.27 shows an example.

Model © After Hours Animation

FIGURE 4.27 An over-the-shoulder shot

Basic Composition Rules

As 3D animation entertainers, educators, or business workers, we do not want to bore the audience. Therefore, presenting compositions that are repetitive and lackluster is not what we want to do. By abiding by the following basic rules of composition, you can make your product exciting:

Golden Ratio The *golden ratio*, also known as the *golden section* or *divine proportion*, is a rule that artists, architects, and designers have used for centuries to help create balance in a frame. The golden ratio describes a spatial relationship between two quantities. As shown in Figure 4.28, if you divide a line into two parts, and the longer part divided by the shorter part is the same as the whole length divided by the longer part, you have created the golden ratio. This ratio is represented by the Greek letter phi and is equal to the irrational constant 1.618033.

a+b is to a as a is to b

FIGURE 4.28
A graphical representation
of the golden ratio

This ratio is used in math, art design, financial markets, and nature. Figure 4.29 shows the golden ratio's presence in a chambered nautilus.

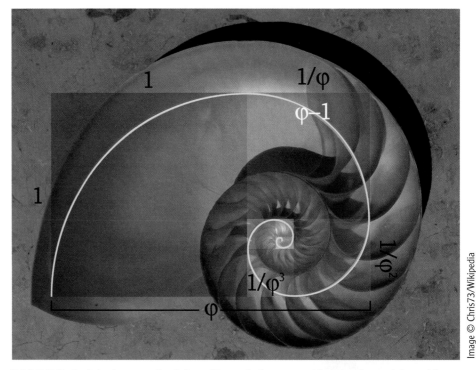

Image © Chris73/Wikipedia

FIGURE 4.29 An example of the golden ratio in nature with a nautilus and the golden section within it

As a 3D artist, the value of the golden ratio is that you can use it to create a balanced placement onscreen of your main subject. To do this, you use a related rectangular shape called the *golden rectangle*. In a golden rectangle, the ratio of the longer side to the shorter side equals the golden ratio, or 1.618:1.

Figure 4.30 depicts the creation of a golden rectangle. First, you draw a square and split it vertically in half, as shown by the light gray line. The square is now two rectangles. Draw a diagonal line, from the bottom-left corner of the new, rightmost rectangle to the top-right corner, as shown by the darker gray arrow. From that point, draw an arc downward to create the longer dimension of the final rectangle. The black line splitting the yellow and white sections indicates an optimal area for placing characters or objects in a basic composition. People find this placement more pleasing than centering the subject. (The split can be on either side of the frame, not just the right side.)

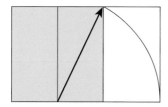 

FIGURE 4.30 The golden rectangle (left) used to create the frame composition in an animated film (right)

Rule of Thirds Imagine a grid dividing your screen into thirds horizontally and vertically. The *rule of thirds* states that the locations where the lines meet are hot spots for placing your subject. These areas are the most appealing to the viewers' eyes. You will see this rule used in film, television, art, and photography. Figure 4.31 shows an image with the grid lines overlaid. Placing the main action on the lower-left hot spot is more dynamic than if the action were right in the middle of one of the grid squares.

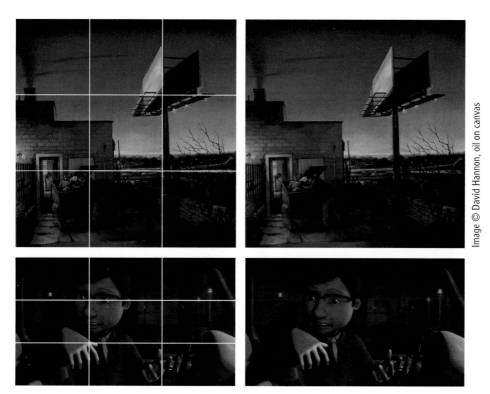

Image © David Hannon, oil on canvas

FIGURE 4.31 The rule of thirds in practice

Head Room and Nose Room   *Head room* and *nose room* are methods of framing a shot that include room for the character or object to look offscreen or to move. Figure 4.32 illustrates nose room. In a medium close-up of a character looking at something in the distance off-camera, you do not want the character's face in the center of the frame, as in the left image. Instead you would allow room on the side of the frame for the character to look across, as in the right image.

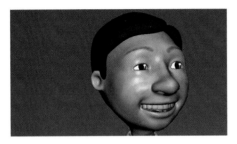 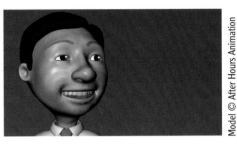

Model © After Hours Animation

FIGURE 4.32 Too little nose room (left) and proper nose room (right)

Nose room does not apply only to characters, but also to objects. For instance, when framing a car chase in which the first car is traveling from right to left, you should place the car on the right side of the screen to allow it visual room to travel (see Figure 4.33).

If you are framing the subject in the center as the subject is looking directly into the camera, you should not leave too much head room at the top of the screen. Excessive head room makes the subject seem weak. You also should take care to avoid cutting off part of the character's head at the top of the screen. You should typically frame the character so that the eyes are one-third of the way down from the top of the screen, as in Figure 4.34.

Model © After Hours Animation

FIGURE 4.33 Good nose room for a car shot traveling from right to left

Model © After Hours Animation

FIGURE 4.34 Excessive head room (left) and proper head room (right)

Directing the Eye

When *directing the eye*, you lead the eyes of the audience to the area you want them to see. As mentioned previously, animation is just too time-consuming and expensive for the audience to miss what was shown onscreen. So directing the gaze of your audience is a must.

There are many ways to direct the audience's eyes. The most basic method is to point at the subject—not literally (you don't want a big finger onscreen flashing "look here")—but via a visual element to lead the audience's eye. Traditional artists have been using this technique for centuries. Filmmakers will use background elements such as a street sign pointing, and artists have used the composition of an image to center the area of the primary element to focus on. Figure 4.35 is the painting The Last Supper by Leonardo Da Vinci, in which you can see the perspective lines of the room, brightness of the background windows and the faces of everyone in the painting leading your eye to the center figure of Jesus.

FIGURE 4.35 Leonardo Da Vinci's The Last Supper.

You can also use light and shadows to make sure you illuminate your subject in a way that enables people to see important details. Figure 4.36, for example, highlights the character's struggling expression and clenched hand.

Image © After Hours Animation

FIGURE 4.36 An example of using lighting to center the subject and draw the audience's attention

Color is another way to direct the eye. You can use a vibrant or contrasting color for the subject you want to highlight. A color that differs from those in the rest of the frame will make the audience look at the subject. Figure 4.37 shows an example.

FIGURE 4.37 The bright red color pulls the viewer's eye to the button on the seatbelt.

Another way to lead the eye is to create a frame within the frame of the shot. You can use a window or doorway to frame a character or subject, for instance, as in Figure 4.38. You can also use tree branches or buildings to frame a small section of the total frame and thereby lead the eye.

Image © After Hours Animation

FIGURE 4.38 The director is using a mirror to frame the character's face within the overall frame.

Depth of field can also be a good way to direct the eye to a certain area of the screen. This optical effect allows a camera lens to focus on one distance at a time. Anything outside the focal distance is out of focus, as in Figure 4.39.

Image © After Hours Animation

FIGURE 4.39 Using depth of field to focus viewer attention

Camera Movements

Camera movements, as you might guess, indicate how the camera can be moved. These physical movements can be used to visually define storytelling information. Camera angles can be just as important to film and television in visual storytelling as the actors giving the performance, and a close-up at the right time in the story will allow the audience to get very intimate experience with a character that a medium or wide shot would not provide. In addition, today's audiences are so used to television and film that if a 3D camera doesn't move like a real-world camera, the audience loses interest due to an unfamiliarity with the visual storytelling.

Cameras can be moved in so many ways, resulting in so many wide-ranging effects on the visual storytelling, that choosing each camera movement can become quite daunting. A solid understanding of your options is key to telling a story. Here are some of the basic camera moves you will need to re-create:

Pan   A pan (Figure 4.40) is a rotation of the camera side to side, horizontally. This move can be created by hand or by rotating the camera on a tripod.

FIGURE 4.40
A camera pan

Tilt   A tilt (Figure 4.41) is a rotation of the camera up or down, vertically. This move can be created by hand or by rotating the camera on a tripod.

FIGURE 4.41
A camera tilt

Roll   This involves rotating the camera on its side or upside down. This kind of camera rotation will allow the camera to roll 360 degrees if needed for effect. (See Figure 4.42.)

FIGURE 4.42
A camera roll

Dolly   A dolly (Figure 4.43) can move the camera forward or backward, toward or away from the subject. This move can be completed by hand, but typically the camera is mounted to a dolly that is pushed. A dolly can be an expensive cart-and-track system or can be as low-tech as a skateboard with a tripod on top of it.

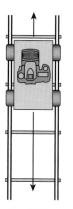

FIGURE 4.43
A camera dolly

Track   You can move the camera along a track to follow the subject, typically from side to side (Figure 4.44). This is not to be confused with a dolly, which moves forward and backward.

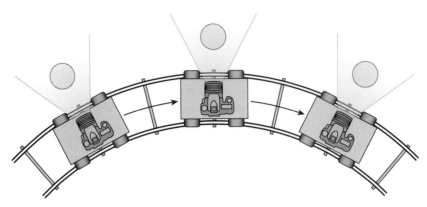

FIGURE 4.44 A camera track

Pedestal   A pedestal (Figure 4.45) tracks the height of an object by moving the camera vertically.

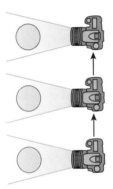

FIGURE 4.45
A camera pedestal

Zoom   A zoom is different from the other camera moves because you are not physically moving the camera, but rather moving the lens to create movement in the frame. Most people have used the zoom feature on a personal camera—you push a button to zoom in on your subject without having to move the camera. In film, television, and 3D animation, you use a zoom only when needed, because it can be distracting to the audience if overdone. The act of zooming a camera physically pushes the camera lens closer to or farther away from its aperture and creates some lens distortion that flattens out the framing and creates an illusion of objects being closer together. Figure 4.46 shows an example of this flattening of an image. The image on the left has a camera focal length of 35, and the image on the right has the focal length set to 200. The background on the right seems flattened out, and the character does not appear as large.

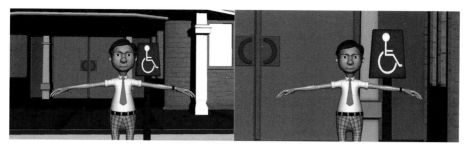

FIGURE 4.46 Two shots of the same character, using a wide-angle view (left) and a zoomed-in view (right)

Handheld   A handheld movement (Figure 4.47) entails holding the camera and moving freely in any direction to follow the action. This movement is good for horror or action films because it allows the viewers to feel as if they are actually immersed in the action. But handheld movement must be used wisely; overuse can be jarring to the audience.

FIGURE 4.47
Example of a handheld camera move

Rack Focus   This involves changing the focus of the camera to push an object that is out of focus into focus, or vice versa. Figure 4.48 shows an example. In the 3D animation world, rack focus can be accomplished in the software's 3D camera but is typically achieved in the postproduction stage with compositing software.

FIGURE 4.48 Example of a rack focus change from one object to another

Editing

Editing is the stage where the story really comes together. In live-action film and television, all of the preproduction planning and the shooting of lots and lots of imagery are put together at the end of the process, in the postproduction editing stage. In 3D animation, the editing must be done in the preproduction stage with an animatic and layout. Either way, the same process occurs, and the same basic rules of editing are used. The following are some guidelines for the editing process.

Cuts

A *cut* is an abrupt change in the imagery that provides the transition to a new shot. This happens all the time in 3D animation as well as in live-action film and television. Most of the time, you never notice it, and cuts help push the story further. But if done incorrectly, a cut can be quite jarring to the audience. It is the editor's job to know when, where, and how to cut in a new shot. There are volumes of books and training material on this one subject, and mastering editing requires many years of practice. To get you started, the following paragraphs outline some basic types of cuts you can make and some you should not make.

Thoughtful Cuts   Never make a cut without a reason. That reason can be simple: something gets in the way of the action, or the actors just stopped being in character because they are being distracted by something offscreen or laughing at another actor, for example. But after you decide to take a shot, stay on that shot until the story demands that it be changed.

Cut on a Look   It is jarring to the viewer to cut from a shot with movement to a shot that has no movement in it. (For that reason, this type of cut is known as a *cut in movement*.) Say, for example, you have a close-up shot of your main character talking. The character hears a sound and turns to look at it. A perfect place to cut would be in the middle of the head turn. In the following shot, the main character's head would be finishing the turn to look toward the source of the sound.

Jump Cuts   Avoid jump cuts! A jump cut is one that changes from one shot to another that has the same composition. For instance, if you start with a medium shot of a character centered in the frame and cut to another medium shot of a character centered in the frame, that is a jump cut. Nothing has changed but the characters. Because that is not enough change for the audience; they will be pulled out of the story. In another kind of jump cut, you move toward a subject but do not change the camera shot enough. For example, going from a medium shot to a close-up, as shown in Figure 4.49, is not a large enough change in the camera to warrant the cut.

FIGURE 4.49 A jump cut from a medium shot (left) to a close-up (right)

Transitions   A transition is an effect used between shots. There are several types: a crossfade (one image fades into the next image), a dissolve (one image dissolves into the next), and a fade (an image fades to a solid color, usually white or black).

A wipe is another type of transition that wipes the screen of one image to make way for the new one. Wipes are very tricky to use between shots. The most recognizable type of wipe, which has fallen out of favor among many creators, is the old moving line across the screen. That method can work, though, as it did in the *Star Wars* saga. In addition, there are more-artistic ways to use the wipe—for instance, you might have a background character walk right across the screen in the foreground, thereby using that character as the wipe. As a general rule, use transitions only sparingly and only for effect.

180-Degree Rule

The *180-degree rule* states that two characters should have the same left and right space onscreen in a sequence. This means that after you set up the scene with the camera, your characters cannot change sides. You can see this rule used in soap operas on television all the time—when two characters are talking, the first character is always on the left, and the second character is on the right until something breaks the action or a new character is introduced. You can think of this rule in terms of a battle scene, in which the good guys are coming from the left and the bad guys are on the right. As you shoot the different fights, you have to keep the good on the left and the bad on the right, or the audience will become confused about who is who.

Figure 4.50 shows an overhead depiction of this rule. After the primary placement of the characters is established, an imaginary line is drawn between the characters. The camera cannot cross that line unless the audience is clued in on the change.

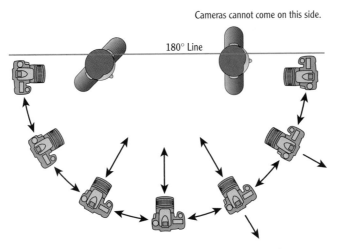

FIGURE 4.50 The invisible line created between characters creates the 180-degree line that the camera should not cross.

THE ESSENTIALS AND BEYOND

The 3D animation industry has borrowed concepts from other fields including art, film, and writing. The principles described in this chapter are only the tip of the iceberg—the basics. You should use this chapter as a springboard to learn more about each topic.

You have seen how principles from fine art tie into 3D animation—for example, the importance of really seeing a subject rather than basing your creations on assumptions of what you think it looks like. You also learned about the basic three-point lighting setup that artists have been using for centuries for painting, photography, and filmmaking.

You have looked at the elements of a basic story and how they can be woven into an original story. You have also seen how the camera can play a role in telling stories visually through a lens. 3D animation is a very immersive industry that will borrow and use concepts from many different fields like art, film, and photography and is creating new concepts of its own everyday, and a 3D artist must become a Renaissance artist of sorts who is able to have their hand in many of these types of concepts.

(Continues)

THE ESSENTIALS AND BEYOND *(Continued)*

REVIEW QUESTIONS

1. Which of these is not part of the Twelve Basic Principles of Animation?

   A. Appeal **C.** Squash and stretch

   B. Straight-ahead **D.** Speed

2. True or false: A story's narrative structure must include all 17 stages of a monomyth, or hero's journey.

3. True or false: A pan moves the camera forward and backward.

4. True or false: The understanding of anatomy is important for a 3D modeler.

5. How many basic elements are needed for a story to hold the audience's interest?

   A. 2 **C.** 3

   B. 5 **D.** 9

6. True or False: It is more important for the audience to sympathize with your characters, not empathize with them.

7. What is the name of the standard basic light setup used in capturing images, whether in photography or 3D animation?

   A. One-point lighting **C.** Natural lighting

   B. Two-point lighting **D.** Three-point lighting

8. Which of these aspect ratios is used in HD television?

   A. 4:3 (1.33) **C.** 16:9 (1.77)

   B. 2.39:1 **D.** 1.85:1

9. True or false: Jump cuts are a desirable type of edit.

10. What is a medium shot of a human figure?

   A. Framing a close-up on the subject **C.** Framing the subject from the waist up

   B. Framing the full environment including the subject **D.** Framing a small detail of the subject

CHAPTER 5

Understanding Modeling and Texturing

Modeling and texturing are two of the primary jobs within the field of 3D animation and are closely tied to one another. *Modeling* is the act of creating a 3D object. *Texturing* is applying the color and surface properties to the model. Every industry that uses 3D animation must start with the creation of a model, which then serves as the foundation for all the other steps in the production pipeline. Texturing is the stage after a model is created, and the application of the texture depends on the geometry type used to create the model.

By looking at each geometry type and workflow individually, you can see the advantages and disadvantages of each and thereby better determine which type to use. In this chapter, you will also look at some of the standard material types and texture maps that texture artists use to create the look of the final model.

▶ **Modeling**

▶ **Texturing**

Modeling

Modeling is an essential part of 3D animation. Everything you see in any 3D animation had to be created (digitized) in one way or another. Typically, a model is either created from scratch or is based on a 3D scan or other form of digitization that is then cleaned up.

Modeler is the job title of an artist who creates or cleans up the geometry of a 3D model. You can think of 3D animation modelers as digital sculptors. Modeling is also typically the starting place for beginners to learn their way around 3D software, because modeling requires you to move around an object, manipulate and correct components of objects, and work with various attributes and properties of the 3D software. However, just because modeling is a starting place for 3D animators to become familiar with the software does not make it easy to master. It takes years of practice to perfect a modeling workflow, create models with efficient and proper resolution, gain an understanding of how physical objects work and are put together, and understand human anatomy before becoming a proficient and professional modeler.

Most people in 3D animation either love or hate modeling, because the technical limitations of the software can make the task feel unnatural to beginning 3D artists. Models created in 3D software such as Autodesk Maya, 3ds Max, and Softimage require artists to move individual components (in some instances, one at a time), which is not a natural modeling experience. New software, including Pixologic's ZBrush and Autodesk Mudbox, has incorporated the idea of sculpture so that artists can work as if pushing and pulling clay. This change has improved modeling workflows and enhanced the level of final detail in the models.

A modeler can use three geometry types to create models: polygons, non-uniform rational B-splines (NURBS), and subdivision surfaces. These geometry types are the mathematical representations of a 3D form. Each has its advantages and disadvantages and component-level differences. You should be familiar with all three types because the one you use will be dictated by each particular project and by the production pipeline used by the studio. In addition, there are many techniques used to create a 3D model. You can model from reference images, use 3D scanning, perform digital sculpting, or start with basic geometric shapes such as spheres, cubes, cylinders, cones, and flat planes. This section presents a closer look at the geometry types and the basic techniques used today, to give you a better idea of what is out there.

Polygons

Polygons are the geometry type most widely used by 3D modelers today. Polygons are straightforward and easy to work with and can be manipulated by a vast array of tools. Polygons are made up of three or more corners known as *vertices* (a single one is called a *vertex*) and the lines connecting those vertices, called *edges*. Most 3D applications create the surfaces we see by filling polygons with *faces*, as you can see in Figure 5.1. Each component (vertex, edge, and face) of a polygon can be *translated* (moved in 3D space), rotated, and *scaled* (changed in size). Polygon faces can be seen in a 3D render. The edges and vertices cannot be seen in a 3D render but can be seen and manipulated in the software itself.

The most basic form of polygon is a three-sided one called a *tri*. The most used type of polygon is a four-sided one known as a *quad*. Most 3D modelers avoid using an *n*-gon, or *n*-sided polygon, which is a polygon with five or more sides.

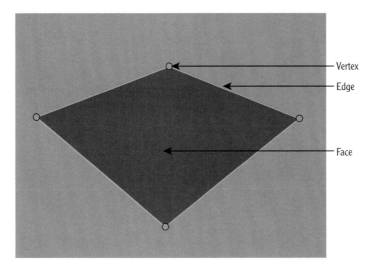

FIGURE 5.1 The three main components of a polygon

THE DIFFICULTY WITH *N*-GONS

The problem with *n*-gons is that the shape might not deform as expected. This shape can also easily become nonplanar and not render as expected. N-gons can easily become a tri or quad with simple poly splitting tools in the 3D software. So it is just easier to not use them in polygon shapes.

Collections of polygons make up a *polygon object* or *polygon mesh*, creating a shape such as a sphere (see Figure 5.2). Polygon objects and polygon meshes can be manipulated as a single polygon, which is what makes this geometry type so popular—anything you can change in or assign to a polygon, you can change in or assign to a polygon object or mesh.

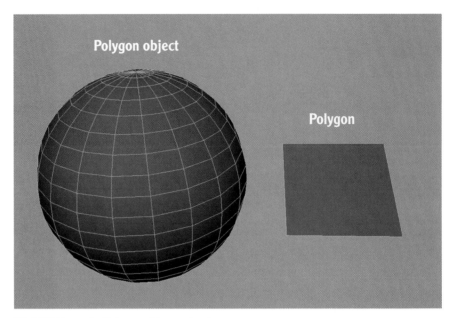

FIGURE 5.2 Polygon object and polygon

Popular tools and techniques that are available in almost all 3D applications enable you to perform the following operations on polygons: dividing, smoothing, extruding, beveling, deleting, combining, and separating. Each is detailed in this section.

Dividing   When dividing a polygon, you create a new edge across its face, as shown in Figure 5.3. Dividing can happen across a single polygon or around an entire polygon object. Dividing an entire polygon object is often referred to as adding an *edge loop*—a set of connected edges across a polygon surface that meet back at the first edge to create a loop. An edge loop is one of the most common ways to create more geometry resolution in a model, which allows for more detail. An edge loop provides the most efficient way to subdivide the geometry of a polygon object because the user defines where the subdivision or additional geometry will be placed.

The way edges flow along a model is called *edge flow*. Good edge flow is organized and typically follows the shape of the object or the muscle anatomy of a creature. Good edge flow aids in the deformation of the model later, in the rigging process. Figure 5.4 shows the edge flow of a human head. The edges flow in circular patterns around the eyes and mouth, which mimics the muscular structure of the face.

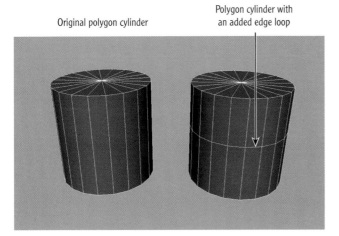

Original polygon cylinder

Polygon cylinder with
an added edge loop

FIGURE 5.3 Adding an edge loop to a polygon cylinder

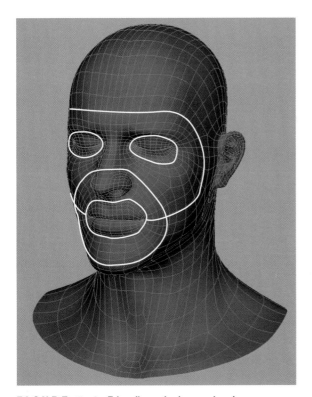

FIGURE 5.4 Edge flow of a human head

Many 3D animation software programs enable you to preview a smoothing effect during the modeling process.

Smoothing   Smoothing subdivides a polygon object and averages the angles formed by all edges of the original geometry. The left image in Figure 5.5 shows a cube that has been smoothed twice, subdividing its faces and changing the cube into a sphere. Each subdivision level averages the angle of the two faces connected by an edge, and in the case of the cube, results in a sphere. The right image of Figure 5.5 shows this progression. The top shape is the original cube that has a 90-degree angle between the two original faces. After a first level of smoothing, the two face are subdivided once, giving us four faces, and which changes the top angle edge to 45 degrees. In the second level of smoothing, each face is subdivided again, and the original top edge angle changes to 22.5 degrees (with the angles formed by other edges changed as well).

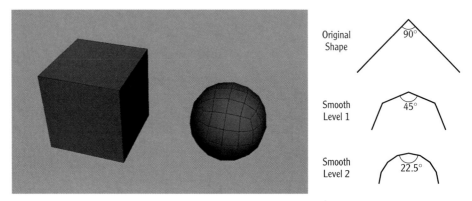

FIGURE 5.5   A cube smoothed to create a sphere (left), and an illustration of the polygon smoothing process (right)

Extruding   Extruding adds geometry to a polygon surface by creating a new surface, offsetting that new surface, and then creating more new surfaces between the offset and original surface. You can extrude vertices, edges, and faces, which makes this technique very useful. Figure 5.6 shows an example of extruding. Cube 1 is the original polygon object. In cube 2, the top face has been extruded and scaled inward. In cube 3, the extrusion is moved up. In cube 4, the top face has been extruded and scaled inward, and then the inner face of that extrusion has been extruded again and moved down to make a hole in the top of the cube.

Beveling   Beveling adds a face or faces that are not perpendicular to the original faces connected by the edges of a polygon model, to give them a slightly rounded shape. Edges created in 3D software packages are unrealistically sharp by default and will look fake if not fixed. Figure 5.7 shows close-up and zoomed-out views of two cubes rendered in 3D. The beveled-edge box (on the right) has a slight highlight along the bevel, which makes the cube look a little more real compared to the hard-edged box on the left. But what if the object you are trying to create has a razor-sharp edge? In that case, you might not want to add the bevel. On the other hand, if you look at a real razor's edge close up, you will see that it flattens off to a beveled edge, which is what allows you to see nicks in the blade—the nicks appear as highlights.

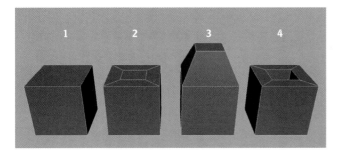

FIGURE 5.6 Examples of extruding a polygon

FIGURE 5.7 A polygon cube without a beveled edge (top) and with a beveled edge (bottom)

Deleting, Combining, and Separating   Deleting, combining, and separating all contribute to making the polygon such an easy type of geometry to use. You can delete any polygon face and then combine two polygon objects together (see Figure 5.8). You can also separate two polygon objects (see Figure 5.9) with no major consequences to the model as a whole.

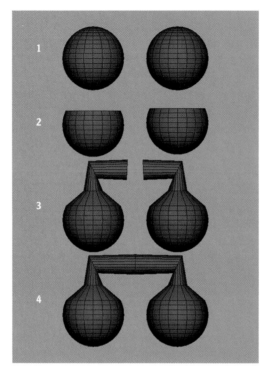

FIGURE 5.8 Deleting and combining polygons.
(1) Two separate polygon spheres. (2) The two spheres with their tops deleted. (3) An extrusion of the top edge loop to create a new shape. (4) The vertices connected together and the two separate objects combined to make a single object.

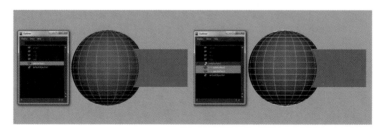

FIGURE 5.9 Separating combined polygons. The sphere and cube are combined in the left image and have been separated in the right image. This is not a function you can see on the objects themselves but in the box beside them listing the objects in the scene.

You must give some thought to the shading of a polygon in the render engine you are using. Shading is created by the normals of a polygon surface. A *normal* is a vector line that points perpendicularly straight out of the surface, as shown in Figure 5.10. The 3D software uses these normals to assign each polygon face its front and back side. The vector is drawn in both directions from the face, and the math algorithm that creates the face via the user's commands differentiates the front from the back side. This distinction is important because many 3D software packages will not render the back side of a polygon unless instructed to by the user.

Figure 5.11 shows a polygon sphere. On the left side of the image, a few normals have been reversed (highlighted). The right side of the image shows the faces that have inverted normals as black, because the render engine by default ignores the faces that are not facing the camera. The reversal of normals can occur for various reasons, such as simple user error, object export and import issues between software, or a software error during the modeling process.

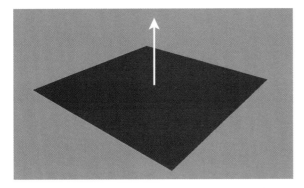

FIGURE 5.10 Polygon face with normal indicated

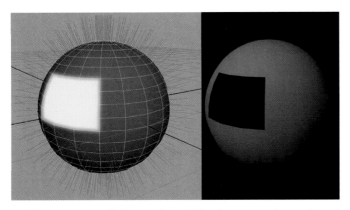

FIGURE 5.11 Polygon sphere with a few reversed normals, as shown in Autodesk Maya's viewport and Render View window

Normals are also used to influence how the polygon object's shading will look. Polygons at the very beginning of their existence were rendered from the angle of the surface normal, which creates flat, or faceted, shading. A new option in polygon shading was created to allow what are called vertex normals to instruct the shading of an object to allow for an angled, smooth effect. The vertex normals will average the surface normals of two connected faces to achieve this smooth shading.

Figure 5.12 and Figure 5.13 show how a polygon and the vertex normals dictate the shading of an object. In Figure 5.12, you can see that the vertex normals of the polygon wedge are pointing directly perpendicular to the surface normals. The sphere looks very faceted and hard-edged. In Figure 5.13, the polygon wedge has a smooth transition across the top edge; notice that the arrows representing the vertex normals are averaging the angles of the two faces. The sphere has soft, or Gouraud, shading and looks very smooth along the surface. The surface resolution is identical in both figures, meaning they have the exact same topology, but Figure 5.13 looks much smoother.

You can see this shading effect on a polygon character model in Figure 5.14. This soft vertex normal allows the 3D artist to avoid having a dense polygon mesh for final rendering.

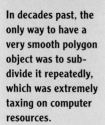

Gouraud shading, named for its creator, allows vertices to reference a polygon's surface normals. This process then averages the surface direction from the vertices and surrounding faces to achieve smooth shading.

In decades past, the only way to have a very smooth polygon object was to subdivide it repeatedly, which was extremely taxing on computer resources.

FIGURE 5.12 Hard-edge polygon vertex normals

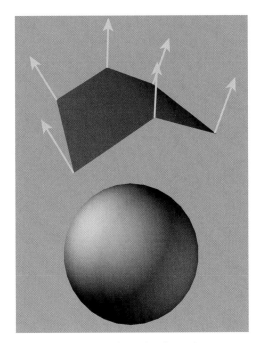

FIGURE 5.13 Smooth-edge polygon vertex normals

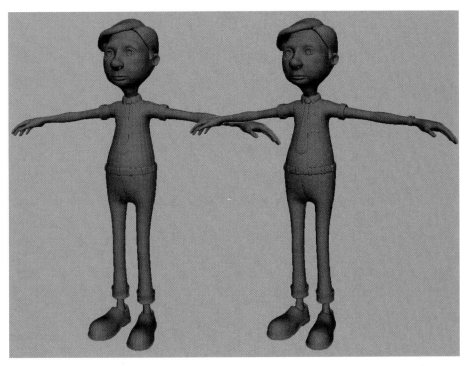

FIGURE 5.14 A polygon model with hard (left) and smooth (right) vertex normals

The density of the polygon mesh, called the *topology resolution*, is an important option in modeling because different industries require different resolutions. The video game industry relies heavily on low-topology resolutions in order to enable real-time interactions during game play. If all of the objects had overly heavy topology resolutions, the game would not play in real time. Film and television, on the other hand, can allow for higher topology resolution because a real-time response is not required, and so renders can take up to a day or two per frame. Still, these industries cannot use an unlimited topology resolution because memory allocations could crash the computer or take too long to render. The vertex smoothing allows an object with a lower topology resolution to render like a very high resolution model.

Figure 5.15 shows two rows of spheres with different shading. The top row has flat, or faceted, shading. The bottom row has smooth, or Gouraud, shading. The numbers across the top of the figure indicate the number of faces in that column of spheres. In the bottom row of smooth shaded spheres, you can see that there is very little difference between the sphere in the 400 column and the one in the 6,400 column. In the top row of flat shaded spheres, you can see the flat faces even in the 6,400 column. This faceted look is usually not desired in 3D animation today.

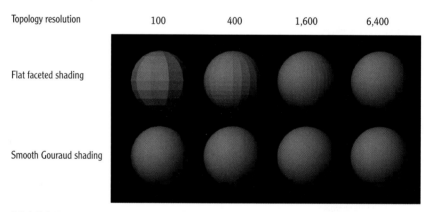

FIGURE 5.15 Examples of different topology resolutions of models with flat shading and Gouraud shading

Polygon modeling is robust but not perfect. You might run into some issues, and it's important to know how to address them. The following paragraphs address some potential problems.

Nonplanar Polygon Faces   By default, polygons should be *planar*, which means the vertices are all on the same plane, as shown in Figure 5.16. If one of the vertices is not on the same plane, you have a *nonplanar* surface, as shown in Figure 5.17. A nonplanar polygon could render in expected ways because the render engine might not understand the shape the user wants. In addition, smooth shading of a nonplanar face will be inaccurate because of the bend in the shape. To fix this problem, you can easily split the quad polygon into two planar triangles, or *tris*, so it will behave and render in an expected fashion, as seen in Figure 5.18.

F I G U R E 5 . 1 6 Planar polygon

F I G U R E 5 . 1 7 Nonplanar polygon

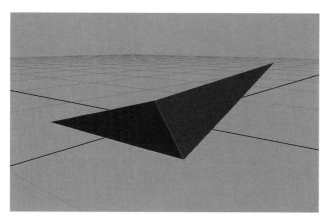

FIGURE 5.18 Nonplanar fix: Split the quad into two tris to create two planar faces.

Laminated Faces   Laminated faces are polygon faces lying right on top of one another. Because a polygon does not have physical thickness, laminated faces can occur—typically in the extruding process. During the smoothing or subdividing of a polygon object, laminated faces will cause errors. Figure 5.19 shows two sets of cubes. The top two cubes are the originals, and the bottom two cubes are the smoothed and subdivided versions. The cube on the left smooths to a sphere, and the cube on the right smooths to a drumlike shape. This occurs because the front face of the cube on the right is laminated, not allowing the smooth subdivisions to round away the edges. Laminated faces occur almost exclusively from user error in the modeling process and can be avoided by careful modeling practices.

Polygon Bowtie Effect   The bowtie effect occurs when a quad or *n*-gon is twisted but remains on the same plane, which will not allow the software to understand which direction is the front of the normal. Figure 5.20 shows two identical polygons, with the polygon on the right illustrating the bowtie effect. On the rightmost polygon, the two vertices on its left side are switched, so the software no longer knows which side is up, meaning it will no longer render properly. This effect occurs from the software not understanding which direction of the face to display due to the surface normal (arrows pointing out of the face) and the twisting effect. This problem is called a *bowtie* because the resulting render sometimes looks like that shape.

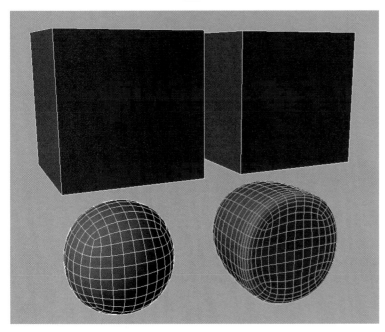

FIGURE 5.19 Laminated faces on a polygon cube will give unexpected results in the smooth subdivision of that object.

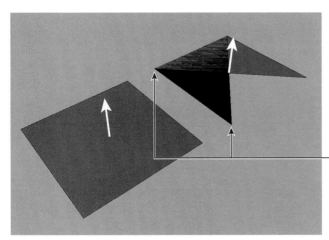

These two vertices switched sides to create the bowtie effect.

FIGURE 5.20 Bowtie polygon example

Two Faces Extruded from the Same Edge   A similar problem can arise when you extrude two faces from the same edge, as shown in Figure 5.21. Because polygons do not have a physical thickness, as you rotate around this shape, you will be looking at the backside of the polygons, and they may not render correctly.

Most render engines used today ignore the faces that are not facing the camera by default. This helps free up computer resources at render time by enabling the software to avoid having to calculate every object and face in the scene.

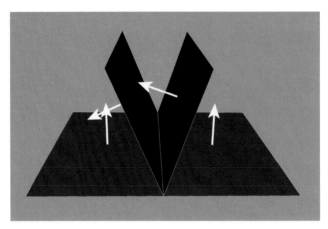

FIGURE 5.21 A double-extruded edge

NURBS

NURBS geometry is a mathematical model type that uses smooth curves as guideposts that will span a surface between them. NURBS models are great at representing smooth, rounded shapes but do have limitations, which makes them more difficult to use than polygons.

In the early days of 3D computer graphics, NURBS were the standard geometry type because of the smooth, round shapes they could create and render. At the time, polygons could not provide smooth shading and would always look faceted without an extraordinarily high topology resolution in the final render. But as computers and software have become more complex and more powerful, polygons have taken over as the standard geometry type. NURBS are still used today in the product visualization and architecture industries, especially to create fast representations of objects that are then converted to polygons or subdivision surfaces to complete a project.

So let's look at few ways to create NURBS. The most basic form of NURBS modeling is to create a NURBS primitive object such as a sphere. The NURBS object has components used to manipulate the object: control vertices, hulls, and isoparms. *Control vertices*, or *CVs*, are vertices that do not lie directly on the curve but can be moved to change the shape of the curve, which will then change the shape of the object. Hulls are lines of CVs that when selected can be manipulated like a polygon edge. *Isoparms* are lines that represent the surface of the NURBS object and can be used to create a new curve along the existing curve to add detail to the surface. Figure 5.22 shows a NURBS sphere with these components.

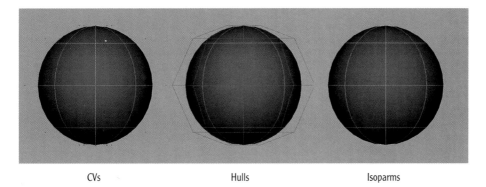

CVs   Hulls   Isoparms

FIGURE 5.22 NURBS components

Another method of creating NURBS is to create a series of curves and then loft or layout the surface along the curves. This method of modeling can create interesting, flat, organic shapes that can be manipulated easily. Figure 5.23 shows an example: the four curves on the left have been selected, and the surface shown on the right is placed to follow those curves. Another method is to create a single curve and then revolve it up to 360 degrees to create a surface such as a cup or glass, as shown in Figure 5.24. You can also extrude surfaces similarly to the way polygons can extrude faces, but along a curve. The first curve indicates the shape of the surface, and the second curve is the path of the extrusion (see Figure 5.25).

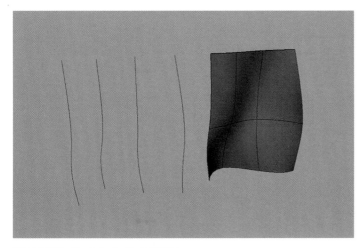

FIGURE 5.23 Lofted NURBS

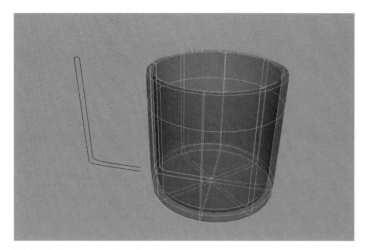

FIGURE 5.24 Revolved NURBS

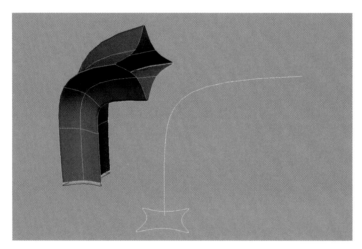

FIGURE 5.25 Extruded NURBS

The difficulty with using NURBS is that they can be only four-sided, which limits the shapes you can create. To be able to create a human head by using NURBS, you must create a *NURBS patch model*, which is composed of many smaller four-sided NURBS patches lined up next to each other. Another challenge is the way NURBS are textured. A NURBS patch model is treated not as one object but rather as many small patches, which makes it difficult to maintain a consistent texture along the surfaces. Unlike polygons, NURBS cannot have faces deleted or manipulated, and you cannot attach separate NURBS objects to one another as you can with polygons. These types of limitations have kept NURBS modeling from being the standard in the 3D animation industry today.

Subdivision Surfaces

Subdivision surfaces (or *subDs*) are a form of geometry that seems to combine the ease of polygons with the rounded, smoothed shapes of NURBS. Subdivision surfaces are whole surfaces, and not patches as complex NURBS objects are. SubDs enable you to create different levels of detail in specific areas where needed without too many problems with edge flow. Subdivision surfaces begin as polygon models and NURBS models, which are then converted to subDs as a last step to add final detail.

Figure 5.26 shows the creation of a subdivision surface. We start with the cube polygon on the left. That cube is then subdivided three times to create the sphere in the middle. The sphere on the right is the result of the cube being converted into a subdivision surface. You can see that the topology needed to create a nice, smooth surface in the subD model is much less than that of the smoothed polygon sphere in the middle, and when rendered, the subD model is a perfect sphere.

The polygon sphere in the middle of Figure 5.26 in an outline form will look very close to a perfect sphere but will never be perfectly smooth because of the nature of planar faces.

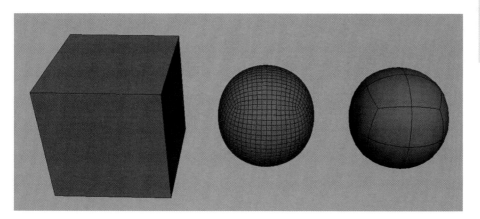

FIGURE 5.26 The cube on the left is the original shape, the middle is a smoothed polygon, and the right is a subdivision surface.

Modeling Workflows

Modeling workflows can be different depending on the type of model you are using, the project's final outcome, and the studio you work for. In this section, you'll look at a few basic types of workflows: from-scratch modeling, primitive modeling, box modeling, Boolean modeling, laser scanning, and digital sculpting. Each workflow provides the same result but takes you along a different path to get there. Modelers typically start with concept art or real-world images of the objects they are to create as references and produce a 3D model in whatever software they are using. All of these workflows do have a high-level structure in common: you start with a low-resolution topology and then add topology as needed for details.

The main workflows are as follows:

From-Scratch Modeling   In from-scratch modeling, you lay out each vertex and draw each polygon one by one until the entire model is completed (see Figure 5.27). This technique is not popular today because of advancements in polygon modeling and editing tools in most 3D applications.

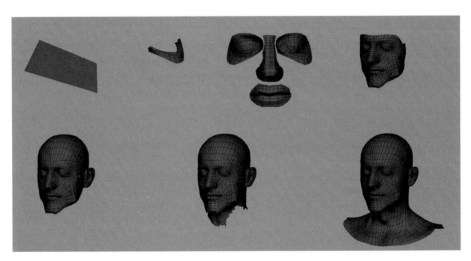

FIGURE 5.27 A few steps of from-scratch polygon modeling

Primitive Modeling   In primitive modeling, you start with basic shapes given to you by the software—for instance, helix, cylinder, torus, sphere, pipe, cube, cone, or plane, as shown in Figure 5.28. You then have to make only minor changes to the primitive model to create an object. This type of modeling is great for hard-surface models such as tables, chairs, pencils, picture frames, simple buildings, and swords. This technique can get you through the basic stages of modeling very quickly. Figure 5.29 shows a chair modeled with this approach, using only cubes. The artist then scaled their proportions to create each part of the object, including legs, seat, supports, and back.

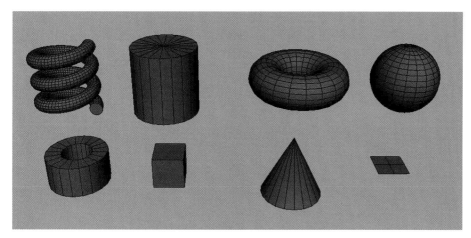

FIGURE 5.28 Preset polygon primitive objects in Autodesk Maya

FIGURE 5.29 Primitive modeling of a chair and a breakdown of the parts used to create it. This chair was created with only cubes scaled to the right shape.

Box Modeling   Box modeling is a popular approach to character modeling and can allow for a quick creation of basic shapes. In this approach, you start with a cube and extrude arms, fingers, legs, toes, and a head. You then add detail to the whole shape by splitting and refining the model. Figure 5.30 shows a few of the steps used to create a character.

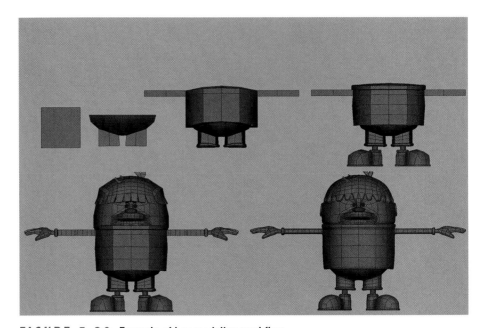

FIGURE 5.30 Example of box modeling workflow

Boolean Modeling   Boolean modeling is an additive or subtractive method of changing the geometry of one object by introducing another object and running a Boolean function. The Boolean function takes the two objects and makes them a new, single object, either by cutting one object out of the other, or combining the two objects to create one, or using the negative space of the intersection as the new object. This type of modeling in not popular in the entertainment industry because of the *n*-sided polygons this method creates. Figure 5.31 shows examples of Boolean functions. The large sphere and cube at the top are two separate polygon objects. The bottom row shows the various Boolean functions. At the left is a *combine* function; you can see an edge flowing along the cube and sphere where they intersect. The middle shows a *difference* function, as the cube leaves a negative shape in the sphere. The right shows an *intersection*, where the negative space of the two objects is left.

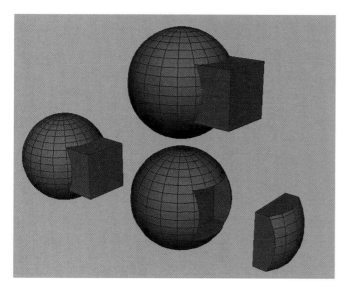

FIGURE 5.31 Examples of Boolean functions on a cube-and-sphere shape

Laser Scanning   Laser scanning is a new type of modeling that starts with a real object that you digitally laser-scan to create the geometric surfaces. The scanning process can be a quick and easy task, but the geometry created is always very messy. The original scan geometry must be cleaned up to be usable in most projects. Figure 5.32 shows a face that was scanned on the left and the cleaned-up head on the right.

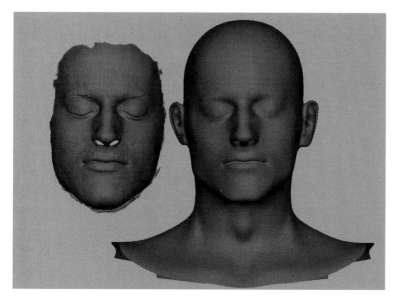

FIGURE 5.32 Laser scan of a face on the left and the clean version on the right

Digital Sculpting   Digital sculpting is a rather new modeling workflow that enables artists to use a massive polygon resolution to create a surface that can be pushed and pulled like clay. This digital sculpting has really changed the workflow for modelers. Up to this point, modeling tended to be very technical, focusing on edge flows and resolution. But this technique allows modelers to jump in and just create the art. Of course, the technical side of digital sculpting remains, but it comes at the end of the process. These digital sculptures are so high-res (in the millions of polygons) that they cannot be animated or used for anything other than just a model. So after the sculpture is created, the modeler has to create a *retopology*—a usable low-resolution model matching the shape and form of the digital sculpture. All of the sculpture's details are transferred by texture maps so that the low-res model will look just like the high-res one in the final render. Figure 5.33 shows a digital sculpture and its retopologized model.

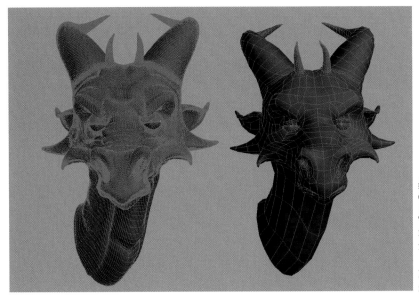

Model provided by Sean Reilly

FIGURE 5.33   A digital sculpture (left) and a low-resolution model (right)

Texturing

Texturing is the process of creating the surfaces and color attributes of models to make them resemble whatever object they are supposed to represent. A person who textures models is called a *texture artist*. However, at some studios, the modeler is responsible for texturing models.

Texture artists must have a good understanding of what makes an object look the way it does, not in terms of its physical shape, but in terms of surface and color. Texture artists manipulate shader properties in the 3D software to achieve the desired result. For example, an unfinished wood tabletop that is brand new is not reflective but has a slight matte sheen across its surface because the wood fibers are not tightly compacted. As the same wood tabletop ages and is used over time, the wood fibers become compacted, which changes the appearance of the surface by making it slightly reflective and glossy.

Texture artists must also be able to mimic the color and patterns of the object they are texturing. Again using the wood tabletop example, every type of wood has a distinctive patterned grain, and the texture artist must be able to create the correct pattern to place on the object. Small details such as knowing the type of grain to place on a wood table are critical to texture artists.

Because digital scans have such high resolution, retopology of digital scans is a great technique for reducing that complexity.

Texture artists should also work on gaining a strong set of observational skills to help them understand how to tell an object's story without saying a word. They need to know where to put flaws, scratches, dirt, mold, and other defects that are important in 3D animation texturing. The creation of perfect objects with perfect surfaces is the default in 3D animation software, but that perfection simply reveals that an object is fake onscreen. Creating defects is what truly sells an object as being real.

Typically, texture artists receive a final model from the modeling department and have to create a UV map for the object(s). They then create the shader with the correct surface properties to represent the object(s). Next they hand-paint or photo-manipulate images in software such as Adobe Photoshop or Autodesk Mudbox to create texture maps for the different properties of the shader, such as a color map or reflectivity map. Texture artists also create renderings of the object to show the lighting team what the object should look like after it is lit and rendered. This section covers these topics of 3D UV mapping, shader networks, and lighting and rendering techniques.

THE MODELING LIFESTYLE

Most modelers at large studios work on only a specific category of models such as organic objects (characters and environments) or hard-surface objects (for example, cars and weapons). At medium and small studios, however, modelers are expected to model whatever assignment is given to them. These modelers must be able to switch back and forth between organic and hard-surface modeling. All good modelers must have an understanding of the modeling tools in whatever application they are using to speed up the process. Also, a strong understanding of anatomy and structure is a must.

UVs

UVs are 2D representations of a 3D object. There is a problem with wrapping a 2D image (a texture) around a 3D object, and UV mapping helps with this problem: UVs are directly related to vertices on a polygon and NURBS, but the UVs cannot be manipulated in 3D space; they are tied to a 2D coordinate plane and edited in a UV editor.

Figure 5.34 shows a 3D model of a human on the left, and the UVs in the UV editor on the right. Notice the relationship between the model and the UVs. The act of UV mapping is often referred to as *laying out the UVs*. This process—although I know it sounds disgusting and awful— is similar to skinning an animal. You are taking the surface of a 3D object and stretching it out to a flat 2D plane.

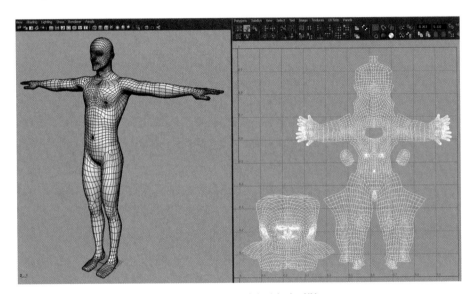

FIGURE 5.34 Example of a 3D human model with the UV map

Most 3D applications provide a few tools and techniques to help the artist create UV maps. UV mapping is typically created after the model is finished. Otherwise, the act of creating the 3D model would make the initial UVs all jumbled up and useless. The 3D software can create new UVs on an object through a series of automated functions such as planar, cylindrical, spherical, and automatic mapping, illustrated in Figure 5.35. These functions "unwrap" the object and attempt to lay out the UVs on a 2D plane. The planar, cylindrical, and spherical function types project the UV coordinates from a plane, cylinder, or sphere, respectively, onto the object, collect the data, and make the 2D map. This type of projection works great on models that are spheres, cylinders, and planes, but on more-complex models such as a human form, these techniques are not enough. Automatic mapping can get you a little further in the process because it projects from a user-defined number of planes, whereas the other mapping types use only one projection to help break down the process into smaller data pieces. Automatic mapping also works well because it does not allow overlapping UVs, which typically are not good.

Overlapping UVs can cause havoc with texture painting, with overlapping UVs the texture painter will have seams that will not be able to be painted out. A texture seam is a definitive line in the texture file that cannot be erased out. In addition, other systems, such as those used to place fur and hair, are based on UVs. Fur in particular will use UV coordinates to allow for texturing and also use the UVs for the initial direction of the fur growth.

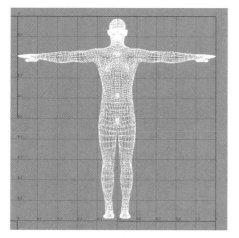

a

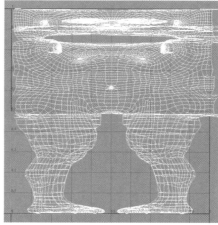

b

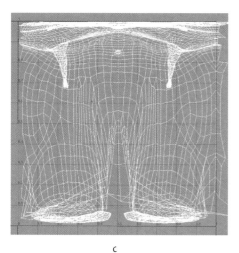

c

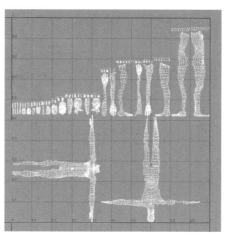

d

FIGURE 5.35 Planar (a), cylindrical (b), spherical (c), and automatic (d) mapping of a human model. The planar, cylindrical, and spherical mapping are not good matches for a complex form such as the human body by default.

UVs are output to an image file called a *UV map* that is used in image manipulation software such as Adobe Photoshop as the artist's roadmap of the UV space for a specific object. This UV map enables the artist to paint the textures of an object and know where he or she is painting on the 3D object.

There isn't yet a way to make good UV maps in any software with just the push of a button. However, the UVs can be started by a computer and then hand-manipulated by the user to create a good UV map. The 3D artist starts with one of the four UV projection types covered already. Then the artist separates, moves, scales, and reattaches the UVs to create a UV map that is uniform and laid out in a way that will make texture painting easy. Figure 5.36 shows an example. This UV map of a human head would be easily recognizable to a new artist needing to paint textures.

This mapping process must take into account uniform spacing of the UVs to help ensure an even distribution of the texture. The UV process often applies a texture with a checkered pattern to the model to verify that the surface has uniformly spaced UVs. Figure 5.37 shows examples of uniform and nonuniform UV maps. The head on the left has uniform UVs; they are all about the same size and are perfect squares, which allows the texture artist to paint confidently. But in the model on the right, the UVs are not uniform, but rather wavy and skewed, which will have the texture artist going nuts trying to compensate for this.

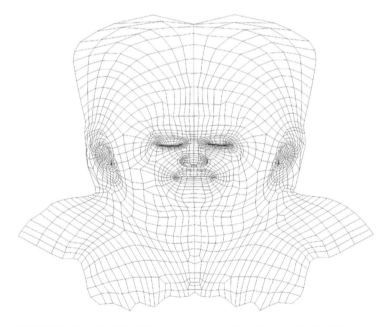

FIGURE 5.36 This UV map for a human head has easily identified major landmarks that facilitate painting textures.

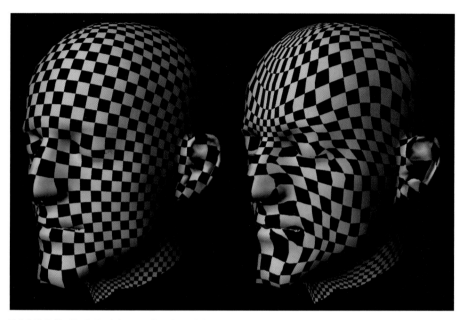

FIGURE 5.37 A human head model with a uniform UV map on the left and a nonuniform UV map on the right

Shaders

After the UVs are laid out, the texture artist assigns the *shader* (also called a *material* or *surface*) to the model. Shaders are the instructions that the software uses to calculate rendering effects, and they allow an artist to define the look of the object and the way its surface behaves in the final render. The look can include attributes such as the object's color, reflectivity, refraction, transparency, translucency, incandescence, ambient color, and specular highlights. Complex shaders offer even more options.

The following are the basic shader attributes:

Color is the color of the object, such as red or blue. This can be a flat color or a texture map.

Ambience is the amount of ambient color that will affect an object's surface. Ambience in the surface property is a simulation of even flat lighting coming from every direction onto the surface (this is not from an actual light source). Figure 5.38 shows an example.

Transparency is how transparent or see-through the object will be. This attribute is used to create effects such as glass.

The terms *shader*, *material*, and *surface* are interchangeable and are often used in the same sentence to mean the same thing.

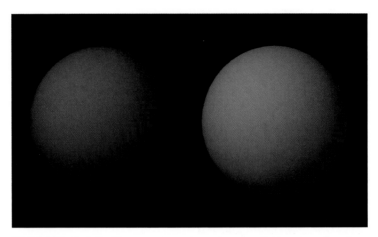

FIGURE 5.38 The two spheres have the same light cast on them from the left side. The sphere on the right has a slight amount of ambience applied; notice that the bottom-right side of the sphere does not fall into complete shadow.

Reflectivity is how reflective the object will be. The reflections can come from raytracing or from a reflection map.

Refraction is the change in light direction caused by a change in speed that occurs as light passes through a solid, transparent object. This causes distortion of anything seen behind the transparent object—for example, when you look through a glass of water and see an object behind the glass appear distorted.

Translucency is the amount of light that can pass through an opaque object such as paper or canvas.

Incandescence is the quality of self-illumination—for example, a computer monitor that is emitting light or a lamp shade with the light on.

Specular highlights are bright spots that appear on an object's surface when light shines on that object. In the real world, these bright spots are reflections of the light source, but in 3D software they are treated as an attribute that is separate from reflections. Treating them separately is faster and more efficient because reflections in a 3D render can be time-consuming to calculate.

Glow is a standard attribute that most 3D applications can simulate to aid in the effect of self-illumination. Figure 5.39 shows an example. The object on the left is bright, like a self-illuminated object, with no halo glow around. The object on the right has the addition of glow, which makes the effect look more realistic.

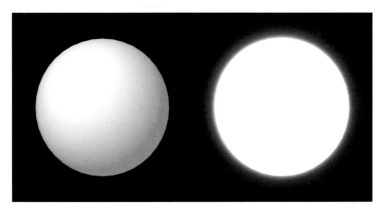

FIGURE 5.39 A sphere with the incandescence turned on (left side) and the same sphere with a glow applied (right side)

Bump simulates a texture along the surface of an object by adding shadow and highlight effects along the surface. Bump maps are gray-scale images in which a mid-gray color represents no change in the surface, black represents inward changes to the surface, and white represents a push outward in the surface. The bump map manipulates the surface normals to change the shading properties and make the surface looked textured. Figure 5.40 shows a sphere on the left with no bump map applied, and the same sphere on the right with a bump map.

FIGURE 5.40 A sphere with no bump map (left) and with a bump map applied (right)

Almost all 3D software packages include a few basic shader types by default, such as flat, Lambert, Blinn, Phong, and Cook-Torrance. In addition, more-complex shaders are becoming more widely used, including subsurface scattering, car paint, and physical architecture. Figure 5.41 shows examples of shaders.

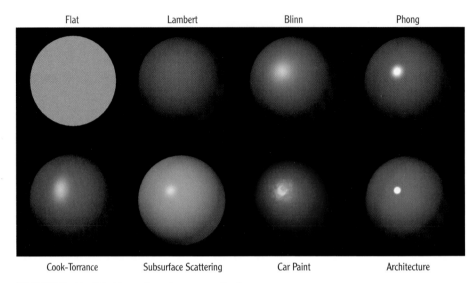

FIGURE 5.41 Examples of common shaders

These shaders are as follows:

Flat shaders, one of the most basic types used today, always return a flat 2D color even on a 3D object. These shaders are good for special flat color maps such as a background image of a sky or for rendering mattes for compositors to use. (Mattes are flat color that can be used to create alpha maps and allow for selections in the compositing software.)

Lambert shaders provide the most basic illumination. These 3D shaders use color but have no options for specular highlights or reflections. These shaders are good for flat, nonshiny or nonglossy 3D objects such as paper or unfinished wood.

Blinn shaders allow for specular highlights and reflections. These shaders provide good control of specular highlights for a range of effects, from a glossy look to high reflectivity. They can be used for many types of materials—plastics, metals, cardboard, and leather.

Phong shaders create a shiny look by adding a sharp specular highlight. This type of shader is good for plastics and other shiny objects.

Cook-Torrance shaders mimic the specular highlights of surfaces with microfacets in them, such as brushed metals. These highlights spread along the surface of an object instead of creating a pure reflection.

Subsurface scattering shaders take into account light penetrating the surface of an object, scattering within the object, and then passing back out of the object. Human skin, milk, and marble are a few examples that can be created with subsurface scattering.

Car paint shaders take into account the complex nature of car paint, which is composed of two or more surfaces interacting with one another. The base layer is the paint that is flat by default but often has flakes that add a specular glitter. On top of that, a clear coat makes the surface look wet.

Physical architecture shaders are physically accurate and simulate real-world illumination properties to re-create many object types: metal (shiny and brushed), glass, plastics, ceramics, and water.

USING ILLUMINATION SHADERS FOR 3D

What we most often refer to as *shaders* are also called *illumination shaders*. Illumination shaders include the most common of all shader types (Blinn, Phong and Lambert). These shaders before rendering will check the direct and ambient light, surface glossiness, and highlight reflection position based on surface orientation and light position. Illumination shaders create the 3D look we see in a render.

Nonillumination shaders are special shaders such as the flat shader that renders as flat 2D color and not the 3D form it is applied to. Another example of a nonillumination shader is a shadow shader that will render only the shadows of an object with no other information like color or specular highlights. This type of exclusive information is used for allowing more flexibility in the compositing stage.

Texture Maps

After setting up shader attributes to simulate the surface properties of an object, the texture artist needs to create the visual information to go into the attributes, such as the color of the object. The texture artist must study the surfaces of objects in the real world to truly understand their appearance. This applies even to fantasy objects, because those still have a basis in the real world.

It is easy to make a 3D object look *perfect* by using just a basic shader, but as a texture artist, your job is to make the object look *real*—or even to create what is called the *plausible impossible*. We see real-world objects every day and are often critical of objects in 3D animation because something feels "off" to us as viewers. This unease arises because objects in the real world are not perfect, even brand-new objects. If you take a brand-new car just out of the paint shop and place it on a showroom floor, for example, as soon as one person touches the paint, that car is no longer perfect. The fingerprint on the paint affects the surface, and it is these small details that make all the difference in 3D animation.

Many factors can affect the surface of a real object, including light, weather, age, and human interaction. Each of these phenomena takes a significant amount of time to leave a permanent effect on the surface of an object, except human inter-action. Light over time will fade and desaturate the color of an object. Weather and age will decompose most objects and add effects to the surface, such as water spots, wrinkling, and shrinking. But human interaction will cause instant blemishes even if not intended—for instance, by leaving footsteps or dropping hairs.

To create blemishes and damage, a texture artist must apply them through *texture maps*, which can be added in two ways—as procedural maps or bitmap file textures:

Procedural Maps   Procedural maps are mathematical algorithms that create various patterns such as cellular, ramp (also known as gradient), grid, wave, fractal, and checker. Figure 5.42 shows some examples.

Procedural maps have three advantages that are worth looking into:

> **Resolution-independent:** Because these texture patterns are created by math, you can zoom in as close as you want without losing any detail in the pattern. This is helpful when you don't know how close you need to get to the object.

> **Seamless:** Procedural textures are seamless, so no matter how much you scale them, you will never see a seam or repeating pattern.

> **Projectable:** Because they are mathematically generated without seams, most 3D applications will allow you to project procedural maps as a movie projector would, toward the object in a seamless manner. This projection technique allows you the freedom to not use UV maps, which in some situations can be useful.

Cellular Ramp/Gradient Grid

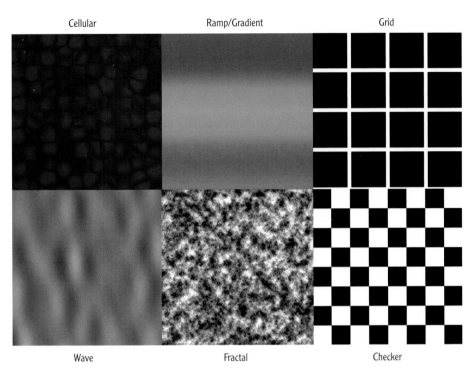

Wave Fractal Checker

FIGURE 5.42 Procedural map examples

The biggest drawback to procedural textures is that they are sometimes difficult to control and place in specific areas of a model when you need to create a custom, realistic texture. For example, if you wanted to add freckles to just the cheeks of a character, a procedural texture would place them everywhere and provide no real way to control their placement.

Bitmap File Textures   Bitmap file textures are the standard picture format that you would use in an image-manipulation program such as Adobe Photoshop or Corel Painter. These are widely used because you have a lot of control of these textures and can even use real photographs as the starting place to achieve realism. The drawback to bitmap images is that they are resolution-dependent, which means that after you zoom into them beyond 100 percent resolution, they will pixelate and distort. This is not a big problem as long as you plan ahead and make the texture resolution large enough for your purposes.

These two types of texture files, procedural and bitmap, are plugged into the shader properties as maps. The standard types of texture maps that you will be creating are color, bump, specular, and transparency. A few other maps are also used often, such as displacement, normal, and reflection maps.

Color maps indicate the color information only for the object you are trying to create. These maps are typically not very exciting by themselves, but once applied and then rendered with all of the other properties, they look good. Figure 5.43 shows a checker map applied to a sphere through the use of UVs.

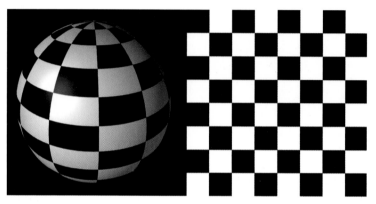

FIGURE 5.43 A color map applied to a sphere (left), and the map alone (right)

Bump maps are grayscale images that affect the surface of the object by adding shadow and highlight to mimic a textured surface. Bump maps do not actually change the shape of an object. Figure 5.44 shows an example.

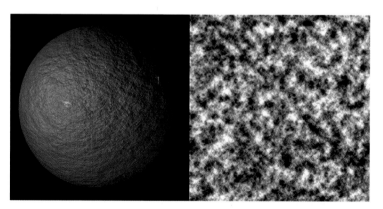

FIGURE 5.44 A bump map applied to a sphere (left), and the map alone (right)

Specular maps affect the way the specular highlights fall along the surface, as you can see in Figure 5.45. Adding noise and scratches can really add a subtle touch to the texture.

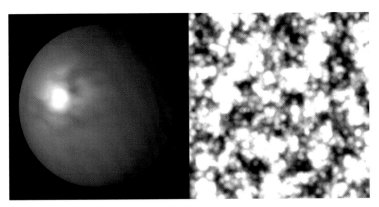

FIGURE 5.45 A specular map applied to a sphere (left), and the map alone (right)

Transparency maps allow for varying degrees of transparency across a surface, as shown in Figure 5.46. They are good for dirty glass or frosted glass or to add color to the glass itself.

FIGURE 5.46 A transparency map applied to a sphere (left), and the map alone (right)

Reflection maps either can create an environment texture to apply to the object to make it look like it is surrounded by that environment or can affect how the real reflections of the object will behave.

In Figure 5.47, the ramp is controlling the reflectivity so that the edges are more reflective than the center.

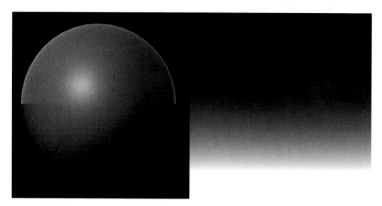

FIGURE 5.47 A reflection map of a ramp applied to a sphere (left), and the map alone (right). The ramp is changing the reflective properties of the sphere.

Displacement maps are grayscale images that displace the actual geometry to create a new shape. Figure 5.48 shows an object that started out as a sphere but became a different shape when rendered with a displacement map.

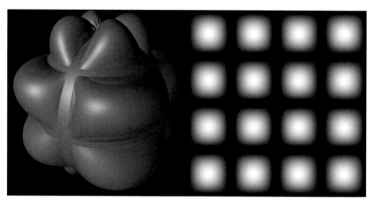

FIGURE 5.48 A displacement map applied to a sphere (left), and the map alone (right)

Normal maps, like bump maps, make a surface look textured, as shown in Figure 5.49. But unlike the bump map, which is a grayscale image, a normal map is a red, green, and blue image. Normal maps are used today in video games to create textured surfaces in a real-time rendering engine. The original black-and-white bump map was not able to create this effect in real time.

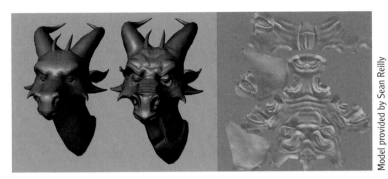

Model provided by Sean Reilly

FIGURE 5.49 A dragon model before (left) and after (center) the normal map has been applied, and the normal map alone (right)

Texturing Workflows

The specifics of texturing workflows differ between people, but the basic steps are similar. There is a hand-painted texturing workflow, a photo-manipulation workflow, a texture-projection workflow, and a paint-directly-onto-the-model workflow. All four are used today. The decision about which one to use really comes down to what you, the artist, are comfortable using and what approach can efficiently create the textures you need.

Hand-Painted Texturing   In this workflow, all of the textures come from the artist, who uses painting software such as Adobe Photoshop or Corel Painter. The texture artist uses reference material but creates the look from their painting skills only. It takes years of practice to be efficient at this type of texturing.

Photo Manipulation   This workflow uses photos to help create textures—for instance, a photo of a wood grain or paint stain. The texture artist creates a library of reference photos to make the final texture map needed. The artist might collect photos from online resources or DVD texture collections, or might go out and take their own photos. The latter is not always an option because of time or travel constraints but usually produces the most authentic results if used correctly.

Texture Projection   This method uses photographs of an object from different angles, projects them onto the object, and bakes the texture to a map. Many maps are created and then (in software such as Adobe Photoshop) corrected into one map. This method works well for the photo-texture artist who can take photos of the real-world object. However, texture projection does not always work if the object is too big or too small to photograph, or for subjects that are prohibited from being photographed—some museum pieces, for example.

Painting on the Object Directly   This workflow is the newest of the workflows and uses software such as ZBrush or Mudbox. These software packages allow for Photoshop-like control while enabling the artist to paint directly onto the object and then export the map out for use back in the artist's primary 3D software. This is the most artist-friendly version of texturing today because instead of somewhat guessing where the upper lip is on a human figure, for example, you can just zoom in to the mouth of the character and paint right on it.

THE ESSENTIALS AND BEYOND

Because modeling and texturing are the foundations of all 3D animation projects in any 3D industry, it is vital to understand your options. You now know the different workflows like box modeling for beginning character modeling and laser scanning to create high resolution topology that you can retopolgize to make an animatable model. Also what geometry types to use, like polygons being the most popular geometry type used today in the entertainment industries and NURBS being used in product design. With a strong understanding of the shader types and texture maps, you can create any look on the models you need. Both modeling and texturing are evolving as technology changes, but a strong understanding of the basics will enable you to move on to new techniques and new workflows in the future.

REVIEW QUESTIONS

1.   Which of the following modeling geometry types is the most popular today?

   A.   Polygons

   B.   NURBS

   C.   Subdivision surfaces

   D.   Geometric Polynoid

2.   Which shaders are good to use for shiny or plastic materials? (Choose all that apply.)

   A.   Lambert

   B.   Phong

   C.   Blinn

   D.   Surface

3. Why is having uniform UVs important?

A. It allows for correct simulations.

B. It affects the texture-painting process.

C. It makes your model's surface look bumpy.

D. It makes rendering impossible.

4. True or false: Beveling will make your edges look too sharp.

5. Which of the following is *not* a NURBS component?

A. CVs

B. Hulls

C. Faces

D. Isoparms

6. What are UVs used for?

A. 2D texture coordinates of a 3D object

B. Placement of vertices

C. Positions for animation corrections

D. Modeling tools

7. What are NURBS good at? (Choose all that apply.)

A. Creating smooth rendering

B. Creating rounded shapes

C. Using curves as a base

D. All of the above

8. What are subdivision surfaces good for?

A. A final geometry type for rendering

B. Fixing NURBS

C. Modeling ease

D. Looking more realistic

9. What is box modeling?

A. Creating each object by individually creating each polygon

B. Revolving a curve to create a cube

C. Polygon modeling that starts with a cube

D. Bouncing cubes in simulation

10. True or false: Laser scanning is a fast and efficient way to create usable 3D geometry.

CHAPTER 6

Rigging and Animation

Rigging and animation could not be more fundamentally different from one another, but they are so closely linked in 3D animation that one cannot really exist without the other. Rigging is the logical side of 3D animation, leaving no room for interpretation of what can and cannot be done. Animation, the movement of objects, represents the art and performance side of 3D animation. It deals with all the gray areas of artistic interpretation of motion, performance, and style. These two opposites can cause many battles between departments, but when rigging and animation artists work together, they can achieve great results. This chapter presents the fundamental tools and techniques used by 3D animators today, from hand-keyframed animation to motion capture, and basic hierarchy rigging to complicated character rigs.

▶ **Rigging**

▶ **Animation**

Rigging

▶

As you learned in Chapter 5, "Understanding Modeling and Texturing," 3D geometry comes in three varieties: polygons, NURBS, and subdivisional surfaces.

All 3D geometry that is going to be animated needs some type of system that provides the animators the control and flexibility needed to move that object in some fashion. This control system is called the *rig*. Figure 6.1 shows examples of rigs.

Rigging artists create the control system for animators to use in the animation process, much like puppet-makers create the control systems for puppeteers. Riggers create this highly advanced control system in such a way that the animators will see only what is needed to articulate the characters and objects in a simple interface. The rigger's primary job is to make the animator's job easier. This is one of the only roles at a 3D animation studio that works specifically to aid a different department.

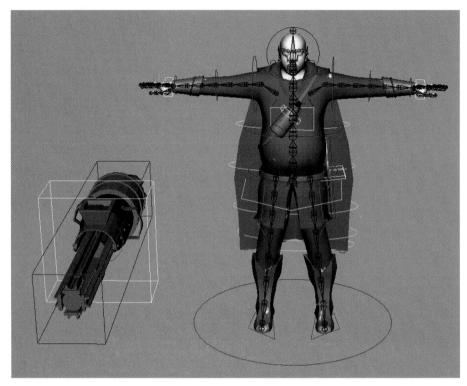

FIGURE 6.1 A rig for a weapon (left) and a rig for a human (right) in Autodesk Maya

The rigging job is highly technical yet requires an artist's fine touch. Riggers need a deep understanding of the inner workings of whatever software and hardware they are using, as well as a firm grasp of computer scripting and expression writing. Knowledge of anatomy, human or animal, is also useful. Because riggers' primary work is to help animators, they need a fairly good understanding of character and object animation in order to know how to create efficient controls.

The rigging artist starts by placing a skeleton made of *joints*, or *bones*, into the character or object. These hierarchy-based pivot points can be selected and articulated, and are positioned similarly to the real bones within our bodies. An alternative to using a skeleton is to use a simple hierarchical system based on parent-child relationships. Next, riggers create controllers that will enable the animators to translate or rotate the joints. The riggers then using *deformers* (tools that change the shape of an object) called *skinning* or *enveloping* connect the geometry to the joint/bone system so that the character's geometry will follow the underlying rig. Finally, riggers create other deformers to allow the geometry to move more realistically, with folds and skin displacement.

Joints or bones in 3D animation do not look like real human bones. Instead, they are a selectable wirelike shape that represents the skeleton system.

The most basic ball-bounce animation assignment that almost all animators must master early in their careers requires a rig in order to work in a 3D application. The geometry of the ball itself could enable the ball to move up, down, and to the side, and even to squash and stretch. But achieving a rolling ball effect through the object's translations and rotations is nearly impossible with the geometry alone. A rotating ball will also rotate the squashed pancake-like shape, resulting in undesirable animation, as seen on the left side of Figure 6.2. The squashed shape will not be flat on the ground and will not look like a flattened ball. To solve this problem, you can easily animate the ball with a simple hierarchy rig to allow for predictable results of translations, rotations, and scale, as seen on the right in Figure 6.2.

The word *translate* in 3D animation means to virtually move an object in the XYZ coordinate space.

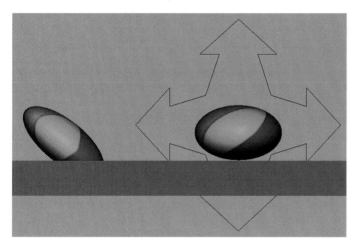

FIGURE 6.2 A ball with no rig will result in undesirable animation deformation and looks stuck into the ground, which is indicated by the gray band (left). A ball with a rig will result in correct animation deformation and rotations (right).

Let's look at some of the tools and techniques available to riggers today.

Parenting

All rigs are based on a hierarchy of systems and controls working in a sequential order to create the articulation of your object. This hierarchy in its most basic form is a parent/child relationship—one object is the parent, and another object is the child. Creating this relationship is called *parenting*. A child object can move, rotate, and scale independently of the parent object, but when the parent object moves, the child will follow. You can have multiple children under a parent, called *siblings*, and can even have children of children, as shown in Figure 6.3. In most 3D applications, you can change this parent and child relationship at any time. You can parent objects to each other, or you can group objects together to move as a unit.

Understanding Grouping and Nodes

Grouping is parenting two or more objects together under a nonrenderable group node. A group node is a translation node that carries only information about movement (translation, rotation, scale). A node is a data component that carries only the information needed. Most nodes are not renderable because they do not have any geometry as a part of their informational structure.

FIGURE 6.3 A parent-child relationship in the Maya Outliner

Pivot Positions

The *pivot position*, or *pivot point*, is the location an object rotates around. In 3D animation, the pivot point is also the position from which the other manipulators will move or scale the object. Setting the correct position of the pivot to create the proper point of manipulation is important in creating a rig.

Figure 6.4 shows an example of a basic hierarchy rig. This rig is just a basic parent-child relationship rig with all of its parts connected. To move the head sphere in a proper way to match predictable head rotations, the pivot point has to be close to the connection point of the body. However, the default pivot point of a sphere is at the center, which will not articulate like a head on a neck, but instead will rotate as shown in Figure 6.5. By moving the pivot point down, you can create the proper motion needed for a head, as seen in Figure 6.6.

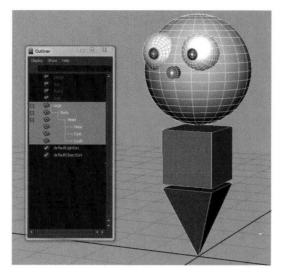

FIGURE 6.4 A simple hierarchy rig in Maya

FIGURE 6.5 A simple head rig with an improper pivot position (in the center of the head sphere), which results in unrealistic articulation

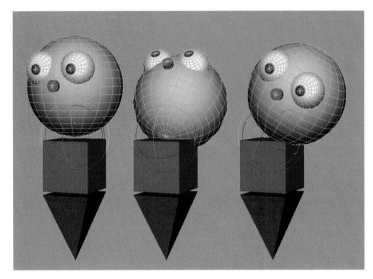

FIGURE 6.6 A simple head rig with a proper pivot position (where the head joins to the body) to allow for proper articulation

Skeleton System

The rigger creates a *skeleton system*, or *joints*, composed of a hierarchal set of pivot points that can be selected and set to carry specific types of deformers with them. Figure 6.7 shows an example of a skeleton. This skeleton system is the basis for any mid-level to advanced character rig. Joints can be used in nonorganic models such as cars and weapons as well to allow for easier selection and deformation.

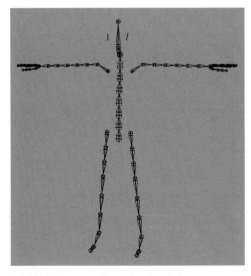

FIGURE 6.7 Example of a skeleton system

Let's look at a few examples of the types of movement that joints can allow in a character. Four basic types of joints can create any type of character articulation:

A **hinge joint** rotates on one axis, as a knee or elbow would. Figure 6.8 shows an example.

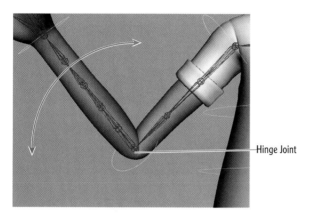

Hinge Joint

FIGURE 6.8 A hinge joint

An **articulated joint** can rotate a small amount if desired, but many of these joints rotating at once can create a large range of motion, as in a spine (see Figure 6.9).

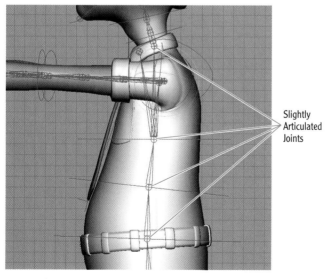

Slightly Articulated Joints

FIGURE 6.9 A few slightly articulated joints

A **pivot joint** rotates around a single axis, like those in the forearm shown in Figure 6.10.

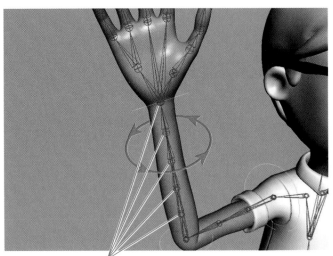

Pivot Joints

FIGURE 6.10 Various pivot joints

A **ball-and-socket joint** can rotate in any direction, as in a shoulder or a hip (see Figure 6.11).

Ball and Socket Joint

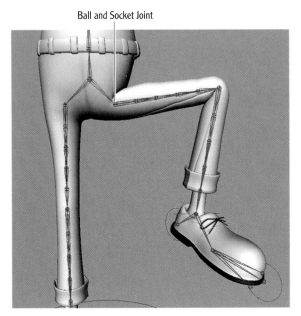

FIGURE 6.11 A ball-and-socket joint

Forward and Inverse Kinematics

The movement of joints can be divided into two categories: forward kinematics (FK) and inverse kinematics (IK). These two types of joint movement provide the animator different ways to approach specific animation tasks.

Forward kinematics is the articulation of joints in their previously set hierarchical order. FK can be thought of as the movement of a poseable toy. You can, for example, move the shoulder, then the elbow, and then the wrist to create the pose seen in Figure 6.12. This forward hierarchy is based on the arm joints being drawn and connected in the order of shoulder, elbow, wrist.

Inverse kinematics is the articulation of joints in the reverse order of their original hierarchy. When using IK, an animator can select, for example, the wrist of a character and move it to a specific position, and the arm will follow, as shown in Figure 6.13. This IK reverses the hierarchy of the original arm to allow the animator to work in a different fashion, as seen in Figure 6.13.

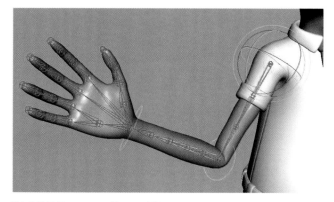

FIGURE 6.12 Forward kinematics in an arm skeleton. The animator would rotate each circle to control the shoulder, elbow, and wrist.

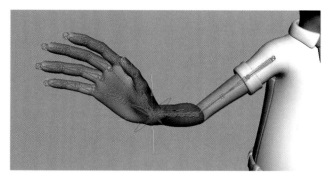

FIGURE 6.13 Inverse kinematics in an arm skeleton. The animator would move the wrist to move the entire arm of the character at once.

FK and IK can be created to allow the animator to switch between these two systems to give the flexibility to create a specific performance if needed.

Deformers

After creating a skeleton system for your character, you need to apply *deformers* to that geometry to allow the geometry to follow the skeleton. Most deformers enable the rigger to create a parenting option at the component level of geometry, not the object level. *Components* are the individual building blocks of an object—for example, the components of a polygon are the vertices, edges, and faces.

Many types of deformers are available today, and not all 3D software has the same type. However, a few standard types are almost always included in 3D software: skinning/enveloping, lattice, and blendshapes:

Skinning or Enveloping   *Skinning*, or *enveloping*, is a deformer that enables a rigger to assign a value to each vertex of a geometry object so that it is affected by each joint of a skeleton hierarchy. This enables the mesh to move with the skeleton underneath it. The mesh is then typically referred to as a *skin*. Many software packages offer different types of skinning, including smooth skinning and rigid skinning.

Smooth Skinning   enables you to individually weight each vertex with multiple values to different joints and allow for smooth deformations, as seen in Figure 6.14. Smooth skinning is the most used skinning method today. It is for almost any type of organiclike objects such as characters, creatures, plants, and tubing or wires.

WEIGHTING

With deformers like smooth skinning you can give each vertex a weighted value to each joint to allow it to follow along with that set value. As seen in Figure 6.14 the lowest vertex indicated has a 0.945 value to Joint 1 and a 0.055 value to Joint 2. This will instruct the vertex to follow 94.5 percent to Joint 1 and 5.5 percent to Joint 2 when the joints are articulated. The typical weight structure is to a value of 1 or 100 percent. There are some instances when it is valuable to allow for more than a value of 1 or 100 percent weighting but not often.

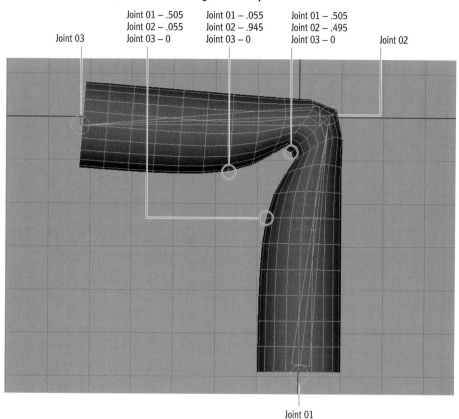

Vertex Weight Value to Specific Joint

Joint 01 – .505   Joint 01 – .055   Joint 01 – .505
Joint 02 – .055   Joint 02 – .945   Joint 02 – .495
Joint 03   Joint 03 – 0   Joint 03 – 0   Joint 03 – 0   Joint 02

Joint 01

FIGURE 6.14 Smooth skinning

Rigid Skinning *Ridge skinning* gives a vertex an all-or-nothing weighting to a single joint, meaning a vertex can have only a 100 percent or 0 percent value weighting to a specific joint. Rigid skinning by default creates rigid and sharp deformations, as seen in Figure 6.15. Rigid skinning is technically a faster deformer tool than smooth skinning, but rigid skinning makes it more difficult to achieve smooth deformations. Rigid skinning can be used for the same type of objects as smooth skinning (for example, characters, creatures, and plant life), but these objects will need to utilize other deformers to achieve a smooth transition in geometry.

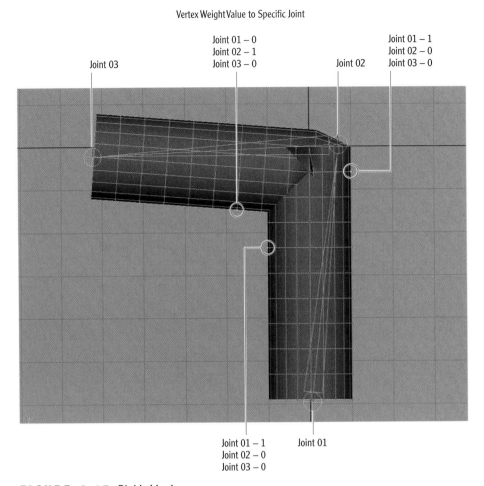

Vertex Weight Value to Specific Joint

Joint 03

Joint 01 – 0
Joint 02 – 1
Joint 03 – 0

Joint 02

Joint 01 – 1
Joint 02 – 0
Joint 03 – 0

Joint 01 – 1
Joint 02 – 0
Joint 03 – 0

Joint 01

FIGURE 6.15 Rigid skinning

Lattice A *lattice deformer* is a cage of vertices that envelops a denser geometric mesh and deforms that mesh in a smooth fashion, as seen in Figure 6.16. It can deform a single mesh or multiple meshes at one time. This is a powerful and useful deformer because it can be used in many ways. For example, you could model a straight fence, but if you want to make the fence have a cartoon straight-line look, you could apply a lattice and deform the fence. You can also create a base human shape and use a lattice to deform parts of the body to create numerous characters with the one base shape.

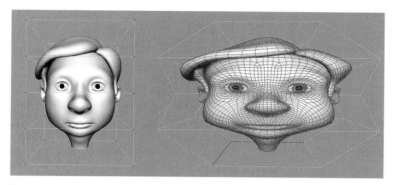

FIGURE 6.16 Lattice deformer

Blendshapes *Blendshapes* are deformers that enable the artist to create an object such as a head, and then duplicate that object and change it (for example, adding a smile to the face) to make a target shape. The blendshape links the two objects together to allow the original shape to deform between the two shapes. Blendshapes can also be used with more than one target shape. This is a tool of choice for creating face shapes and enabling facial animation on a rig like the one in Figure 6.17. Blendshapes are also used to correct skinning in places such as elbows and shoulders, and can be automated to trigger when a character is posed in a specific fashion, to correct bad deformations.

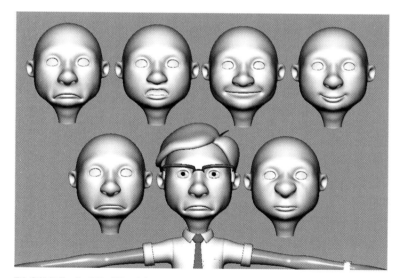

FIGURE 6.17 Blendshape targets applied to a face

Constraints

Constraints are a system for allowing one object to control another object. Constraints can allow you to connect only the translation of one object to another or the rotation, scale, or even the surface of one object to another. Constraints are similar to but mathematically different from parents (the math is beyond the scope of this book) and can give a rigger more control, which means a better solution to creating connections. Most software applications use the following constraints:

Point constrains the translation of one object to another. This enables the artist to attach two or more objects together.

Aim constrains the rotation of one object to aim or point at another object. This type of constraint is great for creating an eye-control system; the eyeball shape will always point at the controller so the animator can lock the eyes of a character on a specific object if needed, as seen in Figure 6.18.

FIGURE 6.18 Example of an aim constraint controlling the eyes of a character. The highlighted green cross is the controller for the eyes, and when it is moved, the eyes will follow it.

Orient constrains one object's rotation to another object's rotation. This enables the artist to attach the rotations of two or more objects. The orient constraint is different from a parent-child relationship, as shown in Figure 6.19. The orient constraint allows the constrained object to rotate on its own axis. In a parent-child relationship, the child rotates around the parent's axis.

Scale constrains one object's scale to another object's scale. In other words, the scale size of one object controls the scale size of one or more other objects.

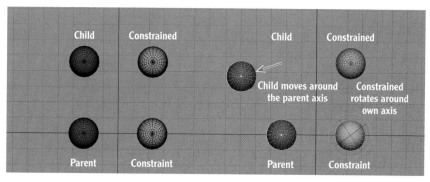

FIGURE 6.19 Example of the differences between a parent-child relationship's and an orient constraint's control of the rotation of objects. The left side shows the original position of the spheres, the right side shows the bottom sphere rotated and how the parent-child behavior and the constrained behavior differ. The child will rotate around the parent's axis and the constrained will rotate around its own axis.

Scripting

Scripting is a tool provided in almost every 3D animation program to enable you to create or add plug-ins or custom tools. Scripting can be done in many programming languages, including C++, Python, Maya Embedded Language (MEL), and JavaScript. Scripting can greatly increase your productivity in 3D animation by allowing you to create your own tools that can help with repetitive tasks.

Creating custom shapes such as stars and arrows, for example, is a time-consuming process requiring you to first make curve controller shapes for the rig. You could write a script that with the push of a button would create these shapes for you, thereby avoiding having to make the shape from scratch each time. Even if you think you might never use scripting, you should learn the basics of a scripting language to help you in your future 3D animation work.

Expressions

Expressions are another way to connect the attribute of one object to another. However, expressions allow for attributes to change under scripted variables dictated by the user. You can, for example, make the translation *Y* of a cube affect the translation *X* of a sphere, much like constraints, but you can then make the cube double the translation values of the sphere. This simple expression would be written like this:

$$Sphere1.translateX = Cube1.translateY \times 2 ;$$

Figure 6.20 shows the effect of this expression. Expressions are a form of scripting, and each program will treat the syntax differently. You can use expressions to add more control to your rigs, particle effects, or anything else in 3D animation.

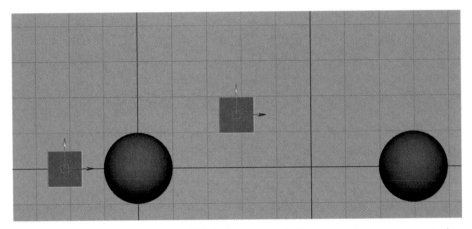

FIGURE 6.20 An expression will link the movement of the sphere to the movement of the cube. When the cube moves vertically, the sphere moves twice as far horizontally.

KEEP IT SIMPLE

The entire control system for a rig needs to be powerful, yet simple for animators to use. The best thing a rigger can do is to create a simple interface that enables a new animator to sit down and quickly grasp the operation of the rig. So after all the controls are created, the rigger might have to create options such as visibility switches to hide certain controls until needed. For instance, having all of the facial controls visible the entire time is typically unnecessary because the face is usually the last part an animator will animate.

The Basic Rigging Workflow

Here is the basic workflow that a rigger follows to organize and create a control rig for any object:

1. Model the character. This step is not always completed by the rigger, but the rigger might be required to fix any issues in the mesh to allow for a deformable object.

2. Organize the objects. In this step, the rigger organizes a scene file so it contains only the necessary parts (the modeling stage can leave unnecessary nodes and objects in the file). The rigger also names all objects for easy selection.

3. Build the skeleton. The rigger creates the skeleton hierarchy and places each joint in the rig.

4. Save the master skeleton.

5. Build inverse kinematics. IK systems are added to the legs and arms and any other parts that might need these systems.

6. Create character controls. These controls need to be easy for the animator to select and to manipulate.

7. Bind/skin/envelop. In this step, the rigger skins the geometry to the skeleton.

8. Fixing the weight points. The rigger fixes any mistakes in the skinning to allow for predictable deformation.

9. Work with deformers. The rigger adds any additional deformers to help with the overall deformation of the object and to provide facial animation if needed.

10. Test the character setup. By testing the rig at this point with animation tests, the rigger can see how the character holds up.

11. Save the master skin.

12. Create a low-res model for rigging if needed. This might be required if the geometry is too dense to allow for real-time animation.

13. Create the facial setup, adding blendshapes if needed.

14. Create a GUI control interface if needed. Extra GUI control interfaces provide a faster workflow for the animator.

15. Save the final rig.

16. Animate the object.

Animation

Animators are the people who bring onscreen characters or objects to life. So what is *animation*? The simplest description is that animation occurs when a group of still images that are slightly different from one another are shown in such a way—that is, in sequential order and at a sufficient speed—that our eyes believe something is moving. So animators must be able to make the 3D characters move frame by frame and in a way that the audience believes the inanimate 3D objects on still frames are alive.

The Broad Application of *Animation*

The word *animation* can be confusing because of its broad application. This book is titled *3D Animation Essentials* and encompasses everything related to 3D animation. This section specifically discusses the animator's role in terms of movement and performance within the larger profession of 3D animation.

In film, the standard frame rate is 24 frames per second. In video, that rate is 30 frames per second. So animators are responsible for controlling the movements of their characters or objects through space 24 times per second to create the performances. A 90-minute film has 129,600 frames, and each frame is touched, studied, and analyzed to make sure it is perfect. This is why animation is so time-consuming.

The math for the total frame count for a 90-minute project is as follows:
24 frames per second × 60 seconds per minute × 90 minutes = 129,600 frames

Animators are typically artists who are not very technically inclined, so just a basic understanding of the software is needed to break into the industry. Today's 3D animation packages have few actual animation tools compared to the tools for other 3D animation jobs such as lighting, modeling, rigging, and VFX. But what animators may lack in technical software knowledge, they must make up for with an understanding of acting performance and observational skills. They also need a strong fundamental knowledge of motion, weight, balance, and timing to make the audience suspend disbelief in what they are seeing and imagine that a character is truly alive. Becoming proficient in animation takes years, and it is a job you will never fully master. This lack of mastery is what most animators find exciting; you will never know everything about human behavior and will always be learning.

In Chapter 4, "Exploring Animation, Story, and Pre-visualization," you learned about the Twelve Basic Principles of Animation, which are important to all types of animation, no matter the medium. In this section, you are going to look at the tools and techniques specific to 3D computer animation.

MAKING THE MOVE FROM 2D TO 3D ANIMATION

All of the tools in 3D animation have been borrowed or adapted from traditional 2D animation. These tools have been tweaked over the years to become the standards in almost all 3D animation programs. When 3D animation was brand new, most studios would hire anyone who was proficient at traditional 2D animation because they could then be taught to animate on the computer in 3D. But as 3D animation has matured, this has not always remained the case. I am not saying that a good animator cannot make the switch from one medium to the other. However, the learning curve for 3D computer-generated animation has become steep. 3D animation over the past 10 years or so has become its own art form with its own language and tools that can take a lot of time to master.

As 3D animation has matured, different varieties of animation have developed in the video game industry: in-game animation and game cinematics (also called cut-scenes). In-game animation is primarily cyclical animation programmed to match the player's controller or keyboard input—for instance, running forward and then sideways, or jumping and climbing. In-game action requires an animator to have a great sense of weight and balance of the animated object or character, but a comparatively small need for overall subtle performance. Game cinematics animation, though, is similar to film and television animation, because it relies primarily on performance to further the storytelling of the entire game.

Film animation has a similar duality, between *creature animation* (the movement of realistic or fictional living beings) and *performance animation* (which communicates the story and the subtler performance aspects). Creature animation must be based on reality or our perception of reality, as seen in *Jurassic Park* for example. We have never seen a dinosaur move but with the study of creatures today we have a good idea of how they would have moved. Performance animation is about great motion and balance of the animated object and characters, but also acting of the characters as seen in most animated feature films from Pixar, DreamWorks, and ImageWorks. These characters are not real and are usually created in a stylized design, but the characters can still have the audience relate and empathize with these characters through their performance.

Most animators will pick one animation area and stay in it, but some animators cross lines. Each of these animation areas requires different skills and techniques, but the tools and principles of animation are always the same.

The animator has one of the most difficult jobs in the 3D animation industry because there are really no right or wrong answers—just interpretations. Animators have to become the characters they are portraying. Animators also must completely understand the shot they are working on to be able to tell the story. This is true even if an animator is working on a scene component other than the character itself. Animators working on a product visualization project, for instance, must be able to show the audience what they need to see in a clean and efficient way. If a simple hammer hammering a nail into a wood block is the animation task, for example, the animator must be able to animate the camera and the nail and hammer in such a way that the audience understands what they need to know. The animator has to use all of the Twelve Basic Principles of Animation to convey this information. The biggest mistake that I see young animators make is they think a shot is animated just because the object moves. The object or character must always tell a story and become alive to be truly animated. Moving objects is easy with a computer, but it takes an artist to make those objects move with purpose and life. So let's look at some of the standard tools 3D animators have to create animation.

Keyframe

The *keyframe* is the most basic tool of any animator. The keyframe is a drawing or pose that an animator creates to be displayed on a certain frame. In 3D animation, a keyframe acts as a marker placed on a timeline. The keyframe gets its name from the frames you work in as an animator. As you know, these frames measure time in film and television. An animator's keyframes are therefore the key locations of poses or positions of your object or character that are used to complete the motion. The computer will then fill in the motion by in-betweening the keyframes. A 3D animator places an object in one position and sets a keyframe. The animator then moves forward or backward to a new position in the timeline, changes the position of the object, and sets a new keyframe. Each keyframe carries the data of the object's position at that time, and the computer interpolates the position of the object over the time in between the keyframes. Figure 6.21 shows a simple example of a walking human character set in two keyframes, 10 frames apart.

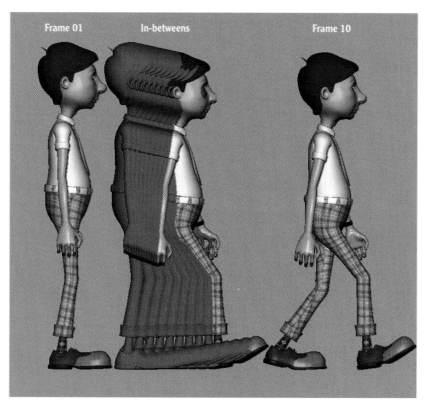

FIGURE 6.21 Example of keyframes and in-betweens. The far left and right side show the character in the keyframes at frame 01 and 10. The middle area shows how the computer added the motion between the keyframes with in-betweens.

Graph Editor

In almost all 3D animation programs, animators can use a tool called a *graph editor* to create and manipulate the interpolation between keyframes. The graph editor uses *function curves* to represent the interpolated movement. Most graph editors are similar in their looks and represent the value of the selected attribute (for example, translate *Y*) in the vertical direction and time over the horizontal. Figure 6.22 shows a graph editor in Maya. Because time is constant, you read the interpolation of these curves from left to right.

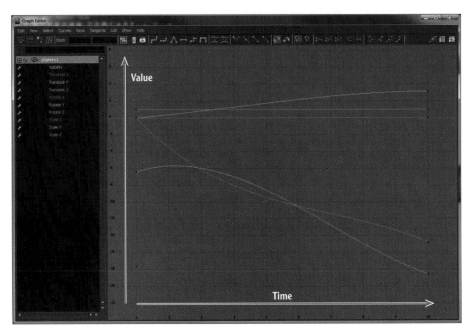

FIGURE 6.22 Function curves in a graph editor

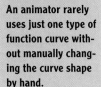

Function curves, also known as *FCurves*, are visual representations of key frames set in time, with the interpolation between the key frames visible.

An animator rarely uses just one type of function curve without manually changing the curve shape by hand.

There are three standard types of function curves in a 3D program:

Step curves hold a value until the next keyframe is present. This type of curve causes each keyframe to hold like a flash card until the next frame pops up. This type of curve might not seem all that useful, but it can come in handy for studying poses in character animation during the beginning stages of blocking a shot.

Linear curves move the object at a constant and even speed. Frames have equal distances between them. This type of curve is useful for fast mechanical motions. In addition, many animators convert the blocking from stepped keys to linear keys when focusing on basic movement.

Spline curves are composed of a slow-in curve and a slow-out curve to create a more realistic type of motion. Spline curves are a good choice if you want your movement to be floaty and soft.

In Figure 6.23, all the spheres have identical keyframes, but the function curves have been changed to show the motion of the different types of curves.

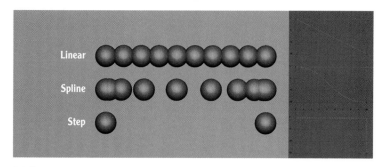

FIGURE 6.23 Linear, spline, and step function curves change the motion of a ball between two keyframes

You can change and manipulate these function curves at any time—and you should. Otherwise, the computer, not the animator, is doing all the animation. Computers will just in-between in the simplest way possible and not understand what you, as the animator, are trying to accomplish. You can change the curves in a graph editor by using tangent handles, shown in Figure 6.24. You might be familiar with this kind of curve-based manipulation in other software such as Adobe Illustrator. You can break the tangents to manipulate the curve in any way you see fit to create the motion needed. The graph editor and curves are a great way to fine-tune your animation and are a standard everyday tool used by animators.

Tangent Handles

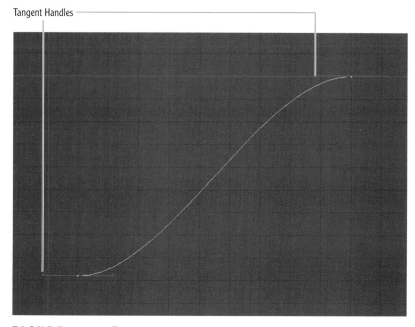

FIGURE 6.24 Tangent handles on a keyframe in the graph editor

EULER ANGLE CURVES, GIMBAL LOCK, AND QUATERNION ROTATION

Using a graph editor and curves to fine-tune your animation can cause problems when rotating an object. Most 3D animation software uses Euler (pronounced *oiler*) angle curves to calculate the 3D rotations of an object, because these curves can be represented and manipulated as function curves. The drawback to using Euler rotation is that each rotation value will be evaluated in a hierarchical way that can lead to some unexpected rotations or even a locking of the object's rotational movement.

When using Euler rotation, the animator has to define the object's movement by indicating a hierarchy of motions along three axes. This hierarchy of rotations can be any one of six options: XYZ, ZXY, YXZ, XZY, ZYX, or YZX. Most 3D animation software has a default rotation order, but it can be changed by the user when needed. Think of the rotating object as a three-axis gyroscope, with three separate frame arms to create XYZ rotations. The rotation order is hierarchical, so the first axis is going to move all of the child axes that follow it.

■ X Axis
■ Y Axis
■ Z Axis
Object to be rotated (arrow indicates the direction that the virtual object would be pointing)

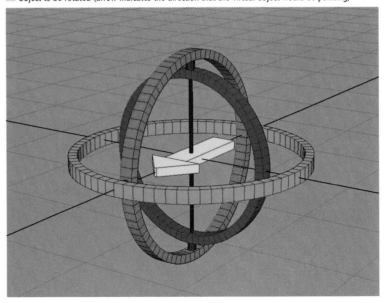

EULER ANGLE CURVES, GIMBAL LOCK, AND QUATERNION ROTATION *(Continued)*

By setting this rotation order, we get two axes that will align and take away the third axis's opportunity to rotate. This locking of an axis is called *Gimbal lock*.

- ■ X Axis
- ■ Y Axis
- ■ Z Axis
- □ Object to be rotated (arrow indicates the direction that the virtual object would be pointing)

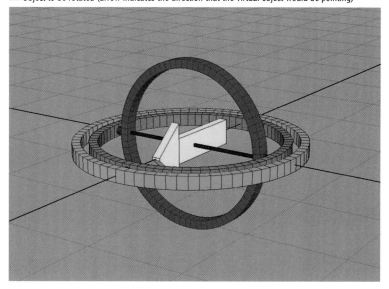

Quaternion rotation is a mathematical way to calculate rotations in a 3D application. This alternative enables an artist to avoid Gimbal lock, which is great, but has its own limitations as well. Quaternion rotation uses four values to calculate the rotation position. The method has two main disadvantages: no function curves are created to enable editing in a graph editor in your 3D animation software, and it is not possible to rotate beyond 360 degrees. Most animators use Euler angles for animation, but quaternion is an option you should be aware of because it may come up in discussions about 3D animation and is an option in most 3D animation software.

Further detail on the phenomenon of Gimbal lock is beyond the scope of this book, but you will know when it happens. When you are trying to rotate an object in a specific way but it just doesn't seem to be working, that is Gimbal lock.

Timeline

The *timeline* enables the animator to evaluate the animation motion through time. Most 3D software packages allow animators to copy, delete, move, or adjust keyframes within the timeline. The act of moving through the timeline is called *scrubbing*. With today's powerful computers, you can typically scrub the timeline in real time to look at your motion. Scrubbing the timeline is similar to the way traditional animators would create a flipbook of their drawings to see the movement they were working on.

Dope Sheet

The *dope sheet*, shown in Figure 6.25, comes from traditional animation's exposure sheet, which would tell the cameraman how to shoot each frame by listing instructions from the animator. In 3D animation, the dope sheet lists the keyframes for objects or controls. You can easily change the position of these keys on the timeline. This tool is stripped down to just the basics, to enable the animator to focus on the timing of keyframes.

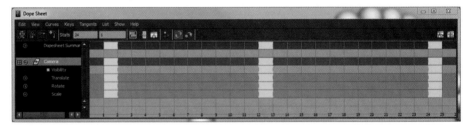

FIGURE 6.25 A dope sheet in Maya. The yellow boxes are the keyframes, which can be moved in the timeline as needed by the animator.

Workspace

The animator's *workspace* is an important tool to learn how to optimize. Having multiple views of your character or object helps track the motion. Figure 6.26 shows four camera views in Maya. Utilizing multiple views can help an animator make selections and see what the character is doing from other angles. This, in turn, helps the animator create correct poses. It is much easier to block in a walk cycle from a side view of your character, for example, than from the front or top view, as shown in Figure 6.27.

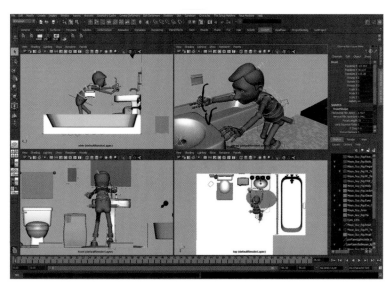

FIGURE 6.26 Multiple camera options in a 3D application

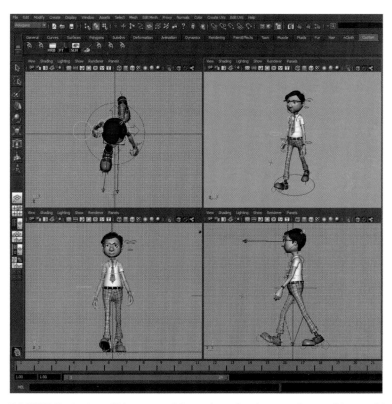

FIGURE 6.27 Side, top, and front view of a character in a walking position

Many animators will work to make the animation look correct from the final camera view, and for the most part, that method is acceptable. In applications for film, television, product visualization, architecture, law and medicine, the motion must look good from the camera angle being used for the finished project. But in the video game industry, you (the animator) do not get to dictate where the final camera is going to be placed. Instead, the action of the game or the character dictates the camera location. For example, the camera might be rotating around a moving character that the gamer is controlling.

Tracking Marks and Ghosting

Another great tool of any 3D animator is a *marker* for tracking the motion on your screen. This visual aid used to be easy to use a few years ago—it was simply done with dry-erase markers. Animators would track motion and draw poses on their CRT monitors with their all-glass screens. However, because LCD monitors are used today, physically marking on the screen has become a bad idea.

But there are still a few marking tools out there for today's animators. One is a software solution that enables you to draw on top of any application. Annotate!Pro, shown in Figure 6.28, is one option for a Windows operating system. The workflow for this type of onscreen drawing is not as fast as most animators would like, because you have to use a hot key to access the software to draw on the screen and then hot-key back to the animation software to make changes. This software approach does work, though, and many animators use it.

The other option that most 3D software allows is ghosting your object. *Ghosting* enables an object to be visible for a certain number of frames before and after the current frame, to let you see the motion across the screen. Figure 6.29 shows an example. This tool is very much like the light tables used by traditional 2D animation artists to see the frames before and after the current one, to track movement.

FK and IK

As discussed in the "Rigging" section earlier in this chapter, FK and IK are tools for moving and posing a character. FK and IK hierarchies can be part of an arm, leg, torso, tail, or wing, but a few types of animations call for a specific type of FK or IK rig. For example, legs of almost all characters are in IK so animators can keep the feet locked to the ground as the body moves through space. If your character needs to place his hand on a table and then keep that hand locked to the table as he moves, an IK arm rig would work best. This is because an FK arm rig would be driven by the body and shoulder, and the hand would never be able to lock into position on the table. Most character rigs enable you to switch between an FK system and a IK system, which is beneficial to the animation.

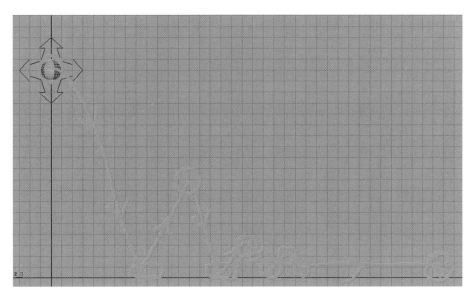

FIGURE 6.28 Annotate!Pro with markings on the screen to aid in motion-tracking animation

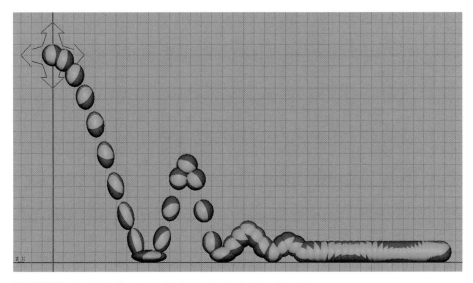

FIGURE 6.29 Ghosting of a bouncing ball to track motion

Video Reference

Video reference is an extremely important tool for animators today. With 3D character animation becoming more and more realistic, studying the movement and performance of an actor (or yourself acting out the scene) is key. Many animators will act out a performance many times, video-record all of the performances, and then with simple video-editing software create a final take to be used for reference. This video reference can provide a lot of information that can be used to create a better animation—for example, basic timing, weight, balance, subtle motion, eye positions, and eye darts. Video reference for other types of animation is just as important, including studying the way an airplane flies, the way a cars turns, the way an animal moves, the way a ball bounces, and more.

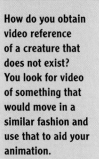

Eye darts are the quick movements of the eye as it is scanning the object you are looking at.

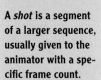

How do you obtain video reference of a creature that does not exist? You look for video of something that would move in a similar fashion and use that to aid your animation.

A *shot* is a segment of a larger sequence, usually given to the animator with a specific frame count.

Blocking is the placement of a character's key poses in a shot or an object's key positions. The animator focuses on basic timing as well as composition.

The Basic Animation Workflow

Here is the basic workflow for a 3D animator to follow in any project:

1. Obtain the assignment of the shot or sequence. The animation lead provides the assignment and the layout file indicating the camera's position or pre-animated camera movements and basic environment. This assignment describes what is wanted, needed, and expected from the shot or sequence of shots.

2. Generate ideas. The animator studies the shot information and pre-recorded voice over dialog, if needed, to get a sense of the kind of performance that can be created with that shot.

3. Obtain reference material. The animator creates or finds video references and will create thumbnail drawings of ideas to create a satisfactory concept of the shot.

4. Block the shot. The lead animator or animation director takes care of the blocking so that the animator will then just have to finalize the motion in the 3D software.

5. Perform finaling. The animator smooths out the motion and adds any final touches to the scene, such as secondary actions including muscle twitches or skin jiggles.

Animation Techniques

The techniques you, as an animator, use will greatly help or hinder the type of animation you are trying to create. Many animators have a favorite technique, but in some situations certain techniques are better than others—not only in terms of the animation created, but in terms of making you a more efficient and faster animator. There are three types of 3D animation: keyframed animation, motion capture and procedural, and each has its own advantages and disadvantages and separate approaches as well.

Keyframed Animation   Keyframed animation is similar to traditional 2D animation. The animator creates a pose or position for the character or object and sets a key at a specific point in time. The animator then creates a second pose or position and sets another key at another point in time. Traditional 2D animation worked the same way, but each frame would be drawn. This is a time-consuming and difficult task and is why most studios have more animators than other roles on staff for a production. This type of animation is used across the different industries and is still the most popular form of 3D animation today. Keyframed animation has four approaches in use today:

> **Pose-to-pose**   Pose-to-pose is an animation principle from the original Twelve Basic Principles of Animation discussed in Chapter 4. This technique allows the animator to lay in key poses (a process called *blocking*) that tell the story of the shot and allow the animator to work on the pacing and flow of the shot. After approval of the key poses from the lead animator or director, the animator will in-between the key poses until the character or object is fully animated. This approach is popular for many animators today because it allows them to show their work to their supervisor at various stages for approval so little time is wasted on having to reanimate a shot. The drawback to this approach is that young animators often do not have enough experience with animation to be able to create strong poses and fully understand what a pose needs in overlap before seeing the action moving. So some time is wasted, having to go back in and fix the overlap in the finaling stage of the animation.

> **Straight-ahead**   Straight-ahead, also an animation technique from the original Twelve Basic Principles of Animation, is the approach of animating each frame sequentially—frame 1, frame 2, frame 3, and so on—until the animation is completed. This was a favorite of many animators a long time ago because it provided a way to create spontaneity in animation; you could have an inspiration mid-animation to create something new and exciting. But as animation became more of a commercial entity, studios were not happy with this approach. Planning out a larger sequence or movie was difficult because there was no way to create the total flow of a larger project. Each animator would animate as many frames as they felt were needed for their shot. This meant that sometimes the animated shots

would be either too long or too short for the project as a whole. Also it was difficult to critique animation because the animator would have finished the entire animation to view, and the only real way to fix a mistake or make a change was to start over.

Hybrid   Hybrid animation is a blending of pose-to-pose and straight-ahead. This workflow offers all of the advantages of the two workflows and gets rid of the disadvantages. The animator creates the key poses for the shot and then typically creates an in-between stage. Then the animator uses a straight-ahead workflow for the end of the process to add in the overlapping action and finaling of the animation. This allows the animator to work on the basic flow and pacing of the shot early on and obtain approval from a supervisor before getting too far. This also allows the director to check the shot to make sure that it fits into the entire project. This workflow is one of the most used approaches in 3D animation today.

Hierarchy   Hierarchy animation is a workflow that is useful in creating cycle animation—an animation of an action that repeats itself over and over. The first and last frame of an animation cycle have to be identical to create the effect. Walking is an example of a good cycle animation of left foot, right foot, left foot, right foot. Many video games use cycles to create the in-game animation of walking, running, standing, jumping, shooting, and dying, for example. But because the animation rig is based on a hierarchy of controls, this approach allows the animator to start with the lower body first, blocking the steps of a walk, for example. Then after the lower body is done, the animator can animate the torso, and then the neck, and then the head. After the body's core is animated, the animator animates the arms, starting with the shoulders, and then moving on to the elbows and then the wrists. This workflow is also a good way for young animators to break an action down and not get bogged down with so many controls and body parts at once.

PATH ANIMATION

Path animation is a technique that allows an animator to set an object on a path and have that object follow the path over a set number of frames. Path animation enables the object not only to translate along the path but also to rotate along the path with banking and twisting. This technique is used within the approaches listed in this chapter.

Motion-Capture Animation　The motion-capture workflow is fairly consistent in the different industries. A system captures a performance or motion and then transfers the data into a 3D animation software package. Motion capture is becoming popular in the video game and film industries because an actor can act out the scene with a director, and that performance is then applied to the 3D character. There are two main types of technology used in this approach, as discussed in detail in Chapter 9, "Industry Trends." The basic type is a marker system, in which an actor wears a suit with a marker set that is tracked and triangulated by a series of cameras to create a three-dimensional data set. That data set is applied to the skeleton of a 3D character rig to drive the position and rotation of each of those joints to create the motion. The other type is a markerless system, in which data is transmitted directly to a computer. Once in the 3D software, the data is applied to a rig to evaluate the motion. The animator at this point cleans up the animation if there are any mistakes in the motion data. Then the animator adds any exaggeration needed. Typically, the hand, finger, and facial performances are not motion-captured but are added by the animator at this time. However, as the technology advances, facial and finger animations are being added to the original capture. Many software options are available, but the core workflow is always the same.

Procedural　In procedural animation, an animator has nothing to do with the motion. Software creates the motion, and the animator just adds in parameters to make the motion respond in a specific way. Procedural animation is very new to the consumer level of 3D animation and is being used more and more in the video game industry. This type of animation can allow background characters or computer-driven opponents to react to the environment and action in a realistic and convincing way. This is one the newest type of animation and is still being looked at by the different industries today. Video games are very interested in this type because it can greatly increase the productivity of the production pipeline by having the computer animate a characters in real time to react accordingly what is happening in the game. The old way was to have an animator animate many different outcomes that may occur during the game.

THE ESSENTIALS AND BEYOND

As you can see, rigging and animation go hand in hand—you cannot have animation without rigging, and rigging would not exist without animation. But despite this cohesiveness between them, they have distinct differences. You can see how technical rigging can be, with its hierarchies, constraints, expressions, and scripting. All of these functions are black-and-white and very logical. Then you have animation, requiring very few technical tools and focusing on performance-based art with no right or wrong answers and all opinions. But with these two polar opposites, teams can create the performances that make us as an audience believe that the characters onscreen are alive or that the car going by the camera is real.

REVIEW QUESTIONS

1. What is a rig?

    A. The deformers of the object

    B. The controllers of the object

    C. The skeleton of the geometry

    D. The control system for an animated object

2. What is a parent-child relationship in 3D animation?

    A. A mom and child object running errands

    B. A hierarchy setup enabling one object to control another object under it in the hierarchy

    C. When an object duplicates itself

    D. All of the above

3. What are joints?

    A. A hierarchy of pivot points

    B. Bones that create a collision object for skin

    C. Constraints to lock bones to the geometry

    D. All of above

4. IK joints would be moved in what way?

    A. Joint by joint, down the hierarchy

    B. By translating the end of the hierarchy to move the rest of the chain

    C. Procedurally with math

    D. By rotating the body to move the arms

    (Continues)

THE ESSENTIALS AND BEYOND *(Continued)*

5. What is skinning?

   A. The removal of skin from the geometry to see what is inside

   B. Adding a skin to a UV to texture the geometry

   C. A specific type of deformer to allow the geometry to follow along with the skeleton system

   D. All of the above

6. How many frames per second are included in a film?

   A. 30

   B. 24

   C. 25

   D. 15

7. Which of the following is not an approach to hand-keyed animation in 3D today?

   A. Pose-to-pose

   B. Straight-ahead

   C. Hybrid

   D. Procedural

8. What is a function curve?

   A. A 2D curve that represents a value over time

   B. A scripting term that describes making animation curves

   C. An outline curve to track motion in the work view

   D. An expression to create a curved animation arc

9. Which of the following is not a function-curve interpolation?

   A. Spline

   B. Linear

   C. Mountain

   D. Step

10. What is the most used animation technique today?

   A. Hybrid

   B. Pose-to-pose

   C. Straight-ahead

   D. Hierarchy

CHAPTER 7

Understanding Visual Effects, Lighting, and Rendering

3D visual effects, lighting, and rendering are the end stages of the production pipeline and will constantly cross paths to create the final look of the project. They are so closely tied to one another that you cannot control one of these processes without the others. 3D visual effects enable us to create natural-seeming and complex motions that would be too difficult to animate by hand. Lighting and rendering are so closely tied to visual effects because the look of the visual effects is dictated by the render engine that you are using as well as the lights that will illuminate the effect. In this chapter, you will look at the basics of each of these stages to better understand them and how they need to work together.

▶ **Creating visual effects**

▶ **Lighting**

▶ **Rendering**

Creating Visual Effects

3D *visual effects (VFX)* artists are jack-of-all-trades artists and are called upon to create difficult effects like smoke, water or hair or nontraditional 3D animation like falling objects from an explosion and tree leaves blowing in the wind. Most visual effects can be created in 2D software, but some cannot be created easily in these programs—for instance, hair, fur, and destructive shattering. 3D VFX artists also create all of the animation that is not hand-keyframed or motion-captured. These types of animations are typically elements such as dust, smoke, fire, rain, hair, fur, fluids, cloth, and explosions. Usually the animations are created by a physics-simulation system that takes into account factors including gravity, wind, and other field conditions. 3D VFX artists must have a firm understanding of all other 3D animation job roles (modeling, texturing,

▶

Destructive shattering **is an effect that simulates objects as they break and shatter. A physics simulation is run to move the shattered pieces and enable them to collide.**

rigging, animation, lighting, and rendering), because they will need all of these skill sets to aid in their day-to-day tasks of creating visual effects.

The simulations that 3D VFX artists create are complex and require a lot of data to complete. Because of this large amount of data, these effects are difficult to manipulate and control and take a lot of time to preview. Recently (in the past five years or so) 3D VFX has become more accessible to more artists and studios as computers have become more powerful and able to handle more and more information.

3D VFX artists create effects using 3D software. They often specialize in one or two of the following categories of 3D effects:

▶ Particles

▶ Hair and fur

▶ Fluids

▶ Rigid bodies (such as falling debris)

▶ Soft bodies (such as cloth)

Many 3D animation software packages have systems for creating these categories of effects. However, 3D VFX artists must be able to make the out-of-the-box effects available in the software look unique to the project they are working on. In the following sections, you'll look at some of these specialties and discuss the 3D animation effects that VFX artists in these areas need to know.

Particles

Particles are points in three-dimensional space that are created and simulated by an emitter and animated with fields or forces. An emitter is a position, volume, geometry or even other particles that create and emit particles into a 3D space; and fields or forces are types of natural forces and motions like wind, gravity and friction and expressions that will move or manipulate the particles. Most 3D software can handle thousands of these particles at one time, which can enable you to create effects not easily produced by hand. It would take forever to animate thousands of points by hand, and a simulation can automate that process for you.

These points by default are just points in space and do not render, but each point can have some type of shader (the properties for rendering a surface), effect, or geometry attached to create a specific look such as dust, fire, rain, snow, flocking birds, swarming bees, or magic pixie dust. For example, to create a swarm of bees chasing a character, it would not be efficient to animate hundreds of bees individually. Using a particle system and attaching the bees to those particles would be more efficient. Particle simulations are used for many purposes other than just dust or magic effects. They can be used for basic crowd or swarm animation, creation of galaxies, and snowstorms.

The following is a basic workflow for creating and controlling particle systems:

1. Create an emitter. The VFX artist can choose from many options to create the emitter—for example, an object, a volume (procedural three-dimensional form), or a position. For example to create pixie dust you could create a position emitter that will emit particles from that particular point.

2. Animate the emitter. The VFX artist sets the emitter's attributes so that a certain quantity of particles are emitted at a particular speed. The VFX artist then adds animation to the physical emitter if needed. This can be hand-keyed, or the emitter can be constrained to another object if needed.

3. Create particle movement. The VFX artist writes expressions or creates fields/forces to manipulate the motion or behavior of the particles in space.

4. Develop the look. Particles can be dots, streaks, blobby surfaces, cloud-like forms, or sprites (flat planes with textures applied to them) and can have geometry attached to them.

Figure 7.1 shows an example of a particle simulation.

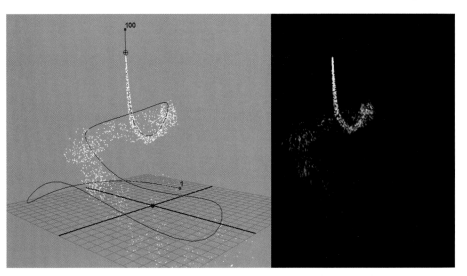

Path animation is a technique that allows an object to be attached to a path and to follow that curve for the length of an animation timeline.

FIGURE 7.1 The scene file with the emitter and particles along a path animation (left), and the rendered look of the particles (right)

Hair and Fur

Hair and fur are systems that will utilize hair and fur creation and rendering with dynamic simulations that create the look of fluid movement of hair or fur. But these dynamic systems can be used as well to create follow-through and overlapping motion for animation—for example, the movement of antennas, tails, and tentacles. Figure 7.2 shows an example of a ball with a form like a tail behind it. The tail is skinned to a skeleton system, and the skeleton system is attached to a hair curve. (Hair curves are created to allow the motion of hair to occur.) As the ball is rotated, the tail is dynamically animated by the hair curve driving the joints.

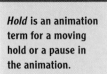

Hold is an animation term for a moving hold or a pause in the animation.

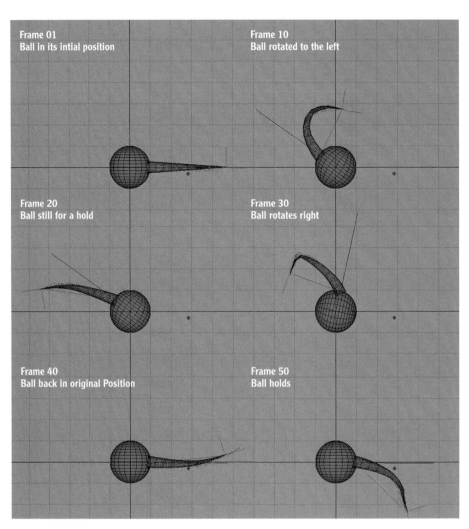

FIGURE 7.2 A secondary animation of a tail is dynamically created with a hair curve to drive the motion of the joints along the tail.

Hair and fur are some of the most difficult dynamic systems to use, control, and render realistically. You will see this effect in many film and visual effects movies, but not really in any lower-budget projects because of the complexity of the render setup and the longer render times. But this effect is one that if done well, can really make a 3D project look very good. Most 3D software has a hair and fur dynamic system integrated into it. A commercial plug-in called Shave and a Haircut by Joe Alter is also available. However, most companies add to these options to create a set of proprietary tools for a specific look. Figure 7.3 shows an example of fur, and Figure 7.4 shows an example of hair.

Model © Jason Higgs

FIGURE 7.3 Fur on a character

Model © Beane Stalk Studios

FIGURE 7.4 Hair simulation and styling on a human head

The following is a basic workflow for creating and controlling hair and fur systems:

1. Create hair or fur. The VFX artist does this by assigning hair or fur to an object.

2. Style the hair or fur. The VFX artist can style the hair and fur to match the look the artist wants: a windblown style, well-styled hair, or even "hair" for grass (with a lot of randomness applied).

3. Establish the color and look. The VFX artist creates color maps if needed to create the color of the hair or fur.

4. Set the dynamics. The VFX artist applies fields or forces and assigns any collision objects needed for the hair and fur to move in the way it should.

Fluids

Fluid simulations are special particle simulations that use an equation (such as Navier-Stokes) to create the movement of fluids. The word *fluid* can be deceiving. It does not mean only waterlike materials, but also smoke, fire, and plasmalike substances. Fluid simulations can render a particlelike look for smoke or fire, or they can be converted into geometry to create a fluidlike surface with proper motion. A few types of software can aid in this relatively new simulation type.

NAVIER-STOKES EQUATIONS

Named after physicists Claude-Louis Navier and George Gabriel Stokes, this equation type describes the motion of fluids. Navier-Stokes equations are applied to aircraft, automobiles, pollution, and blood flow, to name a few examples.

The following is a basic workflow for creating and controlling fluid systems:

1. Create the scene. The VFX artist creates a scene that might contain vessels or other containers to hold the liquid—for example, a nozzle pouring water into a glass. If the scene needs the vessels to be animated, this would be completed at this stage.

2. Export to RealFlow. The VFX artist exports the scene created in 3D software such as Maya, 3ds Max, or Softimage to software such as RealFlow (see the following "Using RealFlow and Caches" sidebar).

3. Create particle movement. The VFX artist creates the movement of the fluid with the aid of particle simulations.

4. Create the geometry. The VFX artist creates a geometry shape from the particles and then creates a geometry cache that will be exported from RealFlow back into a 3D animation software package.

5. Develop the look. Shaders and lighting are applied to the geometry that is exported back to the 3D animation software. This results in the final rendered fluid. Figure 7.5 shows an example.

FIGURE 7.5 RealFlow scene (left) and the rendered image from Maya (right)

USING REALFLOW AND CACHES

A stand-alone software package that is thought of as an industry standard is Next Limit Technologies RealFlow. Simulations are created in RealFlow and then exported into either a geometry cache or a particle cache to be rendered in a separate software package such as Maya or Softimage.

A *cache* is an internal or external data file that stores transformation data (move, scale, or rotate) or deformation data of an object or objects of a simulation. After the cache is created, the software itself no longer has to simulate the movement of the objects. The cache can also be used to transfer the data to other scenes or render the effects on multiple machines at one time to save on render time.

Rigid Bodies

Rigid bodies are solid-form simulations that can collide with other objects and not deform. Rigid bodies react and translate based on attributes defined by the artist, such as center of mass, velocity, and collisions. Rigid-body simulations are a popular type of 3D VFX and are used for basic collisions of hard objects, shattering of objects, movement through space, and ragdoll animations. All of these types of animation can be quickly calculated and are used in many industries such as film, television, video games, medicine, and law.

RAGDOLL ANIMATION

Ragdoll animation is typically accomplished by creating each body part of a character as a low-resolution individual piece of geometry. These geometry pieces are connected by a dynamic constraint system that lets each piece hang on a string connected to the other pieces. These pieces will fall like a rag doll, as seen in the following image. Then the skeleton of the character is parented to the geometry to allow the simulation to run the movement of the rig.

The typical workflow for rigid-body dynamics is as follows:

1. Create the scene. The VFX artist starts by creating the geometry that will be used for the simulation. For example, Figure 7.6 shows a small wall of bricks and a large ball. These objects are basic and low

resolution to aid in the speed of the simulation. In 3D VFX, even if the final geometry is to be high resolution, the VFX artist will commonly create low-resolution geometry for the simulation.

If you had a high-resolution model, a 3D VFX artist would still have to create the simulation by using a low-resolution proxy geometry attached to the higher resolution to allow for fast simulations.

FIGURE 7.6 Beginning scene with no rigid bodies added

2. Assign the rigid bodies. In our example, the VFX artist makes the ball and the bricks active rigid bodies, which means they can be animated only by using dynamic fields and physics. The floor is made into a passive or inactive rigid body, which means that it can be a collision object but is not affected by the dynamic fields, such as gravity.

3. Add fields/forces. The VFX artist adds fields/forces such as gravity to the active bodies. Continuing our example, the ball and bricks are given a gravity field to make them reactive. If you run the simulation at this point, you will see the bricks settle and the ball bounce until it stops. You can make the ball move toward the bricks by setting the initial motion attribute of active rigid bodies. Initial motion is a push or spin of the active rigid body given at the first frame of the simulation.

4. Run the simulation. The VFX artist runs the simulation and adjusts the properties of the rigid bodies to achieve the desired look.

Figure 7.7 shows the simulation effect after adding an initial push to the ball to move it toward the bricks.

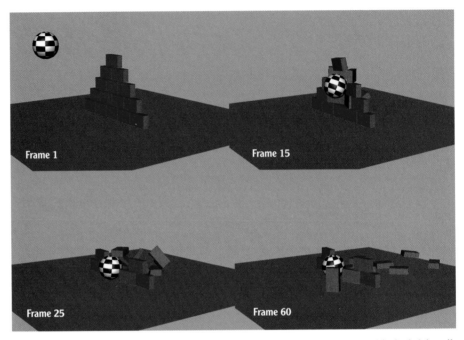

FIGURE 7.7 In this 60-frame progression, the rigid-body ball collides with the brick wall.

Soft Bodies

Soft-body dynamics, also known as *cloth dynamics*, simulates forms that can collide with other objects and (unlike rigid bodies) can be deformed as a part of the collision. Soft bodies are calculated by placing a point or particle on every vertex of a geometric object and then creating a virtual tie to surrounding vertices to maintain a shape if needed. Figure 7.8 shows an example; the dots are the vertices, and the dashed lines are the simulated ties that will hold the geometry shape through the simulation. These types of simulations and deformations are used to create realistic cloth, muscle, fat, stylized cartoon hair, and some fluid-like surfaces. This type of simulation can be very taxing on the computer during the testing stage, depending on the density of the geometry.

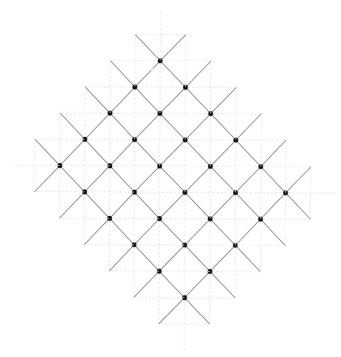

FIGURE 7.8 Diagram of soft-body dynamics

CROSSOVER OF VISUAL EFFECTS SIMULATIONS

Visual effects have crossover all the time in creating the type of simulations needed. For instance, you can use hair to move curtains in front of a window instead of using a soft-body simulation. You can use soft-body simulations to move geometry in the shape of hair to create hair movement and apply hairlike shaders on the geometry. This type of crossover happens for various reasons. An artist might not know a specific system but can fake the effect in a different system, for example. Or creating a geometry plane and using soft-body dynamics to make it move like the surface of water might be easier than creating a complex fluid simulation.

The typical workflow for soft-body dynamics is as follows:

1. Create the scene. The VFX artist creates the geometry needed for the simulation Figure 7.9 shows an example of a chair and circular throw blanket.

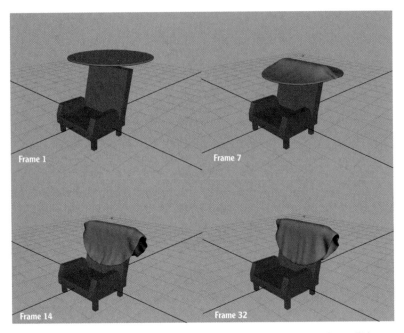

FIGURE 7.9 In this 32-frame progression, the soft-body blanket collides with the chair back.

2. Assign the rigid bodies. The VFX artist sets the objects that are going to be soft bodies and makes any other objects needed to collide with the soft body a collision object. In Figure 7.9, the throw blanket is set to soft, and the chair is set to a collision object.

3. Add fields/forces. The VFX artist adds fields/forces such as gravity and any other physics needed and runs the simulation. In Figure 7.9, the throw blanket is given gravity to fall.

4. Run the simulation. The VFX artist runs the simulation and adjusts the properties of the soft bodies to achieve the desired look.

The Basic VFX Workflow

The typical overall workflow for the effects artist to create a dynamics scene is as follows:

1. Receive the assignment of the shot or sequence. The VFX artist receives the assignment and the scene file with the camera details, environment, and animation from the VFX lead with a description of what is wanted, needed, and expected from the shot or sequence of shots.

2. Break down the scene. The VFX artist breaks down an effect to see how to more easily create the simulation. For example, a VFX artist might need to break a rock wall as the result of an explosion. There are just too many large and small individual pieces of wall to simulate at once, but if broken down into specific-size pieces, creating the effect is much more manageable.

3. Begin the shot breakdown. The VFX artists break the scene into the smaller pieces decided on in step 2 (in this case, breaking the wall into large rock chunks first, simulating their motion, and caching their animation).

4. Continue the breakdown. The VFX artist continues with each step of the planned breakdown, simulating it, and caching the simulation. For example, the VFX artist simulates the medium-size rocks around the cached larger rocks because the medium rocks really would not change any of the larger rocks' momentum and direction. Afterward, the medium rocks are cached. The 3D VFX artist then simulates the smallest rocks around the large and medium rocks and caches them.

5. Perform finaling. Because all of the rocks are cached out, the computer does not have to calculate all of them at one time. The VFX artist can efficiently add the dust and other debris to fill in the rest of the effect to create the final result.

Lighting

3D-animation lighting artists set up the lights in a 3D environment to either show a key object or establish mood. These professionals are very similar to film lighting artists and artistic painters. Lighting artists must be able to create atmosphere and mood in a shot or sequence. They also must create good product lighting to best show every detail of an object without making it look flat and boring. It is also important for the lighting department to create a consistent lighting scheme across a longer project such as a film or television show. Lighting is especially important to a 3D animation project, because lighting must not only convey the narrative and mood of a shot but also visually depict the location, time of day, and even the weather convincingly.

Lighting artists receive scenes that need lighting from the animation team, visual effects team, or the set-dressing team. Lighting artists need a solid understanding of 3D light types and knowledge of whatever render engine they are using to be able to achieve efficient render times. An understanding of how light in the real world behaves is important to be able to fake light behavior in the digital world.

The lighting artist can choose from various light types to create the type of light patterns needed. The artist first creates the intensity and direction of the light and adds color if needed. Then the artist manipulates the shadow properties to match the light-source type. A stage spotlight casts a very intense light with a sharp shadow, for example, but a lamp with a shade creates soft light with blurry shadows. Lighting artists usually work with one light at a time to increase efficiency of render times. After all the lights are in place, the lighting artist will break the scene into render passes to aid in the rendering process and compositing stage. These render passes will allow for faster render times and give more control to the lighter in the compositing stage by breaking the scene into smaller pieces that can be individually controlled. For example, you can render the background separately from the foreground to color-correct the background as needed.

Light Types

The types of lights that the lighting artist has to work with are varied, just as in the real world. However, the basic light types available in almost all animation software are as follows:

Spotlights   *Spotlights* are one of the most used types of light in any 3D animation software. They cast light from a single point, in a single direction, and you can control the cone angle to determine the size of the light. You can also soften the outside edge of the cone shape to create different looks. When using spotlights, the lighting artist has a lot of control in setting up a lighting scheme. Figure 7.10 shows a spotlight illuminating a corner.

Omni/Point Lights   *Omni lights*, or *point lights*, emit light from a single point, in all directions, similar to a lightbulb, as shown in Figure 7.11.

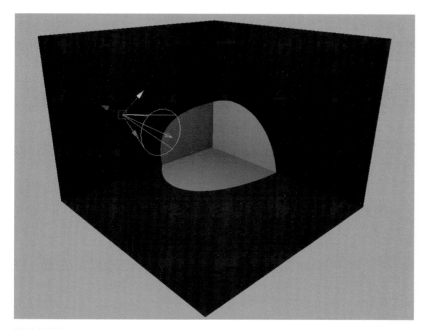

FIGURE 7.10 A spotlight casting light on a corner

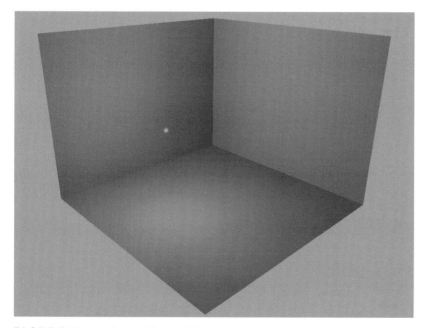

FIGURE 7.11 An omni/point light in a scene

Infinite/Directional Lights   *Infinite lights*, or *directional lights*, create light that is traveling in parallel rays, like that of the sun. Spotlights and point lights both cast light from a single point in some type of cone pattern that will create shadows. But a directional light casts light in parallel rays, like a light source from very far away, and will cast parallel patterns; see Figure 7.12. The infinite/directional light type is great for simulating the sun or moonlight, because it creates the proper type of shadows.

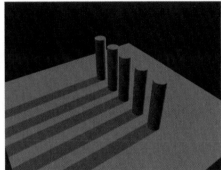

FIGURE 7.12 A spotlight casts shadows on a row of cylinders, creating a V-shaped shadow pattern (left). A directional light casts shadows on a row of cylinders, creating a parallel shadow pattern (right).

Ambient Lights   *Ambient lights* cast light not away from themselves, but toward themselves, at a constant intensity from every angle. These lights were created to help fake global illumination by not allowing areas of your scene to fall into pure shadow (see the "Direct Lights and Global Illumination" sidebar and the "Global Illumination" section later in this chapter). In Figure 7.13, for example, two identical spheres are lit by the same spotlight, but the image on the right also has a low-intensity ambient light to fill in the areas of shadow. This technique was used before computers could handle the more-complex global illumination light techniques used today. This light type is not as widely used as it once was, because of new techniques for creating global illumination, but is still used in specialty lighting to create a specific effect and to create flat lighting when needed, as when lighting a background image that would be placed on a plane to get even lighting.

Area Lights   *Area lights* are the most realistic and complicated of the lights listed here. Point lights and spotlights both emit light from a single point in space, whereas an area light emits light from an area or surface such as a window, computer screen, or lamp shade (see Figure 7.14). This light emission over an area creates soft and realistic shadows, but at a cost of longer render times.

FIGURE 7.13 Ambient light example of two spheres with identical shaders. The sphere on the left has only a direct light, so the back side of the sphere goes into complete darkness. On the right, the sphere has a slight bit of ambient light applied, so the back side does not fall into complete darkness.

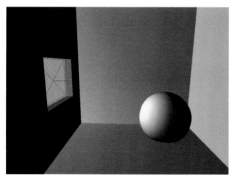 

FIGURE 7.14 An area light in the window (left) and the soft light pattern and shadows that it creates (right)

DIRECT LIGHTS AND GLOBAL ILLUMINATION

Each of the light types described in this section are called *direct lights*. This means that the light rays travel in only a straight line and in one direction. These direct lights do not by default behave like real lights in the real world. A flashlight acting like a direct light will cast light that travels only toward the direction the flashlight is pointing (as in the left side of the following image). In the real world, you would expect to see a flashlight cast light in one direction, but when that light hits an object, it would bounce to illuminate the area

(Continues)

DIRECT LIGHTS AND GLOBAL ILLUMINATION   *(Continued)*

around it (as in the right side of the following image). In 3D animation software packages, we can create this type of light-bouncing and color-bleeding effect, called global illumination, but, again, this is not a default setting.

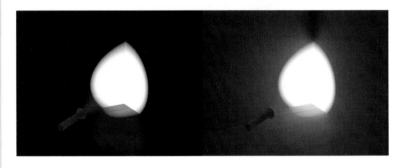

Light Attributes

Lighting artists manipulate attributes to create the type of light source they are trying to simulate, such as a soft lightbulb, a strong spotlight, or a color-gelled spotlight. The following are the most commonly used light attributes available in 3D animation packages:

Intensity   This indicates how strong the actual light is.

Color   This attribute enables the artist to add color to the light source. This can get away from an artist quickly, with too much light color added. In the real world, colored light is created by placing a gel or color filter in front of the source to color the light. This attribute does not turn a light a pure, saturated color, but instead simply adds a color tint.

> The word *bright* is not a scientifically correct way of stating light intensity, but is a good general way of thinking about it.

Decay or Attenuation   Light decay, or light attenuation, is the gradual drop in intensity over distance, which is the way light in the real world acts. 3D software provides options enabling a lighting artist to choose whether to have the light decay. An artist also can specify how that light will decay. Typical light decay options are presented as presets, such as linear falloff or a quadratic/inverse-square falloff. These two types of attenuation allow the light to fall off in different patterns. Most 3D animation software also offers a user-defined falloff, in which the lighting artist can dictate where the light intensity will start and stop by distance. These decay types can be seen in Figure 7.15.

FIGURE 7.15 Linear falloff (left), inverse-square falloff (middle), and user-defined falloff (right), all coming from a spotlight. Each light has the same intensity.

Shadows *Shadows* are important in enabling us to define three-dimensional shapes. Without any shadows, everything would look flat and boring. But shadows are not always desired. Real-world lighting artists for film, photography, and television do not have the option of setting up a light and not having it cast a shadow, but 3D lighting artists can. This option can greatly help 3D artists create the look they want without the problem of unwanted shadows. But shadows in 3D animation do not always look realistic by default. There are two main shadow types to use: raytraced shadows and depth map shadows. Each type has advantages and disadvantages.

Raytraced Shadows These are the most accurate shadow types. They create sharp, perfect shadow outlines. They also enable shadows to pass through transparent objects (for example glass, plastic, and water) and to attenuate. Raytraced shadows will work only if the render options have raytracing turned on. Of the two types of shadows, raytraced shadows are more realistic and soft, but this comes at a cost of much longer render times. These shadows are created by the surfaces of the geometry, which cast rays from every surface point seen from the camera to every light to see if the rays from the surface intersect any objects.

There are very few quality-control settings for raytraced shadows; for sharp shadows, the default setting will be perfect. To create a soft shadow,

▶

*Shadow samples
use an algorithm
to create smooth,
clean shadows.
In the following
image, the left
side shows a low-
sampled raytraced
shadow; notice the
visual noise in the
shadow. The right
side is the same
shadow with a
higher sampling of
the shadow to create
a smooth edge.*

you change the size of the radius of the light. To create a smooth, clean shadow, you increase the shadow samples.

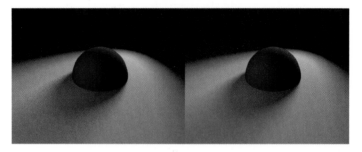

Depth Map Shadows   Depth map shadows are very fast to render and can create good results when used correctly. They can create both sharp and soft shadows but will never render a transparent shadow, which is a big drawback. To create these shadows, each light in the scene casts a resolution-based map onto the scene, and the render engine stores the depth information for the light. Only the geometry closest to the lights, as calculated in the depth map, will be lit and will cast shadows.

Depth map shadows have a few options that determine their final quality. Resolution is the first; this resolution is just like resolution of a texture or a television—the higher the resolution, the more information you have to create a sharp shadow. There is also a softness setting to blur the shape around the shadow to varying degrees. The last setting is quality, which is used to clean the blur to allow for smooth transitions in the blur. Figure 7.16 shows a side-by-side rendering of the different shadow types and their render times.

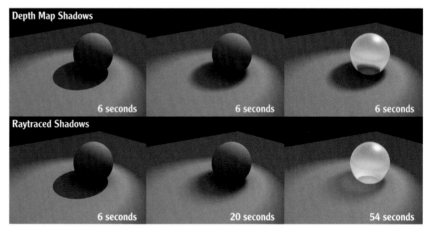

FIGURE 7.16 Side-by-side comparison of depth map shadows and raytraced shadows with render times listed

Linked Lights   Light artists can link lights to illuminate only user-defined objects, which is very powerful in lighting design. A real-world lighting artist cannot make a fill light skip one actor to create the correct fill light on another actor, but a 3D animation lighting artist can. This option allows lighting artists to create very specific looks and moods that are not realistically possible but improve the final shot. In Figure 7.17, one spotlight is pointed at three spheres. The light is linked to illuminate only the two outside spheres. The sphere in the middle is black because it is not being lit by the light.

FIGURE 7.17 Light linking enables a light to be directed to illuminate all or just some of the objects in a scene. All three spheres are the same, but the light is not illuminating the middle sphere.

Lighting Techniques

There are a few basic lighting techniques used in photography, film, television, theater, and painting that can create a specific mood as well as good lighting.

Three-Point Lighting   The most common is three-point lighting (Figure 7.18), which uses three lights:

The *key light* is the most intense of the three lights and is the primary light source. This light by standard rules is placed to one side of the subject and is at least slightly higher than the object.

The *fill light* is less intense and is placed on the opposite side of the key light to fill in the shadow areas cast from the key light. The idea is to slightly fill in the shadow area, not to get rid of shadows.

The *rim, or kicker, light* is placed behind the object to add a rim or highlight area around the object to separate it from the background.

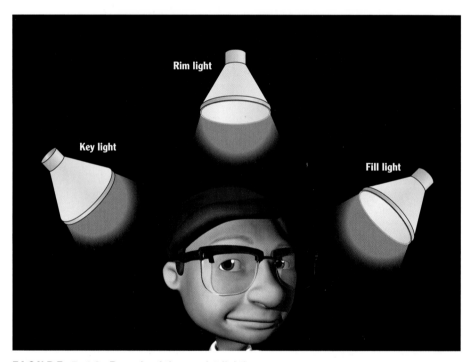

FIGURE 7.18 Example of three-point lighting

Two-Point Lighting   Two-point lighting (Figure 7.19) is like the type of lighting we see every day as the sunlight comes in and the sky's ambient lighting surrounds us as a second light. This lighting setup is similar to the three-point light set, but lacks the rim light.

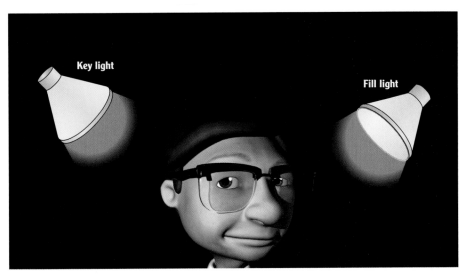

FIGURE 7.19 Example of two-point lighting

One-Point Lighting   One-point lighting (Figure 7.20) is an extreme technique used for dramatic effects. This light setup has only a key light and no fill. This light setup creates a stark transition between light and shadow.

FIGURE 7.20 Example of one-point lighting

Natural Lighting   Natural lighting is lighting from the natural environment that we cannot control. For example, on a cloudy day, the clouds will diffuse the sunlight and wrap the light around the sky to create even, flat lighting with no direct shadows. Or on a sunny day outside, the sun is the direct light source with shadow, but the sky will create a fairly even light source emitted from almost every direction to create a nice, even fill light with a tint of blue from the sky (or even gray fill light on a cloudy day), as seen in Figure 7.21.

FIGURE 7.21: Example of natural lighting to create a sunny-day look

The Basic Lighting Workflow

The basic workflow for a lighting artist is as follows:

1. Obtain the assigned shot or sequence. The lighting artist receives a shot or sequence from the lead lighting artist. The scene file contains the animation, final environment, and visual effects. The lead gives any directions needed for the lighting artist to work from.

2. Start with the main light source. The lighting artist lights a scene one light at a time, starting with the main light source. This main light can be anything—the sun, the sky, a window, a lamp, or car headlights, for example.

3. Add the fill and rim lights. These lights are added to make the subject matter stand out and typically look natural.

4. Apply final touches. Lighting artists add any optical special effects that might be needed in the scene such as lens flares or glows.

Rendering

Rendering, the final stage of the production pipeline, takes the 3D models, rigs, animation, shaders, textures, 3D VFX, and lighting, and renders them into 2D video or still images. These renders are then given to the postproduction team for final prep and output.

A few render engines are on the market today. These include a 3D software package's proprietary render engine, a plug-in that will work within the 3D animation software, or a stand-alone software package that can work without a 3D animation software package. Render engines such as Unreal and Unity Engine also include real-time video game software.

A *render engine* is the software that calculates the final scene and configures the final images.

Basic Rendering Methods

The different render engines all render the basic image in a similar way. They offer two basic rendering methods: scanline and raytracing.

Scanline   This algorithm renders very quickly. The drawback to this method is that it cannot calculate reflections, refractions, or complex global illumination lighting/rendering systems available today in render engines such as mental ray, V-Ray, and RenderMan. Scanline is a great render method for pre-visualization information and quick tests to see how a scene is progressing. The scanline method also works well with cartoonlike, flat, cell-shaded rendering as well.

Scanline rendering works on a row-by-row basis to complete the entire image by first measuring what polygon surfaces are in the scene and then deciding what polygons are visible and not visible from the view of the camera rendering the

Real-time rendering in video games means that the game software and hardware are producing the 3D world in real time, as the player is playing the game.

scene. This act of sorting the polygon objects allows the renderer to not have to calculate what is not seen from the camera, which saves computer system resources. Figure 7.22 shows an example of how this render method works.

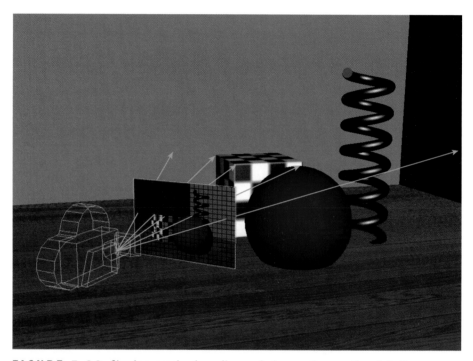

FIGURE 7.22 Simple example of scanline rendering, casting scanlines into the scene and returning information about the pixels that the lines intersect

Raytracing   Raytracing is a much more robust and complete rendering method than scanline, but at a cost. This method can calculate reflections, refractions, and many other complex rendering options in each of the render engines. It casts rays to every pixel onscreen and samples the shape and shader of the object it interacts with. At the sample point, if the shader is reflective, the renderer will create a new ray to cast and sample to tell the point what it is reflecting. These rays can cast until they hit a nonreflective surface (Figure 7.23) or until they reach a user-defined number of ray casts. This ray casting allows the raytracing render method a much larger degree of realism than scanline rendering can achieve, but at a cost of computer resources and time to create the final image.

Figure 7.24 shows an example of a scene rendered in mental ray with a scanline render method and raytracing. Each render uses the same lights and shaders on the objects, but you can see the differences in each image.

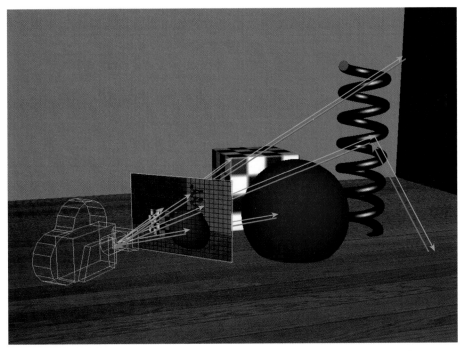

FIGURE 7.23 In this simple example of raytracing rays, the rays are cast from the camera, and if they hit a reflective surface, they will bounce until they hit a nonreflective object. Once the rays stop they will return to the camera to give the data searched for.

FIGURE 7.24 The same scene rendered with the scanline render method (left) and the raytracing render method (right)

Global Illumination

▶

Just as raytracing increases rendering time compared to scanline rendering, global illumination will even more drastically increase the total render time.

Global illumination is a general term used to describe a group of advanced algorithms and methods to create more-realistic lighting and shaders in the render engine at the time of rendering. These algorithms are typically based on raytracing but will add more functions to the rendering algorithm to allow for a realistic final look. This section describes the common types of global illumination methods. Each of these is now integrated into most render engines.

WEIGHING QUALITY AGAINST TIME AND BUDGET

3D artists always have to weigh the overall final quality against the time and money a project requires. When using today's render engines and shaders, a 3D artist has to find a happy medium between perfect looks and reasonable render time. Just because you *can* do something does not mean you always *should*.

Photon Mapping   Photon mapping is a global illumination render algorithm that takes into account raytracing but uses it in reverse. Instead of projecting rays from the camera to calculate the scene, photons are cast from the light source(s) and bounced around the scene, leaving radiance marks on each hit from a photon. Then those radiance marks sample other surrounding radiance marks to determine the final lighting intensity for that sample point of the radiance mark, as seen in Figure 7.25. This type of lighting is costly in terms of render time and overall computer resources because many photons are needed to create the final look. This type of lighting, though, can be very realistic overall in a way that was difficult to achieve just a few years ago. Figure 7.26 shows the left scene lit by one light without photon mapping and the image on the right with photon mapping enabled. You can see the indirect bounce lighting and color bleeding from objects close to one another.

Image-Based Lighting   Image-based lighting (IBL) is a global illumination method that allows the user to create a dome or surrounding sphere to encompass the scene they are working with and assign an image that will illuminate the scene instead of lights. The image used for image-based lighting is typically a high dynamic range image (HDRI).

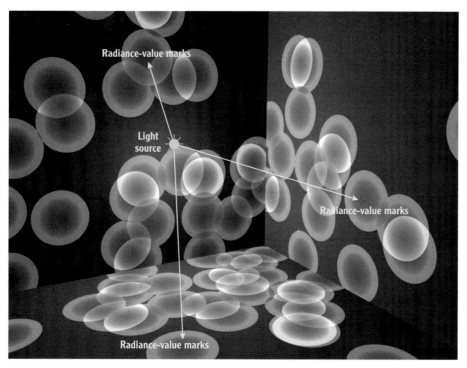

FIGURE 7.25 Simple example of photon mapping. Each of the white circles are irradiance hits that are calculated to create a more realistic lighting system. In practice, hundreds of thousands of these hits are created and smoothed out.

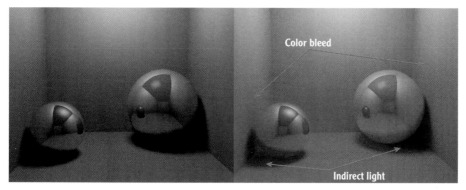

FIGURE 7.26 Lighting without photon mapping (left) and with photon mapping (right). Notice the filled-in shadow regions and the color bleeding from the nearby spheres.

UNDERSTANDING HIGH DYNAMIC RANGE IMAGES

In a regular 8-bit image, the values between black and white are 0 (black) to 1 (white), but an HDRI will allow for more than just the basic 0 to 1 values—it can carry 32-bit floating-point values of 0 to 4,294,697,295. This type of image is typically created by shooting with a camera and bracketing the f-stops up and down from the regular exposure setting. These bracketed images are then combined to create an HDRI in a photo-manipulation program such as Photoshop.

The specific way that the IBL system works varies from render engine to render engine. In general, the camera, from its point of view, casts sample points into the scene, and each of these sample points casts a user-defined number of sample rays randomly into the scene. The sample rays collect radiance data from any surface they hit—typically an HDR image surrounding the subject matter—and return the data of the ray hits to the original sample point. Then the original sample points sample the data from surrounding points to create a final radiance setting and return the radiance data to the camera for rendering the final image. Figure 7.27 shows the dome surrounding the scene, the sample points on the figure in the scene, and the final IBL result.

FIGURE 7.27 An IBL sphere surrounding the subject (left), the camera view sample points created to sample the surrounding area to find illumination (center), and the resulting render (right). There are no lights in the scene—just an HDRI of a sunny sky illuminating the object (resulting in a blue tint).

Advanced Shader Functions

Advanced shaders are being updated yearly to allow 3D artists more tools to add to their toolbox. The bidirectional reflectance distribution function and sub-surface scattering are two of the newest consumer-level advanced shader functions. They have not always been used on the consumer level because they are computer-resource heavy, and regular users did not have computers fast enough to make these functions worth using.

Bidirectional Reflectance Distribution Function   The bidirectional reflectance distribution function (BRDF) defines how light is reflected from an opaque surface. By using this type of shader, you can create realistic anisotropic reflections (Figure 7.28) and Fresnel effects (Figure 7.29) on surfaces that were not possible to produce realistically a few years ago. This BRDF shader model enables you to create glossy reflections with specular highlights that run along the surface direction instead of marking a single spot on the surface.

Anisotropic reflections stretch along the surface of an object because of the microgrooves or scratches along the surface, like that of brushed metal.

The *Fresnel effect* indicates that the amount of reflectivity of an object's surface such as water, glass, and plastic, is based on the viewer's angle.

FIGURE 7.28 Example of BRDF anisotropic reflections in a brushed metal shader

FIGURE 7.29 In this example of the Fresnel reflection effect, you can see that the reflections are greater on the sides of the glass.

Subsurface Scattering   Subsurface scattering enables light to penetrate the surface of the object, scatter accordingly, and then pass back out of the surface. This type of shader is perfect for skin, marble, and milk. Each render engine has a different model of subsurface scattering to allow for faster rendering or more physically accurate calculations. Figure 7.30 shows an example of the subsurface scattering effect on multiple objects to show the effect on different shapes.

The Basic Rendering Workflow

Typically, the lighting artist is also the person in charge of rendering a shot or sequence. Here is the basic workflow for a 3D render or lighting artist to follow for any project:

1. Set up the lights. The artist makes sure that the basic lights are illuminating the scene.

2. Assess the need for advanced lights. The artist determines whether the use of advanced lighting render techniques such as global illumination or image-based lighting are needed. If so, the artist sets up the render to evaluate that system.

3. Establish render settings. The artist sets the render engine's options to allow for production-level rendering. Every render

engine has its own set of standards to allow for this production-level final image.

4. Render in passes. The artist sets up the render passes if necessary.

5. Render the image. The artist renders the image or images for an animated sequence.

6. Composite the render passes together to create the final image. This is done in a compositing software package such as Adobe After Effects or The Foundry's Nuke.

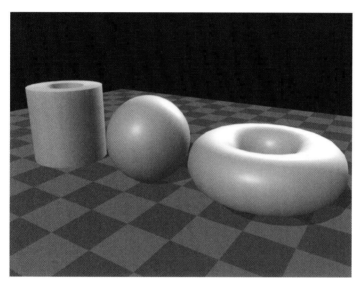

FIGURE 7.30 Example of subsurface scattering on multiple objects

RENDER PASSES

Render passes are processes that break a render into individual pieces. For example, you can break a render down to just color information, shadow information, highlight information, or reflection information to have more control of the final image in the compositing software. You can also break the render into passes per light if needed to allow for post-lighting intensity changes. These passes may at first seem like an extra step to set up, but if done correctly, can be used to correct an entire image in the compositing package so you don't have to re-render a sequence if the lighting was a little off.

THE ESSENTIALS AND BEYOND

3D VFX, lighting, and rendering can be completed one at a time, but each will have an impact on the others and on the final look of the project. 3D VFX that are worked on in a 3D software package, such as hair and fur, 3D particles, rigid bodies, and soft bodies, are becoming more of a standard today thanks to more powerful computers that can handle more-complex simulations. The basic light types typically offered in 3D software have real-world counterparts and can closely mimic lighting in the real world. Lighting is greatly affected by the methods utilized by the render engine; the rendering attributes play a big role in how the final image will look. Having a general knowledge base of all of this information helps 3D artists understand how the final images they are trying to create can be rendered to have the final quality desired.

REVIEW QUESTIONS

1. Which one of the following options is not considered a 3D VFX?

    A. Hair   **C.** Polygons

    B. Rigid bodies   **D.** Fluids

2. True or false: A 3D VFX artist will break a simulation down into smaller pieces to build up the final effect.

3. Rigid bodies create what type of effect?

    A. Soft and flimsy, like collisions and deformations   **C.** Hard collisions with deformations

    B. Hard collisions with no deformations   **D.** 3D particle flow

4. True or false: Fluid effects can be used only for water or fluidlike simulations.

5. True or false: Hair dynamics can be used only for hair.

6. True or false: Direct light will cast light in only one direction.

7. How do point lights cast light?

    A. In parallel rays   **C.** From a large area

    B. From a single point, in a single direction, in a cone shape   **D.** From a single point in all directions

(Continues)

THE ESSENTIALS AND BEYOND *(Continued)*

8. Which of these options is not an advantage to raytraced shadows?

    A. Allows shadows through trans-parent objects

    B. Quickly creates soft shadows

    C. Quickly creates sharp shadows

    D. Creates the most realistic type of shadows

9. True or false: Scanline rendering is a complex render method that allows for reflections.

10. True or false: Global illumination is a single method of creating a realistic final render.

CHAPTER 8

Hardware and Software Tools of the Trade

The hardware and software choices of a 3D animator can be difficult to understand because of the large number of options given to a user. These options provide the user many ways to work and to learn. Power, speed, and storage are advancing to a point that techniques thought impossible a few years ago can now be competed on a normal, everyday desktop computer. So how does a person wanting to get into 3D animation know what tools and techniques to use? It comes from constantly learning. Schools and online learning opportunities are popping up every day. But first, there are a few basics you can learn to get started and to help you dig through all the information out there.

This chapter presents the types of computers that may best fit you as a 3D artist. You'll learn what to look for in a computer and related hardware devices, and what software you may want to use.

▶ **Choosing a computer**

▶ **Using monitors/displays**

▶ **Working with graphics tablets**

▶ **Using 3D scanners**

▶ **Setting up render farms**

▶ **Finding data storage solutions**

▶ **Choosing software**

Choosing a Computer

What computer do you need? Do you really need the computer you want? There is no single correct answer. You need to consider many factors when preparing to buy a computer, including these:

▶ What operating system is best for you?

▶ How fast does the computer need to be?

▶ What types of input and output ports does it need?

▶ What software are you planning to run?

▶ What type of graphics card do you need?

▶ Do you need massive rendering capabilities?

▶ How do you ensure that your system won't be outdated in a month?

All of these matters are covered in the following pages.

You could easily spend $20,000 or more on a 3D animation–capable computer with added software, software plug-ins, and accessories. However, you're unlikely to use all $20,000 of the computer goodness in that new massive machine! So you as a user need to look at your everyday needs for a computer and at your budget, and then go from there. For example, if you are a character animator and will rarely if ever need advanced lighting and rendering capabilities, buying a monster computer would be overkill—because most 3D animation software can run with no problem in real time on a basic computer, so you will not need all that power. But if you are going to be a visual effects artist who will need to simulate complex cloth simulations or heavy particle simulations, you may need a beefier computer to help you quickly finish the simulations. Also, if you are employed at an animation studio or enrolled in an animation school, your organization likely will provide a computer for you to work on.

> ▶
>
> **This book does not provide current speeds and stats for computer equipment because the technology changes so quickly.**

Choosing a Computer Type

There are three primary types of computers you can buy for 3D animation purposes—workstation, desktop, and laptop, shown in Figure 8.1. Each has its pros and cons. Do you need a super fast and powerful computer, a standard everyday computer, or a computer you can take with you everywhere?

Image by Serena Nancarrow

FIGURE 8.1 A workstation (left), a desktop (middle), and a laptop (right) computer

Workstation   A workstation computer is usually the most expensive but will have the most options in upgrades down the line, as well as the most raw computer power and overall speed. The workstation historically was designed for technical or scientific applications but ties in nicely with 3D animation software because of its better options for advanced graphics cards and overall CPU functions. A workstation is typically just a physically larger computer than the other types, and therefore has more power needs than a desktop or laptop computer. But if you are looking for a workhorse computer, a workstation is likely the type you need. Many computer vendors today offer a workstation class of computer, but the options for a workstation are not always on the front page of standard computer consumer websites. You may need to ask a sales representative if they offer one or do a search for *workstation* on the website.

Desktop   The desktop computer is the most common type of computer sold today, and you will have many options available to you when you purchase one. A desktop usually will not be, but can be, nearly as powerful as a workstation. Because graphics cards are handling many of the more complex graphics computing options, today's desktops are more powerful than the workstations of just a few years ago. The desktop in general is more affordable than the workstation, and the various computer manufacturing companies have various configurations that can make for a good overall 3D animation computer. The physical size of a standard desktop computer is smaller than a workstation, but not portable like a laptop.

Laptop   A laptop is a fully portable, self-contained computer that can have varying degrees of power and speed. The biggest plus to a laptop is that it is portable and allows you to work anywhere. A laptop is typically more expensive than a desktop computer or even a workstation because of the small size of the components needed to run it. The research and development is more expensive on laptop parts because of the lack of size and airflow to cool the parts within it. But if you need to be able to have the portability of a laptop, you will be willing to pay a little more for it. Laptops can be just as fast as a really good desktop and some workstations.

Understanding Operating Systems

Operating systems (OSs) are found on any device that contains a computer— including video game consoles, cell phones, smart phones, tablet computers, and servers. Your computer would be a large paperweight without its operating system. An operating system is software that controls and manages the computer's hardware, input/output (I/O) capabilities (see Figure 8.2), and memory allocation. The OS helps other software running on the computer. Without the operating system, a user could not run any other type of software or access any of the hardware. Operating systems you are most accustomed to seeing today have a graphical user interface (GUI) to enable you to see and interface with your computer by using a mouse and a keyboard.

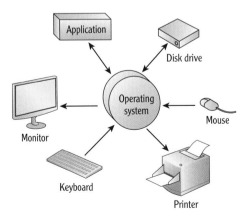

FIGURE 8.2 The input and output flow of an operating system

Each operating system is slightly different from the next in the way that the software code is written. Therefore, a problem can arise in the use of multiple operating systems: your software package of choice might work on only one type of OS, so you could be stuck within that OS. This compatibility problem has become more manageable over the past few years as software companies are writing their software for more operating systems. The best thing you can do as a user is to research the types of projects you are going to work on and try to find an OS that accommodates the software you'll need to use.

The operating system you choose will dictate the hardware you can choose as well, because one of the primary goals of the OS is to run the hardware and allocate memory. So there could be a chance that the new hot graphics card you really want might not be available for the OS you are running.

There are a few mainstream operating systems to choose from, and most users are avid and loyal fans of one OS and will rarely switch to a different OS. Among the most popular OSs on the market today are Microsoft Windows, Apple's Mac OS, and Linux.

Windows   Windows is the most widely used OS in the world. Over the years, the Windows OS has had many versions and upgrades. The most recent version at the time of this writing is Windows 7, shown in Figure 8.3.

As you change jobs and studios, you must be flexible. Each studio is likely to run a different software package or OS.

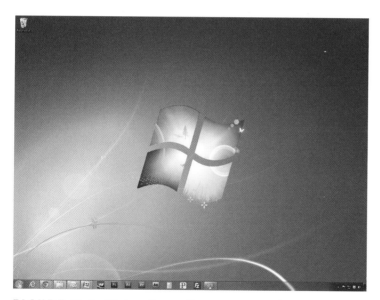

FIGURE 8.3 Windows 7 operating system screenshot

Because the Windows OS has the largest user base of all operating systems on the market today, it enjoys the largest choice of compatible hardware options. That fosters stiff competition in the market between different companies that will lead to better prices when you buy a computer and when you may need extra parts.

THE PROBLEM WITH TOO MUCH

Some of the specific components of the computer that are most important to a 3D animator are presented later in this chapter.

Having so many hardware options sounds like a great thing at first, but can create complications when you build your own system rather than purchasing a prebuilt one. So many third-party vendors create parts and components that choosing the parts can seem almost impossible. Having so many vendors and parts can lead to one vendor's parts not working with other vendors' parts, or a system slowdown with a specific configuration of parts.

Another bonus to working with the most widely used OS in the world is that more software has been written for Windows, so your choices of software and plug-ins is vast.

A computer *virus* is a program that can copy itself and spread through a network, corrupting data in software applications and hardware.

One downside to the Windows operating system is that it is vulnerable to computer viruses. Because Windows has so many options for compatible hardware and software, the potential for computer viruses is greater. A computer virus can be devastating to your system, and you may not know how to purge the virus. Computer viruses come in many forms and can attack different areas of the operating system and hardware, and can over time slow your system or even erase information from the hard drive. So as a Windows user, you must have antivirus software and other protection to safeguard your computer system.

Mac OS   Mac OS X, shown in Figure 8.4, is the latest version of Apple's operating system and is the second-largest operating system used in the world today. Mac OS X is a Unix-based operating system. As with Windows, Mac OS X has had many versions and upgrades.

Mac users are some of the most devoted computer users in the world, and that loyalty is the reason that this OS has survived through the years and now thrives. One of the biggest differences in the Mac OS is that it can run on only Mac computers, which allows Apple to know exactly the type of performance and graphic output of each computer it sells. This means that all of the components in a Mac computer will work together and are easy to fix even for the most basic computer user. The flip side to this is that Mac components tend to be more expensive, and you do not have many options of where to buy the computers and parts.

The Mac OS and Apple computer, originally created as a system that anyone could easily use, has a creative style and design to it. This OS appeals to creative people, including artists and designers, who want to work outside the box. Apple worked with these creative types, making its graphics the better visual option in the computer world.

FIGURE 8.4 Mac OS

Many of today's 3D animation software options can run on a Mac OS and do so very well. But not all third-party plug-ins for that software are available. An alternative with the newer Intel-based Mac computers is that you can dual-boot the machine to run Windows OS on an Apple computer. So with a little extra work, you can have the best of both worlds on one computer.

Linux   Linux is a Unix-based operating system that can be run on a large gamut of hardware. Linux is the leading server operating system in the world. It is also a free open source, which means people from anywhere can create upgrades and push the future development of this operating system. Linux is working its way to the consumer market through many mobile devices. Because the Linux operating system is based on open source code, you as a consumer will see it distributed under names such as Debian, Fedora, Red Hat, and Novell. Each of these operating systems uses the Linux code but is adapted to work in certain industries. Linux is not yet an everyday name in OS choices but is becoming more popular with large studios and businesses each year.

Open source software has its source code freely available for people to study and to improve. Open source does not always mean that the software is available free of charge, however.

Selecting the Components

This is where buying a computer can get confusing. With all of the component options available to upgrade the computer, which do you really need? Unless you are going to build your own computer from scratch, you will most likely be given a set number of options to add or take away from your computer, depending on the vendor. The typical options you should be most concerned with are the processors, memory/RAM, hard drive, graphics card, and I/O. Each of these components, in conjunction with the others, determine a computer's speed.

Processor (CPU)   The processor, or central processing unit (CPU), shown in Figure 8.5, is the brain of the computer. It carries out instructions from software in a sequential order. The speed of loading images, downloading data, and the general overall speed of the computer are based on the speed of the processor. Today we have many options when choosing a processor for a computer.

Photo by William Hook

FIGURE 8.5 A CPU chip

The first option to consider when comparing processors is the clock rate, or clock speed, of the processor. Measured in hertz, this is the rate at which the processor can process data from the hard drive or RAM.

> Computer hardware technology is advancing so quickly that we will see higher-multiple processor cores very soon.

The second consideration is the number of cores in a processor. A processor *core* is a channel that the sequential information is run through to complete a task. On single-core processors, you cannot easily run multiple applications at once, because the computer cannot channel multiple inputs through a single core. Today we have up to 10-core processors, but a typical computer has a dual-core (two-core) to six-core processor. Also these processors can provide *multithreading*, in which the software splits the sequential processes among the processors—for example, enabling virtually 12 processors on a 6-processor core chip. Another way to boost processing is that most computers can have dual processors that both allow multithreading—so, for example, a computer that has dual 6-core processors with multithreading would house 12 physical processor cores, but up to 24 virtual processor cores. The simple rule of thumb is that the more cores you have, the more applications you can run at once.

But certain factors can slow a fast processor—for instance, if the software you are running is not written to allow for multithreading. In the end, the physical speed of the processor working in conjunction with the multiple cores and the software written to take advantage of the processors is what will truly determine the end speed of the processor. Therefore, you should get the fastest multi-core processor you can afford, and if possible, multiple processors. However, do not fret about not being able to buy the best one offered by a vendor. Even a mid-level processor is going to be fast enough for the 3D general user.

The processor is not usually an upgradable component to a computer because it is hard-wired into the motherboard.

Memory/RAM   Memory, or random access memory (RAM) stores the computer's temporary data that the processor will need to access quickly. The RAM has a much faster read and write speed and will allow the processors much faster access to the data than from the hard drive. The more RAM you have, the more applications and processes you can easily run at one time. With 64-bit operating systems, we are now allowed to access more RAM per application than the old 3GB of RAM maximum on a 32-bit computer. Again, the rule of thumb is that the more RAM you have, the better. RAM is also the cheapest and easiest way to upgrade your computer. Adding RAM to a system will not make it suddenly 10 times faster, but will add some speed and overall functionality to the system. RAM comes in a stick format, as shown in Figure 8.6, and attaches via posts on the motherboard.

F I G U R E 8 . 6 RAM sticks

Hard Drive   The hard drive, or hard disk drive, is the component that stores all the data of the computer. There are a few types of hard drives and different configurations for them in today's computers. The most common are Advanced Technology Attachment (ATA), Serial ATA (SATA), Small Computer System Interface (SCSI), Serial Attached SCSI (SAS), and Solid-State Drive (SSD). Most of these names indicate the way the drive is connected to the computer.

SATA and SSD are the two most popular types of hard drives you can purchase today. The SATA is a standard electromechanical hard drive that has a spinning spindle with flat disks called *platters* that hold the data. A read/write head attached to an actuator arm enables the head to access different areas of the platters to read and write data. Figure 8.7 shows a SATA hard drive. The rate that the platters spin and the input and output speed of the connection determines the speed of the drive. You should see a Revolutions Per Minute (RPM) setting for most SATA drives of around 5,400 to 7,200 rpm, and they can reach as high as 15,000 rpm as of today.

Hard drives are typically an easy component to change in a computer.

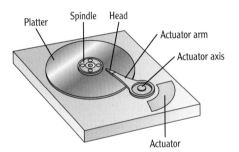

FIGURE 8.7 Illustration of a hard drive

The other type of hard drive, SSD, has no moving parts and is still very new to the consumer computer market. These drives are silent and have very fast read and write speeds. The biggest drawbacks to them right now are a much higher cost and smaller amount of total data space as compared to other hard drives. We have yet to see what this technology will do after long-term use, but many computer vendors are making these drives available to the public today.

One other option related to hard drives is the configuration of the drive or drives. Most hard drives are single drives that hold all the data of the computer, but you can set up multiple drives into a RAID to add data reliability and I/O speeds. *RAID* stands for *redundant array of independent disks* and is achieved

by combining multiple hard drives together to work as one. The benefits of a
RAID system are that the total data stored is distributed over multiple drives,
and the read/write speeds are typically faster than a single drive. There are different "levels" of RAID, such as RAID 0, RAID 4, and so on, each pertaining to
different levels of data protection and read/write speed to the drives (typically
referred to as *striping* and *mirroring* drives).

RAID levels 0, 4, and
5 are the most popu-
lar ones used today.

There are various ways to set up a RAID configuration of hard drives. Software-
based RAIDS allow an operating system to create and recognize a RAID setup.
These software-based RAIDS are easy to set up but can be slower than other
methods. Hardware-based RAIDS are created by attaching the hard drives to a
controller that will control the RAID performance. This option is more difficult
to manage than the other configurations.

A third configuration uses a network-attached storage (NAS) device, a self-
contained device with hard drives inside that will allow for different RAID levels
and functions. These devices are easy to use, set up, and maintain, but can have
slower data transfer depending on the I/O used between the NAS and computer.

Graphics Cards A graphics card is used to significantly aid in rendering or to
actually render images on your screen. Most graphics cards also allow users to
output to multiple monitors, allow for a TV tuner to be attached to the computer, and accelerate 3D and 2D rendering. Graphics cards over the past few
years have been adding RAM and other memory to help the CPU with advanced
graphic capabilities. And today's graphics cards are also boasting a graphics
processing unit (GPU) enhancement to graphics today. Many software companies are now looking to rewrite some of their software's rendering capabilities
and visual graphic workloads to better take advantage of a graphics card GPU to
allow for faster rendering and real-time applications.

I/O The speed at which all of the aforementioned components can handle data
is dictated by the I/O of the whole system. As noted earlier, *I/O* stands for *input/
output*, and the term applies to the Internet connection you are using (Ethernet
or Wi-Fi), the type of hard drive connection, the RPM of the hard drive, and the
type of data ports (FireWire, USB, and so on) for input and output of data to
other devices.

Imagine that you have a lot of water to move. If you have only a small hose to spray
it with, dispensing the water will take longer than if you had a fire hose. That meta-
phor applies to the concept of I/O. Let's say you have a hard drive that can read and

write at one speed, but the data is being input from the Internet at a slower speed. The faster hard drive will be hobbled by the slower speed of the Internet connection. Or if you are trying to edit video on an external hard drive that is RAID configured with 15,000 rpm SAS drives, but you are using a USB 2.0 port to connect your external hard drives, you are at the mercy of the slower USB port speed. As long as you are aware of this one factor, you will be better equipped to evaluate the components you are about to buy.

Using Monitors/Displays

The *monitor*, or *display*, is how most people visually interact with a computer system. The monitor is the unit that displays all of the graphics from your computer, enabling you to interact with the software and other applications through the operating system's GUI.

There are two primary types of monitors on the market today: the *liquid crystal display (LCD)* and *cathode ray tube (CRT)*. Each has its pros and cons in terms of what can be displayed and how they look.

Two newer options have been released but are not yet a consumer staple: the *organic light-emitting diode (OLED)* and 3D without glasses or other viewing devices, called *autostereoscopy*. These two types of monitors are still very new and very expensive. You can also use most modern high-definition (HD) televisions as a display, because the newer graphics cards in computers and HD televisions have input and outputs that are compatible, usually a High-Definition Multimedia Interface (HDMI) or Video graphics Array (VGA).

For a typical user, a good-quality monitor with a decent resolution is all you will ever need. If you become someone in charge of color correcting or proofing digital images for print, you will need a high-quality monitor with color-calibration equipment. Let's take a look at the two primary types of monitors used today, LCD and CRT, shown in Figure 8.8.

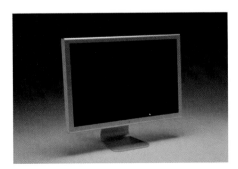 

FIGURE 8.8 An LCD (left) and a CRT (right) computer monitor

LCD   An LCD is a thin, flat display that uses light-modulating liquid crystals to show an image. LCD monitors are the mainstay of many devices and applications, such as computer monitors, televisions, cell phones, MP3 players, and many other handheld devices. They are lightweight, small, have a low energy consumption and have good viewing properties. LCD screens come in many sizes and resolutions and are much less expensive than other technologies.

CRT   CRTs were the main type of monitors until about the early 2000s. The dropping price of LCD monitors and the sheer size and weight of a CRT monitor has hurt the sales of these types of displays. But the broadcasting, photo, and film markets still use CRT monitors because of their greater color fidelity, contrast levels, and viewing angles.

Working with Graphics Tablets

A *graphics tablet* is an input device—the user draws on it, and the marks show on the computer screen. Graphics tablets are used in many places and for many reasons, such as signing your name for a credit card receipt or digital contract, drawing or copying artwork or line drawings, digital sculpting, and other tasks involving a hand-drawn line.

The tablet is composed of a flat surface and a penlike device called a stylus that is used to draw on the surface. The position of the stylus on the tablet moves the computer cursor, and there are options for right-click and left-click functionality. There are also tablet-like LCD monitors that enable you to draw directly on a screen with the stylus. Figure 8.9 shows a tablet-style monitor and a more standard tablet.

Wacom is one of the largest manufacturers of tablets in the world and is very popular in the art graphics industries.

FIGURE 8.9 Wacom Cintiq tablet monitor (left) and Wacom Intuos 4 tablet (right)

Tablets are a great way for an artist to have a more organic and natural feel in creating lines and sculpture on a computer. Before the tablet was available, you would have to use a mouse to create lines and painting, which can feel very unnatural. Early tablets were limiting at first because of their size and lack of pressure sensitivity that many of the modern tablets now have. A tablet is a mainstay in almost any digital artist's toolbox.

Using 3D Scanners

A *laser scanner* is a device that can translate real-world objects into digital data to be used for various applications. The medical, film, and video game industries use this type of technology, as do companies looking to ensure quality control of manufacturing, to perform product prototyping, or to conduct reverse engineering. These 3D scanners can provide an accurate base geometry mesh to begin from if your 3D animated object must perfectly match a real-world object. Figure 8.10 shows the raw geometry data from a NextEngine desktop laser scanner in Autodesk Maya that can allow digital artist to quickly obtain a person's likeness.

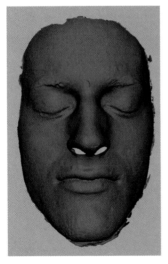

FIGURE 8.10 Laser scan of a human head in a 3D application

There are three types of 3D scanning devices and technologies—contact, non-contact active, and noncontact passive. Each has advantages and disadvantages:

Contact   Contact scanners explore a subject with physical touch. They are typically attached to an arm with a base that does not move. This base gives the scanner a solid position to locate the XYZ 0 position. The arm moves, and the sensor touches the object at various points. Then the arm's rotations are calculated to create a three-dimensional point in space at each touch point. A three-dimensional dataset is created from the many points. Contact scanners can be very accurate but are slow to operate and actually have to touch the object. Very old or extremely fragile objects could not withstand the contact-scanning process.

Noncontact active   Noncontact active scanners emit light, ultrasound, or x-rays that are deflected back to the device to measure the object dimensions. There are a few types of noncontact active type scanners:

> **Time-of-flight**   uses a laser to search the object, and measures the round-trip time between the laser (traveling at the speed of light) and the object to create the three-dimensional form. These types of scanners usually have to create multiple scans of an object to generate the entire 3D form.

> **Triangulation**   uses a laser camera and triangulates the laser point from the field of view of that camera, and then calculates the distance between the laser and camera to determine a 3D coordinate. Again, many scans are needed to create a full 3D scan of an object.

> **Handheld**   is a triangulation laser scanner that is in a handheld form, allowing a user to walk around an object to create a total scan of an object in a single session.

> **Volumetric**   is a way to create a 3D scan from many 2D images. A CT scanner at a hospital is an example of this type of scan. A CT scanner takes many 2D scans of a body part in tiny increments apart from each other, and with the help of software can piece them back together to create a 3D form.

Noncontact passive   Noncontact passive scanners do not emit any form of light or radiation but rather look at imagery from different cameras or at many different images to decipher 3D form. There are two types of noncontact passive scanners:

> **Stereoscopic**   scanners use two cameras slightly apart from one another, and by looking at the differences between the cameras can define a form.

> **Image-based modeling**   uses images of the same object from many different angles, and with the assistance of a user can create key marker points on that object and then analyze the photos to create a 3D form.

Setting Up Render Farms

Render farms are groups of computers that work in tandem to minimize the time it takes to complete a rendering task. If a render takes 10 minutes per frame, and you have 500 frames to complete, a single machine will take 83 hours to render those frames if there are no dropped frames or errors. If you were able to split the 500 frames among five computers, so each machine handled 100 frames, rendering would take only 16 hours to complete. That is less than one day, as compared to almost four days on the single machine. As this example illustrates, render farms are important in terms of saving time and money for a studio of any size.

At a minimum, two computers are needed to create a render farm. However, the smaller the render farm, the less available the machines are for other tasks. To spread the rendering burden as much as possible, you might choose to make every computer in a studio a render machine. Alternatively, you can use a *render rack*, which is a series of rack-mounted computers that do nothing but render frames. These rack systems are efficient but costly to buy and maintain. But the biggest bonus is that no artist loses their day-to-day work machine during rendering (unlike with the nonrack render farms).

You have various options for the setup and maintenance of a render farm. One low-cost option is to have a user go to each computer individually and set up the render job manually to render *x* frames per computer. This is an easy and inexpensive way to create a render farm but can be very labor intensive because of the wait times on login applications, start times, and scene loading. Also, this method makes it harder to ensure that all rendering settings are correct over the different systems.

A second setup option is a network rendering solution that uses a software application to send jobs to the different computers, establishing *x* frames per render job. A person called a render wrangler sends render jobs from the studio's artists into a render queue that then distributes each job to an open computer, as shown in Figure 8.11. The render wrangler can watch the progress of each job and push and pull the lineup of jobs, based on the needs of the studio. This is an efficient way to distribute the rendering, and it is the solution many studios use to maximize rendering efforts.

A third option is *cloud computing*, which entails sending the render jobs to an offsite render facility to have the frames rendered for the project. You pay by job or by frame and typically use a network or Internet submission system. After a scene is ready for rendering, the artist logs in, uploads the scene file to the online server, and then receives an email when the render is completed. This is not a great everyday solution because a lag time occurs between the submission and acceptance of frames, and the service is expensive. But in a crunch time and with limited onsite computers, this option can help a studio render all frames in time.

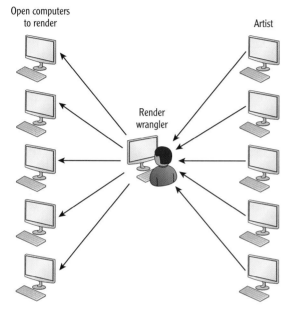

FIGURE 8.11 Example workflow for network rendering

Finding Data Storage Solutions

Data storage is an important topic in any computer-based industry, and even more so in 3D animation. The files that 3D animators deal with are typically very large and take up a lot of space. So how do you store that data efficiently, safely, accessibly, and securely? As a single user of 3D animation, it is relatively easy to back up all of your files with a local system of internal and external storage devices. But in a small to large studio setting, storage is much more complicated. There are multiple users needing to pull from files, input and output speeds to consider, security measures that must be taken, and backup needs to be auto-mated for overall convenience. This automation of data backups is crucial to aid in the reliability of the total storage space, because there is very little reason to have a large mass of data storage if there is no reliability in that storage. There are four storage solutions you can look into, or even mix all of them if needed:

► Local

► Local networked

► Offsite

► Cloud/Internet

Local

Local storage is nothing more than an internal hard drive that holds all of your files. You might add a second internal hard drive in the computer to allow for more storage and a little bit of insurance against data corruption. If the primary hard drive were to become corrupted or the operating system were to get a virus, you would have to wipe the drive and start over. The process of wiping the drive would erase the data stored on it. But if the files were on a secondary drive with no OS installed, that drive would just be a data storage device and therefore could be used in a different computer or once the primary drive was restored. This is not a very high-tech solution and requires the user to manually move files to the drive. In addition, the secondary drive remains susceptible to corruption and failure. So another local option would be to have an external drive set up to back up the files automatically via software. Most OSs have an automated backup system built into them for this very reason.

Local Networked

In a studio setting, multiple artists need access to files, so *local networked data storage* can be a good solution. As Figure 8.12 shows, a single hard drive or computer is set up as the network storage device that the other computers can access. The artist works from this network drive and saves back to it.

The biggest consideration with a network shared drive is the input and output speed of the network. The network needs to be able to move files quickly to cut down on waiting time for file loading and downloading. Most advanced network speeds today allow for real-time video editing of very large files over the network.

The other major consideration is backup. Network storage can be backed up to a separate location, and the backup can also be automated for consistency and convenience. The drawback is that this setup requires double or triple the amount of storage, because everyone is storing to a single location rather than to their own work computers—and this single location needs to be backed up as well.

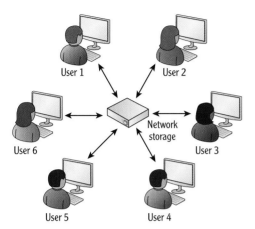

FIGURE 8.12 A local network storage setup

Offsite

Maintaining a network often entails having more employees to administer the network and keep things running, which can be cost prohibitive for small and medium studios. So these studios contract out the storage space to an offsite company that maintains the storage and security of the data. The only thing these studios need to access their files is a high-speed Internet or network connection.

Cloud/Internet

Cloud or Internet storage is an online, offsite solution that a studio can use. However, this type of storage is more geared toward an individual user than a studio. This type of storage is not always as fast as it needs to be for the real-time video editing and large-file retrieval required by a studio setup, but it can work well for very small studios or individual users. More and more of these types of services are becoming available every day, including Dropbox, Carbonite, and Mozy. These services allow you to access your files from any computer at any time. The amount of storage is not as large as on an offsite network setup, but this option can provide great flexibility and access to files.

Choosing Software

Software tools are the ones you will have to become most in tune with over time. There are many types of software that perform many types of tasks, and you will have to learn how to use numerous software packages in your career. But if you can learn and truly understand one of the software packages early on, you should be able to jump into other 3D applications fairly easily, because all of the software packages have the same basic principles and options. Let's take a look at some of the consumer-level software available today.

Comprehensive 3D Animation Packages

Several comprehensive 3D animation software packages are used for modeling, animation, simulation, visual effects, and rendering. All of these packages are used in a wide range of industries: television, games, advertising, architectural rendering, medical simulation, publishing, and graphic design. These are the most popular:

Autodesk 3ds Max   Used primarily for video game creation and architectural renderings, this software can be and is used in many other fields as well. 3ds Max has the largest user group of all software geared toward the 3D entertainment industry.

3ds Max has its own proprietary rendering system, and mental ray is included. (See Chapter 7, "Exploring Lighting, Rendering, and Visual Effects," for more on rendering systems.). 3ds Max can be run on Windows-only operating systems.

Autodesk Maya   Used primarily in visual effects and film, Maya is also employed in many other industries. It has its own proprietary rendering system, and mental ray is included. Maya can be run on Windows, Mac, and Linux operating systems.

Autodesk Softimage   Unlike Maya and 3ds Max, Softimage is not used primarily in one industry. Softimage can be run on Windows and Linux. Softimage has its own proprietary rendering system, and mental ray is included.

Blender   This free, open source 3D application is used more overseas than in the United States and can be used in any industry. Blender can be run on Windows, Mac, and Linux operating systems.

Luxology Modo   Known for its use in the product visualization and architecture rendering industries, modo can be run on Windows and Mac operating systems.

Maxon Cinema 4D   This software is primarily used for graphic design, and many of the tools and plug-ins are geared for this market. Cinema 4D can be run on Windows and Mac operating systems.

NewTek LightWave   This program is used in games and film but not as much as the Autodesk software packages. LightWave can be run on Windows and Mac operating systems.

Side Effects Houdini   Known in the industry for very good visual-effects simulations, this program can be run on Windows, Mac, and Linux operating systems.

CAD

Computer-aided design (CAD) software packages are used to create 2D designs that can be converted into a 3D form. This type of software is used extensively in architecture, automotive design, and product design. The following are some of the popular CAD choices:

Autodesk AutoCAD   This is one of the largest 2D and 3D CAD programs in the world. AutoCAD is used primarily to design architecture and products. AutoCAD can be run on Windows and Mac OS.

Autodesk Inventor   This 3D CAD software is used for mechanical design, simulation, and tooling creation. Inventor is for prototyping and testing mechanical devices before they are built. It can be run on Windows only.

Robert McNeel & Associates Rhino   This NURBS-based modeling software is used in industrial design, jewelry design, rapid prototyping, and graphics design. Rhino can be run on Windows only.

Dassault Systemes SoildWorks   This 3D mechanical CAD software is used worldwide. SolidWorks uses a parametric-based approach to create assembles and models. SoildWorks can be run on Windows only.

Compositing

Compositing software packages are used for layering moving images together to create a final image. These layers of moving images can come from video, animation, and user-created motion graphics. All of the following compositing software packages are used in almost every industry of 3D animation:

Adobe After Effects   This layer-based compositing and motion-graphics software can create professional graphics and effects. After Effects is used in many industries, including television, film, and advertising. Not only can you composite film and 3D animation, but you can color-correct footage, change the timing of footage, rotoscope, mix 2D and 3D effects together, add camera shake, and many other image manipulation effects. After Effects is available on Windows and Mac operating systems.

Eyeon Fusion   Formerly known as Digital Fusion, this node-based compositing software is used in the film and television industry. Fusion is available on Windows and Linux operating systems.

The Foundry's Nuke   This node-based compositing software was originally designed as an in-house compositing package for Digital Domain. Nuke, an industry standard for the commercial and film industry, is available on Windows, Mac, and Linux operating systems.

Digital Imaging

Digital imaging software packages are used for creating or modifying digital images. An artist may paint images completely in the software package or take digital images and change them within the software. All of these packages are used in all 3D animation industries:

Adobe Illustrator   Illustrator is the industry standard in vector image creation. It is primarily used in design but is starting to be used more often in 2D animation asset creation. Illustrator can be run on Windows and Mac OS.

Adobe Photoshop   The industry-standard software for graphics editing, image manipulation, and digital painting, Photoshop is used by many industries for various reasons. As a 3D artist, you will use Photoshop for texture painting, render layer compositing, final image tweaking, storyboard creation, character design, set design, color-chart creation, and many more jobs. Photoshop can be run on Windows and Mac OS.

Autodesk SketchBook   This is an easy-to-use application for digital drawing and painting. Sketchbook is typically used to create quick sketches that you can then take to other software to finish. SketchBook can be run on Windows and Mac OS.

Corel Painter   This image-manipulation software provides the appearance and behavior of traditional art media. The traditional media includes pencils, color pencils, charcoal, oil paint, and watercolor. Painter can be run on Windows and Mac OS.

3D Specialty

3D specialty animation software packages are used for modeling, animation, simulation, visual effects, and rendering. All have a specific, rather than comprehensive, function in 3D animation. All of the 3D animation fields use this specialty software, but each package is used in a specific range of industries:

Autodesk MotionBuilder   This real-time animation production software enables animators to quickly animate characters by using animation layers and to layer animation from different sources onto a character. MotionBuilder also allows motion capture data to be imported and applied to characters. MotionBuilder is available on Windows operating systems only.

Autodesk Mudbox   A digital sculpting and texture-painting software application, Mudbox enables artists to create 3D models without the many technical hurdles found in standard modeling programs. It allows artists to sculpt into virtual clay and to paint color and texture directly onto the model. It also has an automatic pipeline into other Autodesk software such as Maya and 3ds Max. Mudbox can be run on Windows and Mac OS.

E-on Vue   This 3D animation software can create advanced and dense natural environments. Vue uses procedural models to create complex natural shapes such as trees, plants, shrubs, and other foliage. Vue can be used as a stand-alone software package with photorealistic rendering capabilities and can also plug in to Maya, 3ds Max, Cinema 4D, LightWave, and Softimage for animation and rendering. Vue can be run on Windows and Mac OS.

Maxon BodyPaint   A 3D texture painting software application, BodyPaint enables artists to paint directly onto a 3D model in separate layers and map in real time. It will also export the texture maps to then be applied to models in other 3D applications for animation and rendering. BodyPaint can be run on Windows and Mac OS.

Next Limit RealFlow   This dynamic simulation software can create realistic fluid effects and rigid-body dynamic simulations. RealFlow is extremely powerful and fast in the computations of fluid effects that are typically very slow to simulate. RealFlow also has a plug-in for integration into Maya, 3ds Max, LightWave, Softimage, and Houdini. RealFlow is an industry standard for 3D fluidlike effects. RealFlow is available on Windows, Mac, and Linux operating systems.

Pixelogic ZBrush   ZBrush is a digital sculpting and texture-painting 3D software application. This software enables artists to sculpt instead of model their characters or objects, add texture to a 3D object, and quickly sketch out ideas in 3D form. ZBrush can be run on Windows and Mac OS.

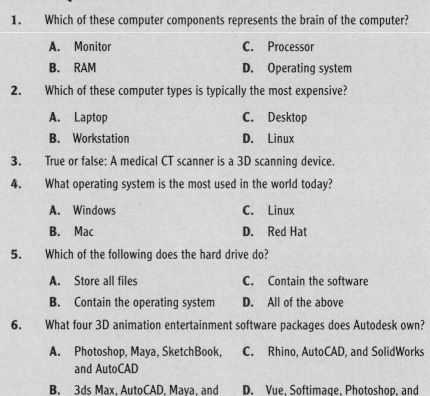

THE ESSENTIALS AND BEYOND

The 3D animation and digital graphics industries are only in their infancy and are changing constantly, which makes them exciting to work in. But because of these constant changes, you must be willing to keep up-to-date on new technology and techniques. The hardware and software is guaranteed to change, and the best thing you can do as a 3D artist is to learn as much as you can about the basics so you can grow as new advanced techniques are introduced. Having a ground-floor understanding of computer hardware will enable you to better understand the new technology as it is released, just as knowing the basics of data storage will enable you to better understand your options when data-storage needs arise. 3D animation is driven by technology, and the technology is driven by the art form, so as a 3D artist, you must be able to learn both.

REVIEW QUESTIONS

1. Which of these computer components represents the brain of the computer?

   A. Monitor
   C. Processor

   B. RAM
   D. Operating system

2. Which of these computer types is typically the most expensive?

   A. Laptop
   C. Desktop

   B. Workstation
   D. Linux

3. True or false: A medical CT scanner is a 3D scanning device.

4. What operating system is the most used in the world today?

   A. Windows
   C. Linux

   B. Mac
   D. Red Hat

5. Which of the following does the hard drive do?

   A. Store all files
   C. Contain the software

   B. Contain the operating system
   D. All of the above

6. What four 3D animation entertainment software packages does Autodesk own?

   A. Photoshop, Maya, SketchBook, and AutoCAD
   C. Rhino, AutoCAD, and SolidWorks

   B. 3ds Max, AutoCAD, Maya, and Softimage
   D. Vue, Softimage, Photoshop, and AutoCAD

(Continues)

THE ESSENTIALS AND BEYOND *(Continued)*

7. Which of the following is the most important consideration in data storage?

   A. File size management   **C.** File types

   B. Reliability   **D.** File allocation

8. Which of the following is required for a local network storage option to be feasible?

   A. Server storage   **C.** Fast I/O

   B. Multiple users   **D.** All of the above

9. What is the minimum number of computers required for a render farm?

   A. 2   **C.** 5

   B. 1   **D.** 15

10. Which of these software packages is not like the others?

    A. Maya   **C.** 3ds Max

    B. ZBrush   **D.** Blender

CHAPTER 9

Industry Trends

With the progression of the art of 3D animation being so closely tied to technology it is created with, it is worth looking ahead to the next big technology push in the 3D animation industry. New technologies are released yearly in many forms—ranging from computer hardware with more speed and faster data transfers, software with advanced capabilities, and technologies that make the workflow more seamless. Some of the new trends being pursued by the 3D animation industry include full-body and detail motion capture, stereoscopic 3D output, point-cloud data, real-time workflow capabilities, and virtual studios. Some of these technologies are in use today but not available to all consumers. For others, consumer use is still over the horizon. Each will provide a faster turnaround on projects and will enable artists to focus on the art of the project and not the technical hurdles of the production pipeline.

▶ **Using motion capture**

▶ **Creating stereoscopic 3D**

▶ **Integrating point-cloud data**

▶ **Providing real-time capabilities**

▶ **Working in virtual studios**

Using Motion Capture

Motion capture, or *mocap*, is the technique of recording the movement of a real person so that it can be applied to a digital character. Chapter 6, "Animation and Rigging," covered some motion-capture techniques. This section details the current technology and where it's going in the future.

Most people today likely associate motion capture with the film and video game industry. We've all seen behind-the-scenes footage showing actors completing motion-capture sessions. But motion capture is used in many other fields—including the military, medicine, and biomechanics—for various reasons.

In all of these industries, two systems—marker and markerless—are used to capture the motion data. You'll look at each of these systems in depth in this section.

Marker Systems

Marker systems apply a set of markers on and around the joints of a performer, as shown in Figure 9.1. A camera system then performs three-dimensional data tracking by triangulating each marker.

TRIANGULATING

Triangulating is the process of determining the location of a point in 3 dimensional spaces by measuring them from fixed points in space. In motion capture camera marker systems this is created by fixing cameras in space and then tracking from the cameras the points of the body. As long as three cameras can see the marker the system can track the point.

These markers can be passive or active, depending on the system. *Passive markers* are made of a retroreflective material, just like the reflective material on running shoes. Retroreflective materials reflect light back at a light source with very little light scattering, so the cameras usually have light-emitting diodes (LEDs) on them. *Active markers* are LEDs that self-illuminate for the optical camera system to track.

FIGURE 9.1 Vicon Motion Capture System

The marker system uses a *capture volume*, a virtual three-dimensional space that is created by placing multiple cameras around a performance space. A 0,0,0 space (the center XYZ location for a Cartesian coordinate system) is created within the software to capture the markers. A performer walks into the capture volume and stands in a T-pose for an initial marker capture. The software takes the initial capture and codes each marker with a name so it can track the markers from that point on. The performer then delivers a performance, and the software assigns translation and rotation values to a skeleton that will be applied to a character rig later.

Marker systems have the following advantages and disadvantages:

Advantages

> ▶ Very high frame-per-second capture rates
>
> ▶ Very accurate capture of position data
>
> ▶ Can capture multiple actors at one time

Disadvantages

> ▶ Cameras can lose track of markers, which means extra cleanup later in the animation stage.
>
> ▶ Capture volume can be very limiting in physical size because of marker visibility from distance limitation of the capture camera.

Markerless Systems

Markerless systems typically allow the user to have more control over where the capture can happen, because the capture space can be larger and not confined to a stage. The typical markerless system is suit-based. A performer wears a suit, like a robotic outer shell, that measures the rotations of each body joint. These systems can use cameras, but often no camera is involved at all. Instead, the suit may transmit data directly to a computer. The suits provide motion capture that is accurate enough for the entertainment industry, but they are not commonly used in medical or biomechanical applications.

Camera-based markerless capture systems are similar to marker systems, in that they use cameras calibrated to a specific point to capture the motion of a performer within a volume. The advantage to camera-based markerless systems is that the performers can wear almost any type of clothing they want. There are even a few motion-capture systems based on the Microsoft Kinect system for the Xbox, which uses a 3D stereoscopic camera system to read and understand motion that is in front of it. Much like the suit-based system, these camera-based markerless systems are used in entertainment and education more than in medicine or biomechanics.

Markerless systems have the following advantages and disadvantages:

Advantages

▶ Larger capture space

▶ Typically faster setup for capture

Disadvantages

▶ Not as accurate, which is important in medical and biomechanical industries

▶ Difficult to capture more than one performer at a time with realistic interactions

Creating Stereoscopic 3D

Stereoscopic 3D is the technology used in 3D movies today to create the illusion of depth on a two-dimensional screen. There are many techniques for creating this effect onscreen or on paper—wearing special glasses, crossing your eyes, closing one eye, using special screens to split light into different eyes, and using color anaglyphs to separate a single image.

Some might consider today's 3D images and movies a passing fad, but with the incorporation of stereoscopic 3D into video games and other applications such as production visualization and architecture renderings, 3D is likely here to stay. So as 3D artists, we need to look at stereoscopic 3D as another tool to help convey our ideas and products to a general audience.

So how does stereoscopy work? Your eyes can be thought of as two cameras that are focusing on the same point, and your brain ties the two images together as one. Your brain interprets the differences in the images as a visual queue to depth, which enables you to see in three dimensions. So to create this effect for television, movies, or even printed images, we need to show two images at once and have the viewer's brain or eyes separate the images to break out the differences and create the impression of depth.

Over time, various tools and techniques have been used to create 3D images. The stereoscope, shown in Figure 9.2, was one of the first 3D viewing devices. Looking through the stereoscope, a viewer would see two prints of the same

2D picture, slightly offset from one another. Each eye would see only one of the images, creating the 3D effect. You might remember a device called the View-Master from your childhood; it is a miniature version of the stereoscope.

Image © DavePage/Wikipedia

FIGURE 9.2 A stereoscope

STEREOSCOPIC 3D'S DATA DEMANDS

One issue of stereoscopic 3D in animation is data storage. Because 3D requires two images to create one final image, a 3D software package has to render two images for every frame of a project. In other words, double the storage is required for all of the frames. This is not a big deal because data storage is becoming cheaper every day, but it's something to think about.

The three main techniques and devices used today for viewing 3D film, video, and television are color anaglyphs, polarized glasses, and shutter glasses.

Color anaglyphs are images composed of two layers—one red, and the other cyan. When wearing glasses with one red and one cyan lens (shown in Figure 9.3), each eye can see only one image, creating the 3D effect. You have probably worn these glasses before. In addition, 3D software such as Autodesk Maya has an anaglyph mode, enabling users to easily see a 3D effect in the work view (see Figure 9.4). Using anaglyphs is an inexpensive way to create a 3D effect, The biggest drawback to this method is the color and overall visual-fidelity loss due to the red and cyan lens that will filter in our eyes.

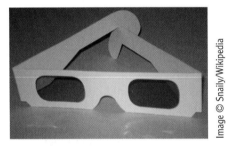

Image © Snaily/Wikipedia

FIGURE 9.3 Red and cyan anaglyph viewing glasses

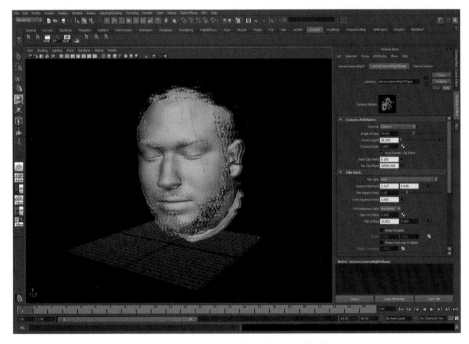

FIGURE 9.4 Autodesk Maya with the anaglyph viewing display on

Creating 3D with *polarized glasses* is a favorite right now for movie theaters. Two projectors project separate images onto the same screen through a polarizing filter. The polarizing filter will separate the light into different types of waves so that the viewer can wear inexpensive glasses with polarized lenses that filter the light, allowing each eye to see only one of the images.

The use of *shutter glasses* is the most popular method for 3D television. The viewer wears a pair of glasses with liquid crystal that can block light passing through each lens. The glasses are then synced up to the television, so that each lens blocks the image on every other frame. Video is played at twice its normal speed—so, for instance, video otherwise viewed at 30 fps is played at 60 fps, with alternating eye images per frame. The viewer sees only the image per eye they are supposed to see to create the 3D effect. This works because of the Persistence of Vision theory discussed in Chapter 3, "Understanding Digital Imaging and Video." Viewers are not aware of the flickering of images. The drawbacks to this method are that when you look away from the television, you will see an odd flickering, and you also have to be in a small viewing range of the television that is not too far left or right of the screen.

Since the 1800s, we have used 3D stereoscopic tricks as sideshow acts or as a gimmicky way to sell tickets to horror films. Until now, reliable technology for easily and accurately creating and displaying 3D images was not available. But today we have various ways to create 3D imagery with minimal quality loss. You can now buy 3D-ready cameras, televisions, and Blu-ray players. The next big push will be HD television with no glasses, called *autostereoscopy*, and no loss of quality, which is going to be a reality very soon.

Integrating Point-Cloud Data

A *point cloud* is a very large set of vertices in a 3D environment that represents the 3D shape of objects. These points can be colored to add texture to the objects. With enough points, you can create a solid surface with as much detail as you want, as shown in Figure 9.5.

This relatively new type of data has not been fully incorporated into 3D animation. Some applications, including Pointools View Pro and Leica Cyclone Viewer Pro, can read and display point-cloud data, but most cannot without the data being converted into polygon or NURBS surfaces. With that conversion to a mesh, much of the detail is lost. However, many other industries are using point-cloud data today, such as manufacturing, medicine, and forensic science.

FIGURE 9.5 Point-cloud data in Pointools View Pro software

The primary way of creating point clouds is with 3D scanning (which is discussed in Chapter 8, "Hardware and Software Tools of the Trade"). Although a few companies have indicated that they can run a 3D point-cloud game engine in real time and provide almost unlimited detail in the objects, we are still years away from putting this type of model in consumers' hands. Offering unlimited detail is what makes point-cloud data an exciting new technology. Having no texture or geometry resolution will completely change the workflow and output quality for the game and film industries.

Providing Real-Time Capabilities

A real-time working environment may be the holy grail of the 3D animation industry. A real-time workflow would enable you to see a completely rendered 3D asset while actively editing that asset throughout the entire production pipeline. Each artist would not have to wait on technical hurdles and waste time waiting on interface updates and slow renders.

Parts of that real-time workflow dream are already a reality. We are able to render video games in real time and the player has complete control of the action of the game at almost all times. But the creation (modeling, texturing, rigging, and animation) of those characters and environments had to be completed by an artist and then painstakingly reduced and optimized to be able to work in real time within the game engine.

We need still more computing power before the real-time workflow can happen. But we do have some real-time capabilities within the 3D animation production pipeline. For instance, real-time high-resolution polygon modeling and texturing are available in software such as Pixologic's ZBrush and Autodesk Mudbox. These two software packages allow modeling and texturing artists to move freely in real time around extremely heavy polygon models to edit the geometry and create color maps directly on that model. This was not even an option only a few years ago. Both of these software packages began by looking at modeling from a different view and recoded their software to use today's faster computers to allow for this real-time interaction. The drawback to these software programs is that they are specialty applications for modeling and texturing, with little to no animation or other 3D workflows.

From a hardware side, dedicated GPU processors on graphics cards and multicore CPU processors are enabling a real-time workflow. Moore's law states that the number of transistors per square inch on integrated circuits has doubled every two years since the integrated circuit was invented. This means that computers double their speed and functionality every two years as well. If Moore's law stays true, by the year 2020, the CPU will have manufactured parts on a molecular scale. This will have a huge effect on the way we use computers and will lead to new types of technologies using computer processing speeds not even imaginable today.

However, even with all of these technology boosts and speed jumps, rendering time in 3D animation has increased over the years. For example, Pixar's *Toy Story* took an average of 2 hours per frame to render in 1995. In *Cars 2*, released in 2011, the average render time per frame was 11 hours. So why are the render times going up instead of down? The answer is in the detail that can be added to today's 3D animation projects. Every time we master a new tool set, we add two or three rendering techniques that are even more complicated for the computer to render. But this striving for real-time render capabilities has pushed the technology to allow for these new complicated render options to be rendered faster and more efficiently and will only continue to push the technology and techniques in the future.

The four main bottlenecks of this complete real-time workflow are rendering with raytracing, complicated shader networks with very high texture maps, animation with complicated rigs and deformers applied to the objects, and animation of complicated simulations for visual effects, all of which are discussed in the following sections.

Real-Time Rendering

Real-time rendering does exist in video games today. The video game engine that you play games in is a render engine showing you anywhere from 15 to more than 100 frames per second of rendered imagery. A lot of cheats and methods exist to allow these game engines to be able to render in real time, such as baking texture maps with some of the lighting and shadow information into the models. This baking of lighting and shadows works as long as the object does not move, because the baked shadow will not move. Reflections are not an easy render option, so cheats of prebaked reflection maps are created. Also there are limits on the resolution size of the texture maps that are applied to objects and characters. There are also geometry limits placed on objects and characters to make sure the process for the hardware to render in real time can be achieved. With each new game system and computer upgrade that is released, the game engines can allow for more-complicated shader networks, texture resolution, geometry resolution, and real-time light and shadow effects because the hardware can process more information.

> Baking textures allows the artist to prerender any of the color information into the texture maps to be applied to the object.

So why can't we get real-time rendering in other 3D animation fields? The answer has to do primarily with *raytracing*—a rendering technique that shoots rays from a camera to sample each pixel. When the rays hit an object in the scene, they are absorbed, reflected, or split with refractions in transparent materials. If reflected or refracted, they will need to create a new ray or rays, depending on what is needed, as demonstrated in Figure 9.6. All of these rays will continue to bounce or split until they are absorbed or the user defines the number of times the ray can move. This process allows for very realistic renders but takes a lot of time to compute. This does not even take into account factors such as translucency, subsurface sampling, global illumination, or raytraced shadows, which all incorporate the raytrace rendering algorithm explained in Chapter 7, "Lighting, Rendering, and Visual Effects."

So where are we today with real-time rendering? A few examples of real-time raytrace rendering have been publicly shown at conventions and on the Internet. Many hobbyists have been trying to create a usable form of real-time raytracing, but with no major universal breakthroughs yet. So we are still just waiting for the hardware to allow for it or for a new breakthrough in the realistic rendering world to emerge. For now, we still have long render times but are getting better results each year, and better render times with those results.

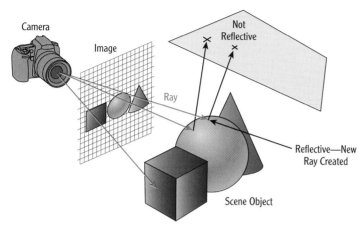

FIGURE 9.6 Example of raytracing

Real-Time Animation

Real-time animation is the act of being able to move a character rig or apply motion capture data to a 3D character in real time. Animators do not like having to wait for character rigs or object rigs to update while they are animating, so for years rigging teams have been creating different levels of detail to enable real-time animation. For instance, dense and heavy deformers that simulate skin movement and skin collisions tend to slow down a rig. These components are not needed until the end of the workflow, when the character is fine-tuned. So animators work on movement without those components. Thanks to today's hardware, that level of detail can remain relatively high while enabling animators to work in real time.

A software solution to real-time animation is Autodesk MotionBuilder, which enables animators to animate and edit in real time with fairly high levels of geometry. Figure 9.7 illustrates the difference between a low level of detail and a high level. MotionBuilder also allows for a simple transfer of motion-capture data to a rig in real time, as shown in Figure 9.8. This means that a director can see what a real actor is doing on the motion-capture stage and then see it applied to a 3D character within MotionBuilder.

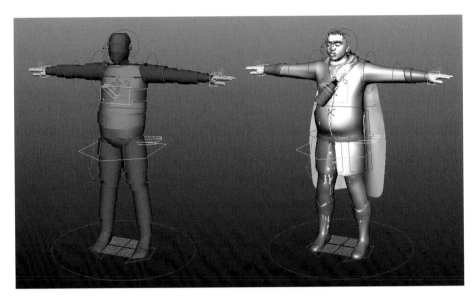

FIGURE 9.7 A low-level geometry rig (left) and a high-level one (right)

FIGURE 9.8 A character in Autodesk MotionBuilder with motion-capture data applied

The one thing that is still a way off is to have no animator at all, and to have the computer create the motion for the character in some way. We are beginning to see this technique in what is called *procedural animation* with software such as Euphoria by NaturalMotion. This software places a virtual nervous system and artificial intelligence into a character to enable it to walk, run, jump, and react in a proper way to its environment. This technology is being used in video games and in some background characters for film and television. But again, as in rendering, we are still far from the time when an animator will not animate our main characters.

Other aspects of animation that would really benefit from a real-time workflow are simulation and visual effects. These effects are very taxing on a computer system. Some effects require millions of particles to be created and simulated, and effects such as cloth and water are even more complicated. Today's companies are able to cache out simulations in hours that would have taken days just a few years ago. (See the "Using Caches to Save Time" sidebar.) So real-time simulations. although not available now, will becomes a reality one day soon.

Using Caches to Save Time

Caches in 3D animation are files that store data from simulated or baked objects. Creating caches can be time-consuming, but once you've cached a simulation, it will not need to be simulated again unless you make a change. Cache files can be very large, depending on the data being stored.

Real-Time Motion Performance

Real-time motion performance is where the 3D animation industry would like to see this technology of motion capture go. It would mean the complete capture of an actor's performance in just one take—the body motion, face shapes, and all appendages including fingers and toes. As of right now, we can capture all of these parts of a human performer, but we have to capture them separately. Most of today's systems can capture most of a performance in one take, but captures are still not as complete as the 3D animation industry would like.

The movie *Avatar* and the video game *L.A. Noire* have both pushed the limits of motion performance capture in their respective industries. *Avatar* created many new real-time capture techniques that allowed director James Cameron to view proxy-level CG models moving in real time on a monitor while the human actors were on the capture set. The digital artists on *Avatar* were also able to motion capture the faces of the real actors in time with the motion capture of the body performances with a high degree of detail, which had not been a straightforward workflow before. *LA Noire*, developed for consoles by Team Bondi and published by Rockstar Games, created a whole new system of motion capture called MotionScan that allowed a great amount of detail in the facial animation that to this point remains unmatched. This system enables you to create 3D mesh deforming in real time with the use of many HD cameras calibrated to a specific area.

THE FUTURE OF LASER SCANNING AND MOTION CAPTURE

A real-time, hybrid version of laser scanning and motion capture enables very fast and accurate 3D scanning to capture shape movement and even texture with an attached camera. Drawbacks are that the quality is not great, you can capture only what is right in front of the scanner, and there's no simple way to attach this laser scanned geometry to a traditional 3D animation rig and geometry.

This technology holds much promise for the television world, however. I have seen tests in which real-time motion capture is taken from people wearing green-screen suits and interacting with human actors on a set, and seen the motion-capture people be replaced with digital characters in real time. This would allow actors to interact with animated characters in real time on a virtual set for a live television broadcast. This is an intriguing technology, and it will be interesting to see what it will do in the next few years.

Working in Virtual Studios

A *virtual studio* is typically a television studio equipped with software and hardware that enables real-time interaction of real people with a computer-generated environment and objects. The background of the real set is a green screen that will be chroma-keyed out of the final image and replaced with the computer-generated background.

The real studio cameras' movements are tracked by the virtual studio system—either through the use of markers on the walls and floors and viewed through the lens of the camera system, via a motion capture system tracking the movement of the cameras, or with the use of a pedestal tracking system for the cameras to sit on that allows all movements of the camera to be tracked. The lens zoom can

Chroma-key is the compositing technique of green screen or blue screen removal.

also be tracked, so as the camera zooms in or out on the real person or object, the virtual 3D environment will also move accordingly.

The film and VFX industries have been creating this type of effect by green-screening the talent and in postproduction adding a new background that is computer generated or from a different location. In contrast, on a virtual set there is no postproduction; it is all done in real time.

There are advantages and disadvantages to this type of system. One advantage is being able to provide a fast turnaround of the final footage because postproduction work is not needed. This system enables actors to have a better sense of the scene they are in because they can see the virtual set on monitors behind the scenes. Finally, it allows television studios to have many different sets on one green-screen stage and thereby cut down on the physical real estate needed to run numerous shows.

Disadvantages of virtual studios include low resolution models and low texture resolution for the environment models, so it can be difficult to create highly photorealistic and complicated sets. In addition, computer-generated characters cannot be animated in real time, making it challenging for actors to interact with the virtual set. And interaction with other virtual elements can be difficult or impossible. The physical green-screen set is self-contained and immobile; it cannot be moved to different locations if needed.

THE ESSENTIALS AND BEYOND

Looking at the industry trends, it is exciting to consider what will come next. Today's trends include motion capture, stereoscopic 3D, and point-cloud data, and the main goal is to have them all run in real time one day. Real time is the big task that developers and hardware engineers are striving for. As 3D artists, we have more tools and faster render times each year, enabling us to focus on more-artistic functions of 3D animation instead of the technical side. That means we will continue to be able to push the boundaries of what is seen and created. This industry is truly exciting to work in right now because the 3D art form is still so young that you could one day create a new and defining technique or workflow that will be used around the world.

REVIEW QUESTIONS

1. Which of these stereoscopic techniques uses red and cyan glasses?

    A. Anaglyph glasses   C. Polarized glasses

    B. Shutter glasses   D. Stereoscope

2. True or false: Real-time raytracing rendering is possible today.

(Continues)

The Essentials and Beyond   *(Continued)*

3.   Which of these new capabilities is the most critical to the future of 3D animation?

    A.   Motion performance   **C.**   Real-time workflow

    B.   3D stereoscopic   **D.**   Virtual studios

4.   Which industry will the virtual studio most benefit?

    A.   Film   **C.**   Television

    B.   Visual effects   **D.**   Video games

5.   Which of these options are advantages for marker-based motion capture?

    A.   Multiple-person capture   **C.**   High-fps captures

    B.   Accurate captures   **D.**   All of the above

6.   What factors make real-time rendering impossible today?

    A.   Lack of sufficient technology   **C.**   The large size of texture files

    B.   Use of complicated render options **D.**   All of the above

7.   What is stereoscopic 3D?

    A.   An illusion of three-dimensional   **C.**   The use of 3D models in a space on a two-dimensional plane   computer

    B.   A reason to wear glasses   **D.**   All of the above

8.   Which video game was first to use MotionScan?

    A.   *Halo*   **C.**   *Super Mario Bros.*

    B.   *LA Noire*   **D.**   All of the above

9.   A virtual studio is what?

    A.   A space that can be virtually   **C.**   A production set that is shown anywhere the production   virtually created in wants it to be   postproduction

    B.   Television set that is set to be   **D.**   The set the actors visualize chroma-keyed out of the life   while on a visual effects set frame and a virtual 3D set is placed in real-time

10.   Which of these options is a disadvantage for markerless motion capture?

    A.   Difficult multiple-person capture **C.**   Fast setup

    B.   Large capture space   **D.**   All of the above

Answers to Review Questions

Chapter 1

1. **B** Although sometimes linked to advertising, product visualization is its own field and is considered a scientific industry.

2. **True** 3D animation is a vague term to describe an industry within 3D graphics. 3D animation will have incorporated animation or motion.

3. **A, C** The video game industry is split into two separate fields: in-game animation and cinematic animation. In-game animation is the creation of all the assets seen in the game during real-time play. Cinematic animation is the creation of the cinematic trailers and cut-scenes.

4. **True** Forensic visualizations are used to help people in the case understand more about what happened rather than to represent fact.

5. **True** Software today can test the structural stability of a design before it is actually created.

6. **D** Each of these points is important in the history of both computers and the computer art form. Without one, the other would not be where it is today.

7. **True** During these two decades, the 3D animation and visual effects industries hit their heyday, and 3D animation filmmakers were able to create visuals never thought of before.

8. **C** Douglas Engelbart invented the mouse in 1968.

9. **D** In 1984, Wavefront Technologies released the first commercially available 3D animation software. Until that time, a piece of 3D animation software was proprietary, meaning it would have to be created by the studio using it.

10. **1995** *Toy Story*, a 1995 Pixar release, was the first fully 3D animated feature film. This film is the first of many feature films released in the 1990s, including *Antz* and *A Bug's Life*.

Chapter 2

1. **A** Storyboards are included in the preproduction stage. Modeling, animation, and lighting are production components.

2. **True** A 3D animation production pipeline is similar to a car assembly line in the way that animation files are worked on by many people in small pieces to create a large product.

3. **C** Visual Effects are a component of the postproduction stage of the production pipeline.

4. **Preproduction** In the 3D animation production pipeline, preproduction is the longest stage because it has nothing to start from. The entire project is created at this stage and time and effort should be taken at the preproduction stage.

5. **D** A concept artist could use any tool to complete the art as needed.

6. **A** The most important part of the production pipeline is preproduction because at this stage the idea is created, and without a good idea, why make the product?

7. **C** Layout is one of the components that resides in different stages and does create a 3D animatic.

8. **B** Asset-tracking sheets are important to keep everyone involved on the same page at all times. With productions getting to hundreds to people it is vital that all involved are up to speed.

9. **A and C** Gnatt and Production Boards are a timeline chart type. Notepads and Napkins cannot be descriptive enough to be a production chart type.

10. **A** A written script typically equals about 1 minute of onscreen time.

Chapter 3

1. **A** Pixels are not always square. NTSC and PAL television formats have a rectangular aspect to their shape.

2. **False** A 16-bit-per-channel image has over 16 trillion colors, and the human eye can see only just over 10 million.

3. **False** The NTSC television frame rate is 29.97 fps.

4. **D** Color correction takes all of these concepts into account. The white point dictates the pure white of an image, gamma correction can cause issues with midtones of an image, and the color may not be true if the mode is incorrect.

5. **True** Raster graphics are resolution dependent and if magnified will lose image quality.

6. **True** The number of pixels in the height × the width is the resolution and with a certain pixel aspect ratio will directly create the shape of the device aspect ratio.

7. **B** To get the number of colors in an image, calculate 2 to the power of the bit depth. In this case, $2^8 = 256$.

8. **A** LCD monitors refresh usually between 60 and 72 HZ.

9. **B** Vector graphics are typically used for line and color graphics. Vector graphics can be used for any art that needs to be indefinitely magnified and still retain its sharpness.

10. **B** The drop-frame timecode allows the timecode to closely match the real-world clock when using NTSC frame rate. Because the NTSC frame rate contains a decimal, it can cause problems with other timecode.

Chapter 4

1. **D** Speed is not one of the Twelve Basic Principles of Animation. The principles are as follows:

> Squash and stretch
>
> Anticipation
>
> Staging
>
> Straight-ahead action and pose-to-pose
>
> Follow-through and overlapping action
>
> Slow-in and slow-out
>
> Arcs
>
> Secondary action
>
> Timing
>
> Exaggeration
>
> Solid drawing
>
> Appeal

2. **False** The 17 stages of a monomyth compose the standard structure found in many cultures. Some stories use all 17 stages, but others use only 1.

3. **False** A camera pan rotates the camera from side to side.

4. **True** The understanding of anatomy is critical to a modeler, to understand exactly why an object looks and moves the way it does.

5. **C** Three basic story elements are required to hold an audience's interest: character, conflict, and goal. Without these basic elements, the story will not be interesting.

6. **False** Sympathy will allow the audience to understand the character but empathy creates a much stronger personal connection by having the audience put themselves in the character's shoes.

7. **D** Three-point lighting is the basic light setup used by photographers and 3D artists because of it ease to set up and get good quality images.

8. **C** 16:9 (1.77) is the aspect ratio of HD television. 4:3 (1.33) is the square television format, 1.85:1 is the standard for most US movies, and 2.39:1 is the ratio of anamorphic widescreen theatrical movies.

9. **False** The jump cut does not use enough of a camera change to warrant an edit.

10. **C** A medium shot of a human figure crops the character at the waist.

Chapter 5

1. **A** Polygons are the most popular modeling geometry used today because of their ease of use.

2. **B, C** Phong and Blinn shaders can be used to mimic a shiny material. These shaders have properties for allowing specular highlights and reflections.

3. **B** The uniformity of your UVs affects the texture-painting process. If you have nonuniform UVs, you cannot paint straight lines.

4. **False** Beveling creates a slightly rounded edge that helps make the model look realistic.

5. **C** Faces are a component of polygons.

6. **A** 2D texture coordinates of a 3D object allow a texture map to be applied to an object.

7. **D** All of the above. NURBS are better at rendering smooth, rounded shapes and enable you to use curves as a base for modeling, like a schematic drawing.

8. **A** Subdivision surfaces are a final geometry type for rendering. These subdivisional surfaces are not great for beginning shapes but are useful for final rendering because of the round shapes they can create.

9.   **C** Box modeling is a type of polygon modeling that starts with a cube as the base shape and adds geometry and definition slowly as the shapes build in.

10.   **False** Laser scanning is a quick way to create a base shape geometry, but the scan data must be cleaned up to be usable, which takes time.

Chapter 6

1.   **D** The rig is the accumulation of all of the controls needed to move the object.

2.   **B** The parent-child relationship is a hierarchical setup through which one object can control another object lower in the hierarchy. This is one of the most basic types of relationships between objects in 3D animation.

3.   **A** Joints are pivot points arranged in a hierarchy; these pivot points can be selected and positioned.

4.   **B** You would move the child of the hierarchy system of joints. For example, you would select the wrist of a character, and the arm (shoulder and elbow) would follow accordingly.

5.   **C** Skinning is a type of deformer that will assign weight value to the vertices of the specific joints to allow the geometry to follow the joint structure.

6.   **B** Film has 24 frames per second (fps). 30 fps is the frame rate for NTSC video, 25 fps is the frame rate for PAL video, and 15 is a typical frame rate for some Internet games.

7.   **D** Procedural animation is an animation technique like hand-keyframed animation is. In pose-to-pose animation, the animator creates key poses and then in-betweens the poses. In straight-ahead, the animator animates the frames in sequential order. And hybrid is a blended version of both pose-to-pose and straight ahead. Procedural animation is animation created by the software not the animator.

8.   **A** A function curve is a 2D curve that represents a value over time, as seen in a graph editor.

9.   **C** A mountain curve is not an interpolation curve type. A spline curve is a function curve that allows for slow-in and slow-out, linear curves represent a constant speed of movement over time, and step curves hold a value until the next keyframe.

10.   **A** Most animators use a hybrid approach to create their animations because it has the advantages of both pose-to-pose and straight-ahead. These advantages are that you can get the planning from pose-to-pose animation but also the spontaneity of straight-ahead between the poses.

Chapter 7

1. **C** Polygons are not a 3D VFX but can be used as one component of a 3D VFX, as in rigid- or soft-body dynamics.

2. **True** To make complex effects shots possible, the VFX artist will break down a shot into smaller pieces and build the whole simulation one effect at a time.

3. **B** Rigid-body dynamics simulate hard collisions in which the object does not deform.

4. **False** Fluid dynamics can simulate a waterlike surface, but also substances such as smoke, fire, and plasmalike materials.

5. **False** Hair dynamics can be used to create secondary animation with collisions and gravity if needed. For example the hair can be used to move a curtain blowing in the wind.

6. **True** Direct light is the default type of light in 3D animation software. Global illumination enables light to bounce and therefore create a more realistic lighting system.

7. **D** A point light casts light in all directions from a single point in space, much like a lightbulb in the real world.

8. **B** Soft shadows are possible with raytraced shadows, but at a cost of longer render times.

9. **False** Scanline rendering is a basic render method that does not allow for reflections. Raytrace rendering does produce reflections. Scanline rendering provides very fast basic rendering.

10. **False** Global illumination is not a single method of creating a realistic type of render, but a collection of different methods including photon mapping, IBL, and advanced shaders. Global illumination creates the look of realism pushed for today in most 3D animation.

Chapter 8

1. **C** The processor is the brain of the computer. Without the processor, the information would not be distributed to the proper components to work.

2. **B** The workstation can cost the most. It typically has the strongest and most expensive parts, which provide great processing power, but at a monetary cost.

3. **True** A CT scanner is a volumetric 3D scanner that scans in slices to create a 3D image of the entire subject.

4.   **A** Windows has the largest user base of the three operating systems—Windows, Mac, and Linux. It also has the most hardware and software options. Red Hat is a version of the Linux OS.

5.   **D** The hard drive is the component that stores the computer's data, including the software and operating system.

6.   **B** Autodesk owns many software titles but does own the four most-used 3D animation software packages in the world: 3ds Max, AutoCAD, Maya, and Softimage.

7.   **B** File size management, file type, and file allocation are all important, but the reliability of your storage is the most important. It does not matter how much you can store if you cannot get to it.

8.   **D** A network storage option needs all three of these options to be usable. Without any of these options, the local network storage would not be feasible.

9.   **A** Two computers are the minimum number needed for a render farm. These two computers would be able to share the responsibility of the rendering duties.

10.   **B** ZBrush is not a comprehensive 3D animation software package. It is used as modeling and texturing software only; Maya, 3ds Max, and Blender are all-encompassing 3D animation software packages.

Chapter 9

1.   **A** Anaglyph is the method of using chromatic colors to allow one eye to see one image and the other eye to see a different image.

2.   **False** There have been companies showing it, but not at a consumer level.

3.   **C** All are important, but a real-time workflow is key because the faster a 3D artist can work, the faster the turnaround of the project and the more time to correct problems.

4.   **C** The virtual studio will most benefit live television streams because it requires no postproduction for 3D virtual backgrounds. The possibility of interacting with computer-generated characters in real time exists as well.

5.   **D** All are advantages of a marker-based motion capture compared to markerless motion capture that is not as accurate and make multiple person capture very difficult.

6.   **D** All are pieces that make real-time rendering impossible today due to the high amount of computing power needed to complete.

7.   **A** An illusion of three-dimensional space on a two-dimensional plane as seen in the movie theaters or comic books for example.

8. **B** *L.A. Noire.*

9. **B** Is a television set that is set to be able to place a 3D virtual set in the frame in real time with the actors.

10. **A** As of today, it is difficult to capture multiple subjects at one time with a markerless system.

Gaining Insight into 3D Animation Education

I am often asked about the educational preparation needed to enter the 3D animation industry. This appendix presents interviews with three professionals in the education community, each of whom has a different take on 3D animation education.

Linda Sellheim is a freelance illustrator turned 3D animation professional, turned educator. She has worked for a variety of public and private, for-profit schools and now works for Autodesk as the academic segment manager for primary and secondary education.

Larry Richman has worked for the Art Institute of California–Sacramento for the past two years and for other private, for-profit schools for the past ten years.

Steve Kolbe is a 3D animation industry professional who is teaching at a large, state-funded, liberal-arts university, the University of Nebraska–Lincoln.

Linda Sellheim

I'm the academic segment manager for primary and secondary education at Autodesk, and we create learning content, we work with schools, we support how … teachers are using [the software], and try to help them bring it into their classrooms and use it. So that's kind of what I'm doing now. We work not only in North America, but we're doing a little work in the UK and hoping to expand our most recent project, which is the Digital STEAM Workshop (Science, Technology, Engineering, Arts, and Math), a curriculum using all of the software sold to the secondary market from Autodesk.

My background: I am trained as an illustrator. I went to the Art Center College of Design prior to the digital revolution. So my skill sets are storytelling, drawing, painting—my original skill sets. I worked as an editorial illustrator out of college and then moved into working in animation and film and special effects in the very early days, which was fascinating, and I got my first little addiction to computers watching that go on, working with people [and companies] like Douglas Trumbull and Hanna-Barbera, at a very interesting time to see the shift happening. From there, I worked in the toy business; for a while, I worked for Mattel and a company called Galoob. It was a very interesting experience, also learning more about production and manufacturing. And I've had a long career, as you can tell. I had lived in San Francisco during some of that work and came back to LA to open the gallery [Xtremz Art to Wear] and was doing clothing and costuming, which has sort of been a hobby for many years, and I needed a change so I turned it into a small business. It seems I have always moved between the worlds of 2D and 3D and at times to the act of physically creating things as a creative outlet. I worked with fabric for a while, then at some point along the way, I got a digital camera to start taking photos of the work that I was doing and I rolled into a complete technology slide, closed my business, went back to graduate school, became fascinated generally with all of the technology that was going on—particularly in relationship to games and game engines and how those were being used in different ways—and finished up graduate school, freelanced in games while I was teaching, did that for about eight years, and eventually ended up at Autodesk.

How does Autodesk fit as a part of the 3D animation education system?

I think one of the things that we can do at Autodesk and as our education team, we can really help bridge industry and education. I work with secondary education, and they're probably the least informed group about the potential for education and career opportunities using Autodesk software. It's really exciting for me to talk to groups of high school teachers and have them realize how many incredible and interesting jobs there are in games, film, animation, broadcast. You know, most high school teachers don't come from that kind of a background, so it's really exciting when I tell them there are many jobs using Maya and 3ds Max. So it's great, because most teachers and students think that it's just character animation or designing characters, or they're not aware of all of the intricacies that go on in the business and that an animator doesn't necessarily do modeling, and the differences between games and film, and how things are modeled, textured, and animated for the different industries.

With your history in the 3D animation industry, 3D animation education, and now with a 3D software company, what are some of the biggest changes you have seen in 3D animation education?

In the educational field, I see at the postsecondary level that teachers have more experience and are better prepared than they were even five years ago. But at the secondary level, I see the tools starting to make their way into the classroom and the interest, but the teachers not being prepared. One of the things that I think we really need is a cultural shift in the way we help these teachers with professional development, to bring the tools into their classes to help educate students about these opportunities—just like everyone knows Facebook wasn't around 10 years ago, and look at all the jobs that have been created with technologies like that in film and games, and all the places in medical and everywhere, where these technologies are being used. These students are going to need to be prepared for a different kind of mindset in the way they work with tools, so I think the cultural shift we need to see is—in secondary—preparing these teachers through professional development and to facilitate the tools in the classroom, meaning they don't need to be experts; there's no way they're going to know all the abilities of a tool like Maya or 3ds Max if they are not using it regularly. So really, the students learn fast once they become interested, so it's helping students, and helping teachers engage students in a good pathway to move on with the technology so they can go on to college and university and even possibly careers in production right out of high school.

Do you feel that students should look for formal or informal training in 3D animation?

I think with what they're receiving in high school now, most likely yes, they would need other training. As you know, there are some very innovative programs in a few places. I've seen some amazing work, but it's more of an anomaly than the norm. So I think there are so many opportunities for students—and that going back to what I talked about, the cultural shift of moving these secondary teachers to the guide on the side, and you know, as their students become interested in the tools, there are great online resources. I mean, we live in a world right now when you can go to YouTube and look up just about anything and find someone who's done a video on it. And more formal things, as far as moving on, I think college and university is probably more of something students need now with this than maybe 10 years ago, when there weren't formal programs.

Do you feel these formal school systems should be training specialists or generalists within the 3D animation field?

Well, that's a tough one.…When I was teaching, one of things that I did move on to do over those years was [to run] a program for a for-profit school—a game art and design program. And it is really hard, because the generalist jobs are fewer; those are more small-company jobs for something like a Maya lighting generalist. I'm thinking of some of the things my ex-students are now doing, but I really think that the industry jobs are probably more specialized in terms of things like animation. We just don't have the time in schools to train students to the skill level they need to be at everything. I think it's very rare you'll find someone who's an incredible animator, incredible modeler, lighter, and texturer, along with compositor and everything else. I mean, when you think back to the days when I was in college, we spent four years learning just how to design and hone our drawing skills and understand design, composition, color—the human form—and now students are doing that plus all the technology, so I think probably more-specialized skills will help students, get out of school and get those jobs.

What questions do you think students coming out of high school looking to go into a formal training program should be asking of a school they're looking to attend?

Well, I think they really need to do their research, having their ideas about what they're interested in. I mean, obviously, there are different kinds of programs, there are more experimental new media and schools that have very traditional tracks and great animation programs. I think that they really need to check the faculty, see what people have done, you know? It's a very personalized relationship once you get into school, as you know, and you become very involved with your instructors.

Just to get real specific about questions, I think that they should look at who's graduated from the school, what they're doing, what the outcomes have been, so that they understand the success level of the students getting jobs out of school, what kind of jobs, maybe do an informational interview with some of the graduates working in the industry, so that's a big one. What's the background of the faculty, where do they come from, what's their experience? And then really research that program and find out if it meets the needs of the industry that you're looking at. Students can do all kinds of great research now, so I'd say, before you write the check, make sure you're really sure you get what you need.

What advice would you give to students who are already in a formal educational system?

You only get to do this once. Make sure you get the best use of every minute of it....Not that you won't learn the rest of your life, because I think we're all in a continuum of lifelong learning....But in a school environment, when you're with your peers, and you know you can dialogue and share your ideas and learn, it's just, it's a phenomenal space, and if you're in it, use every second of it because you won't go back there again in the same way. You won't have those peers. Working in the real world has its challenges, and it's great—I have a great job— but that learning environment is special.

Do you feel that graduate school is important for 3D animation today?

I think graduate school is always important…sometimes working in between, rather than going directly from [college to graduate school] is good, depending on your skill level. I think sometimes it gives students those extra couple of years to hone their craft because, like I said, before we used to spend four years at a university in the arts and creativity, learning just about design and color and form, etc., and now students are learning technology on top of that. So it really depends on the individual, but I always think that graduate school is an amazing place for growth and honing skills, and I'd recommend it to everyone at some point in their life.

Do you think that students should work on personal films or on a skills-based demo reel during school?

I think again it depends on the student and their interest and then, you know, their peer group. I think learning to work on teams is incredibly important, so something like a small project [like] a small film, where you can really show that you can work with a group of people to develop something is a great skill, and I know the industry is interested in those things.

Is there anything else that you would like to tell people looking to go into the 3D animation industry right now?

From where I sit, with a company like Autodesk, I just think it's an exciting area to go into, with not just traditional film and games being [the only] places to go. There are also just amazing opportunities in things like medical visualization, and the crossovers in architecture and engineering and animation and architectural visualization—there are just so many open doors and so many places technology is being used and the ability to be able to visualize and create with these tools is pretty exciting, so I think the changes we'll see in the next five to ten years will open many doors for students.

Larry Richman

I went to Rider University for my undergrad and majored in business and administration with a focus in marketing. I went to work doing sales after school and realized that I had interests in the arts, specifically in animation. I moved out to Los Angeles, started working in television for a few years, working in mostly postproduction and working with the art department, and from there I realized I wanted to get into it [animation], went back to school for computer animation at the Art Institute of California–Los Angeles. While I was in school,

I interned at Sony Pictures Imageworks and did some freelance projects. I got a job while in school with a small telecommunications company [The Savemore Group], where I did some of the graphics, some of the marketing, and animated a commercial for them. I was doing a lot of freelance for mostly web page companies doing vector illustration, and a little bit of concept and 3D. At the same time, I started teaching some principles of 3D for Learning Tree University and some other basic animation production stuff. From there, I went to Brooks College, teaching beginning 3D and material and lighting and was offered a lead instructor position of animation at Brooks, which transferred to a department chair in animation. I was there for just about two years. From there, I went to the Art Institute of California–Orange County as the, for a very short time, assistant director of media arts and animation, and game art design. I was promoted to the academic director for those same two programs [media arts and animation, game design] and while I was there, I also helped start the visual and game programming major and started the visual effects and motion graphics major. I was there for just under six years and then left the Orange County campus to take on the dean of academic affairs role at the Art Institute of California–Sacramento.

What type of educational institution do you work for?

The Art Institute of California–Sacramento is a private, for-profit institution. I was formerly with the Orange County campus of the Art Institutes. Both of these campuses are part of a larger educational system owned by Education Management Corporation (EDMC).

What advantages do you see within your school system for students who want to go specifically into the 3D animation industry?

The curriculum is based, really driven, by preparing students for entry-level employment in the animation industry. It's formulated through meetings of a professional advisory committee, meeting with the professionals working in the field who advise on curriculum, and then the curriculum is designed to really build from basic skill sets throughout the bachelor's degree in preparing students for that entry-level employment. It's working from a base knowledge of little to no skill sets, and each step builds on that curriculum, so we really focus on entry-level employment and developing those specific skills, on being able to be employed upon graduation.

What major changes have you seen over the past few years in 3D animation?

I think the major of the changes I've seen in 3D animation over the past few years are those related to the technological advances. There's been a lot done in adjusting the pipeline to make things easier for the artist, while adding more realism and detail to the end product. In terms of curriculum revision, the educational system (in my opinion) has been proactive and semi-reactive, but is trying to be proactive in terms of all the changes that are going on outside the educational theater, in terms of the ever-changing technology needs. The technology variation outside, and how to make that work within the educational system, making sure that you're not just focused on technology specifically, but the foundations behind it. So it's really trying to focus on the theoretical while understanding how it's applicable to the specific skill set.

How long is your current program at the school? How long does it take a student to graduate?

The bachelor's program, if a student were to go full-time, taking five classes a quarter, including the general education classes, a student could be done in three years. But that's really based on the number of units a student attempts in an individual quarter. The curriculum is designed for a student going full-time to complete in three years, and that's going to a full-time year-round program without summer off and based around a quarter system.

What do you feel students should be looking for when choosing a school to study 3D animation?

I really think the fact that the school has an understanding of industry needs. You know, it's very important to learn the foundation skills and to understand animation and related topics from the theoretical standpoint, but if the intent is for—let me back up a second and say it depends on the intent of the student—but if the intent is to work in industry specifically, the student should be looking for a curriculum that has an understanding of what the industry desires and is constantly looking back to what the industry needs are asking for and are referred back to industry in terms of curriculum development or vision. If the student's desire is to create fine-art animation or to create pieces that are not necessarily geared specifically toward working in the industry, then a base-knowledge curriculum, where they can develop foundation skills or theoretical skills and work from there would be what they want to look for.

What advice would you give students coming into a formal education, and what should they be taking advantage of while they're in school?

I think a really important thing to do is to understand that as much as they might love it—you know, love animation or love drawing or working on the computer—it is going to be hard work. They need to prepare themselves for critiques that…are intended to make their work better, [and know that] they're not personal attacks. They really need to have an understanding of the difference between criticizing the work and criticizing the individual.

And the other part is to take advantage of the resources while they're in school, of their peers and faculty. And their faculty and peers' connections within industry. There is such a great base wealth of knowledge that comes from the faculty who teach at the schools, in terms of working in the industry or creating the works of animation for themselves, and they need to go beyond the classroom and talk to faculty and look for areas for them to develop outside specific assignments. I would go beyond that and say students need to take the skill they developed in the classroom and through the formal instruction, and create assignments for themselves outside what's asked for specifically, and then bring it back to the faculty for critique—you know, bring it back to those professionals, those teaching professionals, who have that knowledge and can help them grow. And that should be an ongoing, continual thing, where students are always taking it beyond what's just required and pushing them to the next step.

Do you think that students should work on personal films or a skills-based demo reel during their time at a formal educational institution?

That is a great question. And the one thing that I will say is, if you ask two people what should be on a demo reel, you will probably get eight different answers. I think it really depends on what the student wants to do. In CG and the industry over the years, you won't get a straight answer on that. Either way will work, so long as the skill set is developed....If the student is looking for a job in industry, then the [demo] reel [should be] tailored for the job that they're looking for. So in other words, if they choose to make an individual short film, the skill sets that are demonstrated during that film [should be] highlighted to the reel that they are showing an employer...[because] different employers are looking for different things. Some employers will say that when shown a short film, they're not sure what the student's skill set or desire truly is. Other companies will say, hey, this person has a broad area of knowledge, and they can be applicable to a number of different areas and be of more value to them. If the work is good, then it can be harnessed into whatever the outcome is at the end. So the important thing is that it's good animation or modeling, and the other elements of making a 3D piece, whether you make a short or a skills-based reel, if it's not put together well and not executed with all the foundational principles, it really doesn't matter what it is.

Do you feel that graduate school is important in 3D animation today, or what do you see as its role within 3D animation today?

It really depends on where the student wants to be. I've had students who have gone straight from a bachelor's degree to working in the industry and do very well in that. If their desire is to go beyond the entry-level position and eventually to work toward a lead or director role, then graduate school could play a strong role in that....Really, graduate school is going to be based on where a student wants to see themselves; if they see themselves going right into industry in an entry level and working up from there, then undergrad may be sufficient. However, some people are going to need even further development of skill sets in that area, and grad school is going to help play that role.

Is there anything else that you think people should know when looking into going to school specifically for 3D animation?

I think really understanding the production pipeline is essential, and what the different roles are. Feature films, television shows, commercials aren't done by an individual. They are done by teams, each person on the team playing an important role. So I would say more than anything…the frequent thing that I hear back from industry is this person may have a great skill set, may be a great animator, a great modeler, etc., but if they don't have the ability to work with others, then they're really not an asset to that company. Many individuals with attitudes will get phased out of the industry relatively quickly because it's such a team-intensive process, and the ability to work with others is so essential. The other part is knowing that you have a love and a desire for that industry, you're going to be doing this all the time for a job. If it's something that you don't think you're going to love, knowing that it's work, you need to really consider that. It's got to be something that you're passionate about and go beyond. You know at the end of the day, just because you clock out doesn't mean you stop looking at your own animation and others' work and constantly try to develop and improve yourself as that animator or artist.

Steve Kolbe

I currently work at the University of Nebraska–Lincoln. I've been doing that for just right at three years now. I come from working in film, television, commercials, and games and whatnot in the industry, for about 12 years prior to this. I started off in advertising and graphic design when I was in school. Actually, before that, I was a physics major. I gravitated really into this sort of work. It was far more exciting than advertising and much more creative. Back when I was learning it, there were no schools teaching. I kind of taught myself 3D. I was about the only person in Omaha, Nebraska doing [those things], at least commercially. I grew fairly quickly in that realm. Also, because there were not many others around me doing it, there wasn't a whole lot pushing me to get better at it. I found myself plateauing very easily. So I decided after a couple of years to go back to school. I went to the Art Institute of Dallas. I got a quick little computer animation degree because I already had a four-year college degree, and

*I was able to skip past all of their prerequisite classes and basic general educa-
tion stuff and get right to what I wanted to see. I used that to get my first job
in the industry on the computer animation side, anyway, on Jimmy Neutron. I
just moved through the industry and eventually started growing a family and
wanted to have a little more time with them, and California did not agree with
us as far as raising a family goes, and we wanted to move back home. Luckily,
we were blessed enough to find this position open and jumped at it.*

What type of school is the University of Nebraska?

The University of Nebraska is obviously a very large, tier 1, land grant research
institution with a very major sports program involved with it as well. [Tier 1 is
a top ranking in a university or college ranking system that consists of many
different criteria. —ed.] So, all that is to say, there's a lot of money coming in
from various resources the school has access to. Not just our film school, which
I'll get to in a moment, but the university in general. The education system is
very, very large. Obviously, it's a gargantuan university broken up into separate colleges, and each college is further broken down into separate schools.
So specifically...I am an assistant professor for the Johnny Carson School of
Theater and Film, for the College of Fine and Performing Arts, for the University
of Nebraska–Lincoln. It's a very large business card.

This brings me to another important point, though. I do work for not just
the University of Nebraska–Lincoln, but for the Hixson-Lied College of Fine
and Performing Arts. That college is named after the Hixson-Lied Foundation,
because the Hixson-Lied Foundation actually donates a ton of money to that
college...which goes to the three schools: the School of Music, the School of
Art and Art History, and the Johnny Carson School of Theater and Film. And
the Johnny Carson School of Theater and Film is named as such because of the
Johnny Carson Foundation, since he is a graduate of the film and theater and
broadcasting degrees here at the University of Nebraska and has donated 13 million dollars over the years to our school in particular. In fact, they just donated
another million dollars last Friday. That million dollars is set aside as a separate
trust fund essentially for us to just draw interest off of for scholarships.

*What kind of advantages or benefits do you see for students wanting to go into
3D animation specifically with your type of school?*

The first advantage would just be the sheer size and the amount of revenue
that comes into this university and the resources that then allows us to have.
Like I said, we're a research facility, which means we are very heavily into the
sciences. That's part of our charter from 1869. The university is involved in real-
world research, rather than theoretical or what have you. That brings a ton of
grant money into the university. It makes the university very noticeable. But

that also means there are quite a large number of scholarships….That's just in addition to the rest of the stuff we have going on. Oftentimes, people will come to this side of the university for a much more rounded education because they kind of want to do, say…film and theater performance. They would like to maybe direct movies one day, but they also want to be able to have a trades skill and go perform as well. Or they'll do film and business…or we've got one who is actually a triple major. She is film, English, and biochemistry. It allows them to pick and choose their majors and minors and be able to fabricate a much more rounded education, essentially.

Our school in particular is not an animation school per se; it is a film school primarily. I was hired to begin an animation focus. Right now, because I've only been here for about two or three years, we have not had a chance to recruit that many people who are deeply interested in animation. Most of my classes focus around 3D as a digital effects tool: adding, like, the whole *Jurassic Park*–type of stuff, being able to add a character to a live action scene, being able to just enhance a scene with a digital…explosion done in a compositing package, but then 3D particles are added from a 3D package, or a 3D crowd scene and scenes like that.

What changes have you seen in the educational field for 3D animation since your time as a student up to now?

As far as computer animation is concerned…no one was teaching it when I was a student in the early, early 90s. There really wasn't anyone teaching digital effects, unless you were at a hard-core film school, and even then it was more about the creation and the films because the hardware and software was so expensive at the time and so difficult to use that it was not something other schools could really wrap their head around to be able pay for and to be able to teach. I mean, render times back then were just stupidly large. We weren't even rendering at full HD or 2K or 4K. [2k stands for the pixel resolution of 2048×1080, and 4K equals 4096×2160. —*ed.*] Just trying to do an NTSC rendering setup at 720×486 was—you were camped out at the machine hoping it didn't crash for days. Now, drawing from that, hardware and software have become so cheap, in a sense, that you can do film-quality effects from a home machine now that you've only spent say $3,000 on it instead of $300,000.

What do you think students should be looking for when choosing a school to study 3D animation?

One thing that always annoyed me in the industry and in hiring people was that even after going to an animation school, they still had no idea really what the different roles were in the industry. Especially kids coming right out of high school that just go, "Umm, animator!" Do you know what an animator does? You do realize that not everyone is an animator, right? There are very specific roles that people are assigned to because it's very much like the industrial revolution, Henry Ford sort of assembly-line function of filmmaking, whether it's for games, television shows, or feature films. Smaller studios may need people who can do multiple things. Those are oftentimes the easiest places to find jobs. The more you know how to do, the better off you will be.

So when you're choosing your school, I would choose a school that is not going to attempt to pigeonhole you….You want to learn as much as you can. It's great if you know from the outset that you want to be a texture artist. That's fantastic. Congratulations. I love it. But don't let that be the only thing you take from that school. You've got to learn other things. If you really like playing in Photoshop and a little bit of 3D because you're texture painting, learn how to do matte paintings. Learn how to be a compositor as well, so you can actually sort of put the final touches on your texture maps. Any time you can help out in another realm in a studio is just another arrow in your quiver that you can pull out and use to maintain employment and rise through the ranks that much faster. So I guess if you were really going for something in the animation world specifically, I would choose a school that allows you to work and get to those goals, but also within your budget. There are some really expensive animation schools out there.

Do you think schools should train students to be specialists or generalists?

I would say both. Everyone is going to gravitate to a specialized skill set that they just tend to like more than others through their education. But they should definitely be forced to learn other disciplines. Just because someone's a modeler doesn't mean they shouldn't learn to animate as well. As I said before, it's something else you can do to help out on a production. I think it makes you a better modeler, knowing how something has to be moved. Conversely, I think it makes you a better animator if you know something has to be rigged.

Do you feel graduate school is an important function in 3D animation today?

That depends. Do you want to teach or do you want to work? If you want to teach, then by all means do it. If you want to work, I really see no point whatsoever in going to graduate school, especially if you did an undergraduate degree in a comparable major. If you're going to school like you guys are doing at Ball State, where you're teaching more than one 3D [field] or more than just digital effects, I think graduate school is overkill. Just because of the name *graduate level*, it's that much more expensive. I think people are much better served by being told there's nothing wrong with getting another undergraduate degree. Or why do you even need the other degree? Go get some classes, even if you don't finish the school, get the classes you need to, and go work. There are online classes, there's Animation Mentor, there are classes at community colleges. Go get the classes you need. I tell students all the time, just because you're here at this major university, and you can't find the time to take more drawing classes right now, doesn't mean that wherever you end up living isn't going to be offering…some community classes near you. You just need to practice drawing; go do it. It doesn't mean you need to get a graduate degree in art or another undergraduate degree in art or anything like that. Don't pigeonhole yourself into thinking that "Oh, I've got to have that other degree in order to do it." I've never ever in the industry ever looked at someone and went, "Wow, they have a graduate degree, they're obviously going to be a better animator." No, that means they may know a little bit more about animation, but it doesn't mean it makes them a better animator.

Do you think students should work on personal films or a skill-based demo reel during their time in school?

That kind of depends on the student and what they want to do or their focus. I like both realms. It depends on if they're a storyteller or not. Just because you're in animation doesn't mean you're a storyteller. A majority of animators just thrive on the shot they have been given and they're going to wrap themselves into that shot and tell the story of that shot. But if they had to come up with a script or a story idea on their own and actually follow through from beginning to end, most of them would not be that way.…I have a student right now whose focus is digital effects, but he's also adept at telling stories. He's cowritten a script, but it's all digital-effects focused, for him to be able to show off his digital effects work. So it kind of crosses both boundaries. It's like doing a short film, yet it's also going to be like a cut-together skills-demo reel.

What advice would you give students coming into formal education in 3D animation today? Are there specific things you would tell them to do or not do?

I tell them to do their research and try to narrow it down to what focus you think you want to do and just be aware that's probably going to change once you actually start learning what you think you want to do. College, if anything, is not only *learning about what you want to do*. It's also about trying to *figure out what you want to do*. People change majors all the time; they change focuses all the time. They'll take a sound-editing class and say, "Holy cow, this is actually kind of fun. I like going out to record a wild sound and being able to affect it and put my thumbprint on a film or what have you on a project." There's nothing wrong with all of a sudden changing focuses, because you actually found something you had no idea you would fall that much in love with and use that as your focus or just another skill set. Prepare for change. Just because you want to be an animator, or a texture artist, or a layout artist right now, it doesn't mean that's what you're going to want to be after you start learning more about other stuff.

Any other advice you would like to give to someone who is looking to go into or is just now going into 3D animation?

Good god, it is not glamorous in any shape or form. I mean, it's a lot of fun. You're going to make some really close friends and some really big enemies. That's what happens when you do what you have to do in animation. Be prepared. When I say not glamorous, I mean you have to be prepared to work over 100 hours a week for weeks on end. Be prepared to not have your weekends for months on end. There's a reason that Hollywood kills marriages. It's because it takes away all of your time doing these projects. They are spending millions and millions of dollars to make these movies, and you are getting paid to generate that by a specific point in time, or it costs them millions and millions more. Just be prepared. That's not to scare anyone away. But it kind of is. Be prepared for the number of hours it takes. I mean, I've hired recent graduates and let them go within a few weeks to a month after they were hired because they just sat there and said, "I'm not going to work this weekend. I'm not going to do these hours." Well, if you don't, I will bring someone in who does. I don't have to keep you. This is a job.

Beyond the depressing news of those hours and things like that, it's not all gloom and doom....You're going to make some incredible friends. And that comes from being with this group of people for 100 hours a week or what have you, for weeks on end. They become your family. Like a family, you'll argue, and like a family, you're going to have some really fun times. There's nothing like still being with 20 of your best friends, all hammering away on the computer, trying to finish your own scene and trying to get stuff out the door, and suddenly a nerf fight breaks out or someone just starts giggling, and everything is just really funny because you're that freaking tired. Those sorts of things happen just like they do probably with high school students who read this and their best friends late at night. Those sorts of things do happen, but there's a lot of work that has to be involved. You're going to end up trusting these people you work with more than you trust anyone else, because they're being given a shot just like you are. And their task is to get it done on time, just like yours is, and when you need help on a shot, they're going to be there. When they need help with a shot, you're going to be there. It's very rewarding as well. It just also comes at a cost. That's it.

Learning from Industry Pros

This appendix is made up of interviews with professionals in the 3D animation industry. These people work in completely different fields and at companies of different sizes, and their interviews will give you insight into the needs and wants of various companies and how they go about looking for potential employees.

Brian Phillips is the founder and creative director of The Basement Design + Motion, a small boutique studio in Indianapolis, Indiana. He has been an art director at other small boutique studios and has taught as an adjunct instructor at various universities.

Jim Rivers is the hiring manager for Obsidian Entertainment, a large size video game developer. Previously, he was the career services advisor at the Art Institute of California–Orange County.

Rosie Server is a senior recruiter at Sony Pictures Imageworks, a very large animation and visual effects studio. She has also recruited for ImageMovers Digital and Lucasfilm and has worked for 9 LLC and Omation Animation Studio.

Brian Phillips

I got started as a 3D artist working in architecture. It was quite rewarding at the time. I was the first person to translate construction documents into something tangible. I did that for about seven years, but hit a creativity ceiling. I had some friends doing cool work in advertising and thought that would be a better industry for me. So I left architecture to start my own design studio. I was officially on my own in 2004, and have been working in advertising ever since.

What are you looking for on a demo reel from an artist?

For me, I am really looking for someone to bring something unique to the table—somebody who just has a certain style or a polish to them that we don't currently have in our studio. What I am really interested in is the creative process. So what I am really interested in seeing…are breakdowns of projects, of how they [the artists] do things, even if it is not on the reel. What is most appealing to me is somebody to work through the creative process and has polished work and brings unique style to the table. I don't like seeing tutorials. Reels are great to hook you in, but you need to have more depth in your work.

When you are hiring for an artist position, what are you looking for during an interview?

Drive, willingness to learn and share information. I want somebody who culturally fits into the studio. If you get an interview, it is obvious that you are polished enough, so at that point in your interview, it is really about your personality and who you are and how you approach things and how you approach your work, and how easy you are to talk to—which really would seal it for me with an artist.

Do you look for a specialist or a generalist?

Mostly generalist, mainly because of our size. We are not in a position to hire just a character animator or just an illustrator. My designers are illustrators; my art director is an animator; I'm an illustrator and an animator; my 3D artist is a motion graphics artist, character artist, and modeler. We have to wear a lot of hats around here just because we don't have the projects or budgets that bigger studios have. The way we solve problems and the way we approach them with our work tends to be collaborative because we're all generalists. We are working to get there and that answer may change. But at this time, we need generalists.

Do you think formal education in 3D animation is important today?

Yeah. I think it's important because I can relate it back to my education, where I didn't have the luxury of learning from second-, third-, or fourth-generation animators. I learned tools, and when I got into the industry, I realized the tools were secondary to the fundamentals and techniques. You get a lot of that if you go to the right school. I also think schools are good places to network. Typically, your teachers will have connections to the industry and can help you, so I think school is really important.

Do you think the educational community is doing a good job today preparing students to work in the 3D animation industry?

I think it's regional. I'm in the Midwest, so I can't answer that question for the West Coast or East Coast, because I don't know. So I can't just give a generalization and say the educational community isn't doing a good job, but from the portfolios I have seen in the Midwest—there's opportunity to improve.

What do you think schools can do to have students prepare them to work in the industry?

I'm not sure I'm qualified to answer, but I believe schools could take a more project-based approach and build their curriculum like an actual studio.

Students need exposure to the studio environment and pace. I think that's critical to teach somebody animation or any real artistic craft. Just sitting in a room by yourself with somebody showing things on a projector is not an effective way to do it. It needs to be studio-based. You need to have industry touches, so whether that's people teaching from the industry, or you bring in people from the industry to help and oversee, critique, I think that's really important.

What schools do you feel are educating students well today to go into the 3D animation industry?

Honestly, I don't give as much credit to the school as I do the student. I'm a firm believer that anybody can get into the industry, regardless of the school you go to. The roads are just paved differently. Ringling and CalArts are producing great talent. I think Savannah is a great school. The Art Institute, Ball State and Huntington University are doing a great job at preparing students.

Which do you think is more important: technical skill or conceptual skill?

I think they're both equally important.

When you are hiring for a new artist position, where do you post job openings for your studio?

We don't really do a lot of job postings. Our hiring is done through our connections—our friend or people we went to school with. That's how we have grown. If I need to go out and find someone, I'll look at portfolio sites.

Out of these next three traits, prioritize them in order of importance for somebody who's looking for that first job: raw talent, networking and who they know, and personal drive.

To me, it's personal drive. That's really where growth comes from. That's where your work ethic comes from, in my opinion. Afterward, I would say pure talent, because I think if you have the drive and you have pure talent, you're going to have a successful career and be a successful artist, and you're going to contribute to the studio. Networking through who they know—that from my perspective isn't that important at all.

Is there anything else you would like people to know when looking into the 3D animation industry?

I would say if you want to get into the 3D animation industry or motion graphics, the most important tool is drawing and is the most often overlooked when you think of 3D animation and any type of graphic design. The fundamental techniques in drawing and communication and just being able to sit in a room with a group of people and draw something out and write something out that can communicate your idea quickly is so important, and just having that fundamental tool set as an artist, and a pencil and paper, I think, is often overlooked by young animators and young artists trying to get into the industry. They instantly jump on the tool and they forget about the planning process. In our studio, everything starts with pencil and paper or a whiteboard. I think that's so important and so critical now, if you want to get into the industry.

Surround yourself with people who are like-minded and are trying to achieve the same thing, and don't wait on your school to provide you your education. You almost have to go out and grab it. I've seen a lot of times where students would get frustrated with the school. You just have to take ownership of your education, and you get with a group of people and say let's do something, let's make something. I think the making stuff outside of your school is what gets you the attention and the experience you need.

Jim Rivers

I started college late. I was in my 30s, and all the kids around me were 18, 19. While I was there, we really didn't have a career services department at the Art Institute [of California–Orange County]. We had a lady, but if she didn't like you, she wouldn't help you—that was pure and simple. While I was a student, I was always the one helping all the kids. I do call them kids, because I could have fathered some of them. They were young, and they didn't know anything, and no one would teach them anything. I had to take it upon myself to teach these kids how to network, how to write resumes, how to approach people. Finally, when I was going to graduate AI, the Art Institute, the president of the school at the time, Jenny Gonzalez, pulled me aside and asked if I would like a job, and I agreed. I actually never thought of going that route—I wanted to be an artist—but I was watching all the younger guys and all the nastiness they were going through, and I was like, I had responsibilities, so I couldn't do it. I worked for the Art Institute for three years and I was really good at my job, training career service advisors from other schools, and I had a 96 percent placement rate.

One afternoon, one of [Obsidian Entertainment's] owners, Chris Avellone, walked into my studio, and he said, "Hey, I want you to do exactly what I want." I heard stories about him because all of his friends and my friends were friends, but I never actually met the man. I said, "Okay, I'll do exactly what you want me to do," because apparently he'd gone to other colleges, and instead of listening to what he had to say, they would just give him every candidate they had, and he would end up having to do all the work, and that's not what he wanted. I did exactly what he said, and I gave him four candidates to interview, and he hired two out of the four, so that was pretty good. After it was all said and done, he pulled me aside, and said, "Hey, look. We don't really have *anyone at Obsidian Entertainment. Do you want a job?" and I was thinking to myself, "Hell, yeah, I want a job!" I took the job, thinking I was tough sh#$, but the first 90 days at this job turned into complete mayhem. I had no idea what I was really doing. I was kind of guessing, but because I like people, and I believe in the company, it kind of gave me that ability to grow and become the recruiter, and plus, they have very supportive owners who let me be the recruiter that I wanted to be. I'm very community aware. I want the developers coming through schools right now; I want them to be prepared when they get out. I'm very college friendly, and I go to all the schools, and I make sure they know what they are getting into. What a college recruiter will tell them compared to what really is the truth is like night and day. I've been with Obsidian Entertainment for almost four years. There isn't any place in the world I've enjoyed working at as much as I've enjoyed working here. I want to keep pushing our developers and keep them focused.*

What do you look for in a portfolio or demo reel?

I'm past demo reels. The only demo reels I want to see is if they are animation, but as far as art goes, I would rather see stuff that was well put together, well shot, well documented, all in game engines, mind you. For example, say you are a character artist. When I open up your web page, I want to see the concept piece. I want to see your reference work. Then, I want to see all your low-poly models with or without lines to see the polys. Then I want to see your high-poly models, and then I want to see your textures. I want to see your textures well managed. So if you had 1024 by 1024 and had tons of gaps all over the damn place, I want to know why you couldn't figure out how to make all that space work. I also want everything documented. I want to know poly counts and tri counts. I want to know your texture sizes. I want to know what textures you use, because everybody uses the big three, but now with technology being the way it is and the ability to start trying other shaders, pretty much, I want kids to not only think inside the box, but outside as well. Also, to start thinking about the box next to their box. Also, a lot of times I'd even have artists say, this kid is better than me. That's what I look for as well.

When you say "game engine," does it matter which game engine specifically, if they are applying to your studio?

No, the reason they have to know an engine is because if they want to go into games, I expect by the time they have sent me stuff, they have been with their friends, they have modded games, they've built stuff in games. So they should understand an engine. I mean, Unreal [Engine] 3, Crysis [CryEngine]—they're free. There's no excuse anymore. When I went to college, we didn't have access to this stuff. Now, all of the tools are out there for you to use, to be able to make better games, because we know how hard it is to make them, so we expect them to know as much as possible.

When you are hiring for an artist position, what are you looking for during an interview?

For me, in an interview I look for a personality fit for the culture of the studio. I'm not a programmer. I'm not a designer. I'm not an animator. I'm not an artist anymore, but I do understand what I'm looking at when I'm reviewing work. For example, say I like your work, and I do pass you on to an interview, I will interview you for your personality. If you and I are talking on the phone, and you're smug, I don't want you working at my studio, because that kind of personality is contagious, and I don't want it there. Now, when the team gets to interview you, they dissect you. They find out everything about how you see games. How you build games. That's what they want to see. Programming, they want to see your math, your abilities. It all depends, all of us are different pieces in the recruitment process.

Do you look for a specialist or generalist?

Specialist. Absolutely, we are triple-A's.[Triple-A video games are games with high budgets that are expected to sell well, such as *Fallout: New Vegas, Crisis, Halo,* and *Call of Duty: Modern Warfare 3. —ed.*] If I hire you as an environment artist, you are going to be an environment artist. If I hire you as an animator, you are going to be an animator. If you want to make games with your friends in a garage, and you get to do five roles, then it's good to be a generalist, but in triple-A land, if I invest in you, I need you to be what we want you to be, and that is it.

Do you think formal education in 3D animation is important today?

Not for the art itself, but for the maturity of the candidate, it's great. I've seen time in and time out with some candidates, that their work is awesome, but they lack the same maturity as someone with a higher education. When you're working the long hours most of us do work, you need as much as you can to keep it together.

Do you think the educational community is doing a good job today preparing students to work in the 3D industry?

Depends on what school we are talking about. There are some schools out there that, yes, we fight over some of their candidates. That's how well they prepare them. Now there are some other schools that, honestly, kids come out of there and the best thing they will ever do is be a color corrector at Kinko's.

Which schools do you feel are educating students well today?

The top of my food chain is The Guildhall at Southern Methodist University (SMU). The master's program is fantastic. For undergrad, DigiPen is one of the best. The kids are pushed very, very hard. Everything we see out of them is pretty top notch. FIEA [Florida Interactive Entertainment Academy] is another good master's program. I really like them a lot. Rochester Institute of Technology—we like them very much. Occasionally, you get AI [Art Institute] kids that are great. For artists, like concept artists, Laguna College of Art Design, Art Center [College of Design in] Pasadena, the Academy of Art [University] in San Francisco; you will never get better artists than out of those three schools, as far as in concept or illustration. For animation, Ringling, Animation Mentor, [but] the only thing with Animation Mentor is that all the reels kind of look alike. For programming, SMU, Rochester, MIT all have solid programs for programmers. I try not to be real judgmental on schools, but I have some that I hate, and I have some that I like.

Which do you think is more important: technical skill or conceptual skill?

In animation, they will never have to concept anything (in triple-A). They are given their storyboards and characters, and they are told, walk cycle, jump cycle, etc. What I look for are people who understand the Twelve Principles of Animation, who actually know how to make a performance work, who know how to exaggerate a little bit, but not to go completely out of their mind. I just look for people who understand gravity is there, weight. I love when kids [make a] soldier and they act like their weapon doesn't weigh anything. Those are the things I look for. They can't get that if they don't have a solid technical base skill.

When you are hiring, where do you post job openings for your studio?

I kind of cheat. I've learned how to use LinkedIn in my favor, where it doesn't cost me anything. I get myself into every group I can—every industry group, and there are thousands of members in all of them. Then I post banner ads on all their things for free. I get a lot of ad time out of that. Then I also go out there, and I shake hands. I go out and tell people about what we do. I'm not a big fan of advertising, because honestly most of the time I don't get what I want for the money I've spent, and the only way I'm going to get what I want is if I take it to the road and take it to them.

Please prioritize these next three traits in order of importance for somebody who's looking for their first job: raw talent, networking and who they know, and personal drive.

Networking, personal drive, and then talent. Many times, the people who have talent will lack the other two things. They have it, but they don't know what to do with it. I've seen it so many times, it's not even funny. I'll have a kid who is the greatest artist ever, but has the personality of a paper bag. The individual didn't know how to promote himself, or he didn't know how to get out there and had no drive or want or reason to actually go out and do such a thing.

For example, I do this presentation on resumes, websites and cover letters. Well, I sent that presentation to 12 different studios to different recruiters who I'm close with, and I said, "Hey, chime in, so I can make this a universally cool presentation." And a majority of what I said was correct, but every now and then, somebody would chime in and see this differently, or [say] my student doesn't approach it from this point, so when I do the presentation, I start off with everybody's studio is different. This is where research is very, very crucial when you're out job hunting, because where I think it's okay to do this, some people would find that very offensive and rude. There would be three different recruiters sitting on a panel, and we would be answering questions, and it would be three different answers.

What resources would you like people to know about when looking for a job in 3D animation, or what else do you consider important?

Networking is everything. People do not realize how big networking is. If you look at games from the big picture, we're actually a really tiny industry. Everybody knows everybody else, and they know each other's business. Let's say, if another company is looking for a certain thing, and I have a whole bunch of that certain thing, or I've met a bunch of kids at a networking [event], or I met a bunch of industry folk who have lost their jobs, the first thing I'm going to do is say, "Wait a minute! I know this company that has openings right now. Why don't you apply over there? Or, send me your resume, and I'll ship it in there for you." We do things like this for each other more times than you can imagine. But networking in my mind is top of the list.

Is there anything else you would like people to know when looking into the 3D animation industry?

Study life more. For example, they do animation, but their performance is very Frankenstein. In their head, they see it, but they just can't seem to do the finishing touches on it. I want people to try harder. I want people to realize that this is not an easy industry, and you have to be the best of the best. If your artwork or your animation or your design does not look like the games you are playing, then you are not doing it good enough, period. Back in the day, we would look at somebody and feel they are close enough, but we don't do that anymore—we don't have to, because there are 50+ schools out there that have some game-related industry. Whatever degree, there's 25,000 candidates out there [and] less than 2,000 jobs. I have all the time in the world to be picky and choosy. The thing is, the schools need to push their students harder. Do not be afraid to fail their kids, because I wouldn't. My kids, I told them straight out, if you don't do what I say, I will fail you. And guess what? They did all their homework.

Rosie Server

I pretty much started right out of high school. I probably wouldn't be a great example to your students because I didn't go to college. But I interned for Bon Jovi's postproduction studio right out of high school. I actually started in sound because my entire family works in the sound industry. Audio recording was pretty much what I did. I was working with timecode and I set up edit bays. I would set up microphones and host the talent when they came. I did that for about a year, and my stepmom happened to work in animation, at Omation, and she said they needed a PA [production assistant]. She asked if I was interested and I was only 19 at the time. So I said, "Yeah, sure, why not?" So I moved out, lived on my own, became a PA, and kind of worked up the ranks over there. I was the PA for probably a year at Omation and I became a coordinator and just moved up the ranks from there. And the nice thing was, I got to start in the beginning, when they had early storyboards and concept art. I worked directly with Phil Cruden, the art director. I got to see the show [the film Barnyard*] from beginning to end. I worked in almost every single department in my time during that show. Through the connections I had made at Omation, I found out about a job in LA for* 9, *the movie. Due to my background in sound, they asked me to become the editorial coordinator because I knew a lot about postproduction. I signed on to that, and they asked me to actually be the script supervisor. I did not know a thing about writing a script, but I figured, "why not!" I did that for a few months, and it just wasn't really for me. I had already been kind of burned out in production at Omation because of such crazy hours, and* 9 *was just not what I wanted to do. You know, I was only about 22 at the time. It was just too much work and not enough pay. My friend Robin deGrasse who had worked for Omation had gone up to Lucasfilm Animation, and she was looking to quit for personal reasons. She asked me to come on board to be her replacement. So of course, you know, Lucasfilm comes calling, you say yes. I said, "Sure, why not?" and dropped everything. Somehow in the HR paperwork, they messed up my title. I was supposed to just be a coordinator, and they brought me on as a recruiting sourcer, which is the first level of recruiting. I had never recruited before, and I have never done anything like that. I had told them the mishap, but they decided to have me source anyway. So it's kind of a weird thing how I got into recruiting, by accident! Within a year, I had gone from a sourcer to a recruiter. While there I worked at all of the divisions: ILM, Lucasfilm Animation (US and Singapore), Lucas Arts, and Skywalker Sound. I did a little bit of everything. I recruited for live action, animation, games, international candidates. It was a great experience. I was there for about four years. From there, I had an opportunity to go to ImageMovers*

Digital. I went over there for about 2 years until they unfortunately closed down. That's what brought me over to Sony Imageworks. I've been here recruiting since 2005.

What is your title at Sony Pictures Imageworks?

Right now I'm a senior recruiter. I had started as a contract recruiter working from home and they made me a staff recruiter after about 6 months.

Do you personally interview candidates?

I do. I do the pre-interview for all the artistic TDs [technical directors]. I can only go so far with an interview because I'm not an actual artist myself. I don't think they would want me actually working on the movies! However, I do the pre-interview, so it's basically just seeing if their personality fits. Artistically, I know what to look for in a demo reel. I know what each show is looking for in a candidate. When it comes down to technical questions, the CG supervisor would be the one to ask.

What is it you look for in a candidate when you conduct an interview?

I definitely look for personality traits. We look for key words that might make them seem like they're high maintenance or not team players. For example, if they constantly complain about a job they had. Possibly irritated with an employee or a supervisor. You're supposed to be showing your best and you shouldn't be complaining.

You mentioned earlier that you also look at demo reels. What is it that you look for specifically on demo reels that will make one reel stand out compared to the others?

I say it all the time: always put the best work in the beginning, because usually we're looking at a lot of demo reels—whether they're DVDs or demo web links—usually we're going one after another. If we're not impressed in the first minute, we don't even watch the whole thing. Basically, for experienced artists—it's kind of hard for students—we see what kind of shots they worked on in a movie. If they were hero shots. If it looks like the shot was complicated. If it's just a still shot of someone, it's not quite that difficult, depending on the environment that they're in. It also depends on if it's an animated feature or it's a visual effects show. At Sony, we hire for both. Supervisors on VFX shows will only want to hire artists with experience on VFX shows. If you only have animated feature experience, you are not as appealing to them.

Do you look for specialists or generalists in 3D animation?

Usually for digital effects and animation, it has to be a specialist. It's rare that we hire a generalist. It is good that they can do other skills or departments. Typically our needs are going to start in one department and move to another. You're not going to do both at the same time. So we definitely look for people who just specialize in one type of department. Whether it just be animation, or modeling, or effects, or what have you. I think for a generalist, it tends to be more toward game studios. When I worked at LucasArts, they definitely looked for people who can do more than one skill. That seems pretty common for games, but not for visual effects and animation.

From experience throughout your years as a recruiter and in the many studios that you've worked for, do you see a formal education in 3D animation as important?

Definitely. I can tell a difference in demo reels. I can tell when someone has gone to college and when someone has not. Not to say that when you're self-taught you can't be terrific, because I've definitely seen that as well. For instance…Kris Costa, who was at Omation. He is one of the lead modelers at ILM [Industrial Light & Magic]. He was self-taught. He was actually a banker before he became a modeler, but he taught himself how to do it. His work is amazing. I think it's good to have that formal education. Working with professors is similar to working with a CG supe, director, or lead. They guide you towards the look they are envisioning as opposed to what you may want something to look like.

Do you think the education community is preparing students to come directly out of school and go straight into the 3D animation industry?

I've only been doing this since 2005, so about six to seven years now. It's definitely gotten a lot better over the years. When I first started, I felt like a lot of the schools were still new to it. I feel like over the years with internships going on, career advisors have gotten used to what the recruiters and hiring managers want to see. I think the schools have improved on their techniques.

What schools do you feel are educating students well to go into the 3D animation industries that you're recruiting for?

It depends on what department. I think for animation, we tend to draw a lot of people from Animation Mentor. Ringling has a lot of really good animators. We find that those are kind of the two big ones that we pull from. For concept art, I would say Art Center [Art Center College of Design]. SCAD [Savannah College of Art and Design] has really been stepping up their students as well. Technology of course: Texas A&M, Clemson, MIT.

Which do you think is more important for a 3D animation artist today, technical skill or conceptual skill?

If you're just an animator, definitely your technique and knowing your range of motion. Technical, it depends on the studio you go to. I know when I was at ILM, animators had to know how to rig as well. That's not really standard across the board. ILM really expects a lot out of their artists. At Sony, you don't have to be quite as technical to be an animator. For TD type roles, you definitely need to know the technical aspects of it, like Python, C++, Mel, etc. Right now it seems like Nuke is the standard for compositing and for lighting it tends to be Maya. Katana was just for Imageworks, but ILM has taken it on as well. So hopefully it will spread to other studios. I think for the TD roles, it is definitely more technical, but for the more artistic roles like animation and modeling, it's more the aesthetics than the actual technique.

When recruiting for a new position, where do you post job openings for your studio?

The usual ones are VFX Pro, 2-Pop or LinkedIn. Facebook has been really good because it's a free site with different groups you can join. It's the same with LinkedIn, with groups that you can join that have specific job boards. We do post on CreativeHeads.

Are there any resources people should know about when looking for a job in the 3D animation industry?

That's a good question. Definitely be on the lookout for different events. For example, we're going to be at CTN Animation Expo. It's a great opportunity to meet recruiters firsthand. SIGGRAPH is a must. For gamers, GDC. Those are definitely events your students should go to, because it's a great way to meet recruiters. Most of the time, they have supervisors with them. You're not just stuck in a pile of emails. You're actually there talking to them, so I would say that's the best advice I could give as an outside resource. Also look for internships. Most studios have internships nowadays. It's important to know when can you apply and how are you eligible…just being up-to-date on all that stuff.

Out of these next three traits, prioritize them in order of importance for somebody who's looking for that first job: raw talent, networking and who they know, and personal drive.

I would say raw talent is number one. If you're talented, you're talented. It comes across in your demo reel and in your resume. I would say networking is number two, especially if you're a new student coming out of school, if you have another artist recommending you, you definitely have one up on top of everyone else. If you have the connections to recruiters at different studios, it's more of a direct way to get into the position that you know. As you go on through your career, it's who you know. It tends to be more who you know and not what you know.

Personal drive.

Personal drive. You know, they're all important, but that one's probably the last. It's hard to say it's not important, but definitely having the raw talent and the networking are the two most important things. Having that drive is important, especially as a student. Because I feel like they have more drive than anyone in the industry. As you become a more seasoned artist, you kind of lose that drive, and it definitely shows. I know myself, personally, I like dealing with students a lot more than senior artists because they're more excited to do the job that they're doing.

Is there any other advice you would like the people reading this book to know?

I think for students, the best advice I could say is, like I said before, put your best work in the front of the demo reel. If you're applying for visual effects and animation, it's really important to have just that one department that you're looking for. It's good to have a variety of skills, but for those two industries, visual effects and animation, they like to know you're going toward one department. If you come in and say, I want to do everything, we'll say. "Well, that's great, but we want to know [specifically] what you want to do." With games, it's the exact opposite, so it gets a little confusing. In games, they want to see that you do want to do everything.

For resumes, it's kind of the same thing. Sometimes you have to tailor a resume to go toward the company you're trying to apply for. It depends on the position you're applying for as well. Look at the job description. See what they're looking for. If it says they're looking for someone who knows Nuke and Maya and all that, make sure you put that on your resume—of course, [only] if you actually do know it. Keep networking and remember that even though you're in school, you're going to probably eventually work with the people you've been with in your class. Keep close ties with them. Don't burn a bridge early on because you will eventually work with that person again, or they will work somewhere you want to work…So always keep that in your mind, that it's a very small industry.

INDEX

Note to the Reader: Throughout this index **boldfaced** page numbers indicate primary discussions of a topic. *Italicized* page numbers indicate illustrations.